ENTREPRENEURSHIP AND ECONOMIC TRANSITION IN CENTRAL EUROPE

Jean-Paul Larçon
Editor

ENTREPRENEURSHIP AND ECONOMIC TRANSITION IN CENTRAL EUROPE

Kluwer Academic Publishers
Boston/Dordrecht/London

HEC School of Management,
Paris

Distributors for North, Central and South America:
Kluwer Academic Publishers
101 Philip Drive
Assinippi Park
Norwell, Massachusetts 02061 USA
Telephone (781) 871-6600
Fax (781) 871-6528
E-Mail <kluwer@wkap.com>

Distributors for all other countries:
Kluwer Academic Publishers Group
Distribution Centre
Post Office Box 322
3300 AH Dordrecht, THE NETHERLANDS
Telephone 31 78 6392 392
Fax 31 78 6546 474
E-Mail <orderdept@wkap.nl>

Electronic Services <http://www.wkap.nl>

Library of Congress Cataloging-in-Publication Data
Entrepreneurship and economic transition in Central Europe / Jean-Paul
  Larçon editor.
        p.   cm.
    Includes bibliographical references (p.) and index.
    ISBN 0-7923-8279-X
    1. Structural adjustment (Economic Policy)--Europe, Central.
  2. Europe, Central--Economic conditions.   3. Privatization--Europe,
  Central.   4. Entrepreneurship--Europe, Central.   I. Larçon, Jean-
  Paul.
HC244.E57   1998   98-39133
338.943--dc21   CIP

Photograph Copyright - "Roger-Viollet"
Technical Support - "Tessier-Ashpool, Ltd."

Printed on acid-free paper.

Printed in the United States of America

To my daughter Anne-Sophie

Contents

Contents

Contributors

Sergio Alessandrini is Professor of Economics at the faculty of Law of the University of Modena. He is also Lecturer of European Political Economy at University L. Bocconi of Milano. In recent years he has carried out research on economic regionalism and European integration, with particular reference to the transition economies. He is a scientific advisor for the restructuring of the education system in Central European countries within Phare and Tacis programmes. Among his recent publications are: Economic Regionalism and World Trade System, Giuffrè editore, Milan, 1994, (with G. Sacerdoti) and The EU Foreign Direct Investments in Central and Eastern Europe, University L. Bocconi, July 1997.

Attila Chikán is Professor and Head of the Department of Business Economics at the Budapest University of Economic Sciences. He directed the research program the findings of which are presented in chapter 5. He teaches Business Economics, Theories of the Firm and Management of the Value Creating Process. His special fields of interest include economic and business policy and the management of value creating process, focusing on manufacturing and logistics. He holds a number of national and international academic and business functions.

Erzsébet Czakó is Associate Professor and Deputy Head of the Department of Business Economics at the Budapest University of Economic Sciences. She was the Deputy Director of the research program the findings of which are presented in chapter 5. She teaches Business Economics and Strategic Management. Her special fields of interest are the content of and approaches to competitiveness researches, competitiveness of various sectors and higher education in business.

Franck Debié is Assistant Professor in international management at HEC School of Management, Paris. Trained in history, geography and management, he has specialised in political and social sciences. His work is on peace processes, related political and economic transition and public governance. His fields of study are the Balkans and the Middle East. He teaches on political risk, international governance and European affairs in the HEC School of Management, the Ecole Normale Supérieure, Institut d'Etudes Politiques de Paris and Oxford University.

Saul Estrin joined the London Business School in 1991, where he is a Professor of Economics and head of the Economics subject area. He was formerly a Senior Lecturer at the London School of Economics, and has visited Cornell University, Stanford University and the University of Michigan Business School. His research concentrates on the process of economic reform and transformation in Central and Eastern Europe. He has particularly focused on questions of privatisation, company restructuring and different ownership forms.

Jean-Paul Larçon is Professor of Strategy at the HEC School of Management, Paris, where he teaches international strategic management. A former Dean of HEC and Professor Emeritus at Warsaw University of Technology school of business, he participates actively in the HEC research and educational programmes in Central Europe and the Community of Independent States. His current work focuses on business strategies in economies in transition.

Petr Musílek is the Deputy Head of the Banking and Insurance Department at the University of Economics, Prague (VSE Praha). A teacher of finance at VSE, he has also experience in the investment banking department of Bank Austria Vienna. He has published numerous books and articles focused primarily on the financial markets

Ingeborg Nemcova is Associate Professor at the department of Economic Policy, University of Economics, Prague (VSE Praha). She is an Engineer of Economics, Candidate of Science, and Alexander Hamilton fellow at USC, USA (1991-92). She teaches Economic Policy, Privatisation and Transformation at VSE and Charles University. She introduced Community of European Management Schools (CEMS) course of Economic Policy in Prague. She is the President of the Czech Fulbright alumni association.

Kjell A. Nordström is Assistant Professor at the Institute of International Business, Stockhom School of Economics, and Director of IIB education. His research concentrates on global competition, international strategy, the internationalisation processes and particularly the modes of involvement in Eastern Europe for corporations of advanced industrial countries.

Christian Ragacs is Assistant Professor at the Vienna University of Economics and Business Administration. He received the Theodor-Körner Price for his Contributions to Growth Policy in 1997. His fields of research are Theory of Economic Growth, Labour Economics, Theory of Income Distribution, History of Economic Theory in the 19th Century, Applied Econometrics, with an emphasis on Time Series Analysis.

Maria Romanowska is Professor at Warsaw School of Economics (Szkola Glowna Handlowa) and head of the Institute of Management. She is the author of many books on corporate strategy and strategic alliances. Her current research interest is in the process of concentration within Polish economy. The data base of the Institute of Management allows systematic monitoring of large Polish industrial groups: their behaviour and an analysis of the way they compete or co-operate with foreign companies in Poland.

Styrbjörn Torbacke, is a former research associate at the Institute of International Business of Stockolm School of Economics, is now the head of the computer department of Kraft-Freja in Stockholm.

Jan-Erik Vahlne is Professor of International Business and was formerly Rector of the Stockhom School of Economics in Riga, Latvia. He is now at Chalmers University of Technology, Gothenburg, Sweden, preparing the establishment of a new business school. He has published widely on many aspects of international business.

Martin Zagler is Assistant Professor at the Vienna University of Economics and Business Administration since 1994. He received the Stephan-Koren Price for the dissertation entitled "Contributions to the Theory of Endogenous Growth under Market Imperfections" and the Theodor-Körner Price for his Contributions to Growth Policy in 1997. His fields of research are Intertemporal Macroeconomics, Endogenous Growth, New Keynesian Economics, Monetary and Exchange Rate Economics.

Laszlo Zsolnai is Director of the Business Ethics Center, Budapest University of Economic Sciences. He is also Visiting Professor of Ethics in the joint MBA Program of the IMC Graduate School of Business, Budapest and the Case Western Reserve University, Cleveland, Ohio. He is the initiator and co-ordinator of the Inter-faculty Group in Business Ethics of the Community of the European Management Schools (CEMS). Dr. Zsolnai has more than 100 publications on interrelated topics of economics, ethics, and human ecology.

Preface and Acknowledgements

HEC Foundation has a strong tradition of supporting research programmes in management sciences. The Foundation believes that research in international management is a key factor of success for companies and a key element in management education at HEC School of Management, Paris.

Research programmes of the Foundation associate HEC faculty to corporate members of the Foundation: Adecco, Arthur Andersen, HEC alumni association, Bain & Company, Banque Nationale de Paris, Bain & Company, Cartier International, Crédit Lyonnais, EDF/GDF, Ernst & Young, Casino Group, Gemini Consulting, Hewlett Packard, Lazard Frères & Cie, L'Oréal, Mars & Co, Paribas, Pernod Ricard, Price Waterhouse, Procter & Gamble, Publicis, Schneider, SNCF.

This book is the result of the HEC Foundation research programme on "corporate strategies in emerging countries". The programme covers diverse emerging business environments: Latin America, Asia, Central Europe and CIS. Most of these emerging markets have previously demonstrated a high level of uncertainty: economic fluctuations, social turbulence, political instability, and economic nationalism. However, in spite of recent financial crisis in Mexico (1994), Central and Eastern Europe and Asean (1997), they are still very attractive to foreign direct investors resulting from the development of the private sector, new investment codes, the development of regional trade areas and high growth potential.

International management experts face interesting dilemmas for investigation and action on emerging countries. These economies offer a unique opportunity for companies to quickly build a strong presence in new fast growing markets thanks to privatisation, growth of international trade, investment and globalisation. Yet, this opportunity implies risk and flexibility; firms have to adapt their strategic vision, management processes, and human resource policies to local conditions.

Former research has thus helped in identifying common characteristics such as the management of risks, transfer of technology, restructuring of the value chain on a world basis and new patterns of co-operation between local and international companies. Present research focuses on the specificity of economic transition in Central and Eastern Europe and the relationship between the changes in the economic environment and the opportunities for entrepreneurs, strategies and management processes.

The HEC School of Management has a strong established presence in the region since 1989, training MBA students, professors, managers from the Czech Republic, from Hungary, Poland, Lithuania, and Romania as well. This experience contributed to put the research into perspective and to follow the rapid pace of transition.

The HEC Foundation would like to thank all the professors and administrators involved in the development of HEC Central and Eastern Europe Centre who lent to support the research: Jean Klein, Dean of faculty and research, Jean-Marc De Leersnyder, associate Dean for International affairs, Jean-Luc Gulin, deputy General Director, Gilles Laurent, former associate Dean for research, Bérangère Pagès, managing director corporate relations.

The HEC Foundation also benefited from the strong support of the Community of European Management Schools (CEMS) founded in 1988. The CEMS is a European initiative to encourage excellence in management based on a partnership between 50 international companies and 15 leading European management schools.

We are glad to have among our authors professors not only from western schools such as Stockholm School of Economics, U. L. Bocconi (Milan), Vienna University of Economics and Business Administration, but also from the three outstanding Central European institutions that have joined the CEMS in 1998:

- Budapest University of Economic Sciences (Hungary),
- The University of Economics, Prague (Czech Republic),
- Warsaw School of Economics (Poland).

We are also glad to have the contribution of Saul Estrin of London Business School, one of the leading European experts on economic transition.

The HEC Foundation and the editor would like also to express their special gratitude to:

-       Bernard Ramanantsoa, Dean of HEC School of Management, Paris: since the beginning of the programme, his commitment in developing research on transition in Central and Eastern Europe was of immense help.

-       François Vachey, Vice President Human Resources of L'Oréal and President of HEC Foundation Development Committee: he initiated the research programme on emerging countries and helped focus our work on key issues for practitioners and researchers.

-       Nicole de Fontaines, Secretary General of CEMS and Jaroslava Durcáková, Vice-Rector for International Relations of the University of Economics, Prague: they helped considerably in mobilising researchers of the CEMS network.

HEC Foundation and the editor want also to express their special thanks and congratulation to professor Attila Chikán of Budapest University of Economic Sciences: in July 1997 he took the post of Economics Minister of Hungary's' new government headed by Prime Minister Viktor Orban. Attila Chikán is in favour of liberal economic policy, he wants both to assist foreign investors and help the growth of small and medium enterprises, and he will also prepare Hungarian economy and companies to EU accession. Professors and industrialists of the HEC community wish him the best success.

Antoine Bracchi
Honorary Chairman, Ernst & Young and
Chairman of the Board, HEC Foundation

Paris, November 1998

Introduction: Organisation of the Book

Jean-Paul Larçon
HEC School of Management, Paris

Economic transition is part of a transformation process involving major changes at the political, economical, social and psychological level. In less than ten years most countries of Central and Eastern Europe, at the exception of those affected by the war in former Yugoslavia, have re-established a democratic political life, moved rapidly from centrally planned economies to market economies and opened internationally their society and economy. Most of these countries after years of severe economic depression have now recovered and are increasing their participation to European business sphere and world trade.

Privatisation in CEE countries has been the core mechanism of the transformation process; and the transfer of property to private owners radically changed the goals, values and behaviour of all economic agents and decision-makers: employees, pensioners, consumers, companies, stockholders, managers, bankers, municipalities, government agencies.

For some foreign enterprises, CEE countries might be still perceived as a foreign distant, and uncertain environment but for others, ranging from small European family businesses to multinational companies (MNCs), the region in transition is just another facet of the enlarged European domestic market and business environment. Newcomers to the region do not usually face difficulties in operating in this neighbouring cultural environment, but one of the major challenge for foreign companies is to adapt their management goals, structures, processes and human resource to rapidly changing local market and local business system. Successful companies in Central Europe have simultaneously been highly responsive to local specific transitional dilemmas and opportunities and integrated their regional approach within a broader framework of a global strategic management perspective.

The objective of this book is to clarify the mechanism of transition in Central and Eastern Europe (CEE) and to highlight its consequences in term of entrepreneurship and corporate behaviour.

Key issues, such as privatisation, development of financial markets, participation in word trade, restructuring industries and companies, foreign direct investment and international joint ventures, are quite similar from one country to another. If problems are similar, solutions are not differing so much even if the pace of transition varies a great deal as well as short-term priorities.

The more the process transition continues, the more similarities and convergence can be find in the evolution of local economic and business environment.

The two first chapters consider the region globally and emphasise two important features:

- First the emergence of an entirely new political and business environment, which has already opened the door for new and successful business strategies of international companies,

- Second the success and limits of privatisation: success by the irreversibility of the reform and the sharing of privatised economy, yet serious limits in term of efficiency. In chapter 2, **Estrin** argues that mass privatisation did not create the appropriate ownership structures and corporate governance and that it might lead to severe difficulties for efficient restructuring.

New business environment, privatisation, restructuring: in chapter 3 to 9 through analysis these aspects are dealt with in depth, using the most characteristic national examples. CEE countries are not homogeneous: they differ from historical, political, cultural point of views. Some are relatively rich like Slovenia or the Czech Republic, other much poorer like Romania and the Baltic Republics. Four countries are the concentrated on: Czech Republic, Hungary, Poland and Romania, a total population of 83 million inhabitants with three leaders of transition: The Czech Republic, Hungary and Poland and a late comer Romania.

In chapter 3 **Nemcova** draws the lessons of Czech Privatisation and confirms Estrin quote opinion looking at the positive and negative results of Czech voucher privatisation. She explains the links between voucher privatisation, the power of Investment Funds and the relationship between Funds and

Czech leading banks. She concludes on political success of privatisation and serious shortcomings in term of restructuring and corporate governance.

In chapter 4, **Musilek,** discusses the Prague Stock Exchange and a technically well adapted system of trading but which is lacking of serious regulation. The financial market is not yet in a situation to directly serve the needs of Czech companies looking for capital for long term growth.

In chapter 5 **Chikán** and **Czáko** concentrate on the issue of restructuring and competitiveness. They point out the four key areas that have influenced competitiveness: changes of the economic mechanism from shortage economy into a market one, the social acceptance of the changes, the characteristics of economic policy and the management of the firms. The authors see the substantial improvement of the performance of Hungarian companies as the result arising from market forces than government economic policy. They also identify managerial skills as a key element of differentiation between Hungarian high and low performing companies.

Continuing in Hungary in chapter 6, **Zsolnai** probes the ethical fabric of a transforming economy. The social reception of market economy in Hungary as well as the ethical attitudes and values of managers that are still in transition and may involve a lot of ambiguities and ambivalent feelings. The ethical posture of Hungarian companies differs strongly according to two dimensions: the intensity of competition on the local market and the degree of exposure to international competition.

In chapter 7 **Romanowska** explores the links between economic growth and Foreign Direct Investment (FDI). Poland, the largest economy of the region is now also the leading host country for FDI. Romanowska points out FDI as a key success factor in the transition process thanks to the transfer of resources and technology, the development of exports, and the positive influence on Polish companies' competitiveness.

In chapter 8 **Alessandrini** investigates the links between social, political and economic transition in Romania. The absence of political stability and a lack of clear direction in term of economic policy have had a very negative impact on Romanian transformation. Real progress in privatisation and in the establishing the legal framework for a market economy is recent and the Romanian government has still to face the difficult challenge of privatising and restructuring large SOEs and public utilities.

Final chapters study three specific aspects of transition: the role SMEs, the strategy of MNCs, and the impact of EU enlargement on business strategies.

Chapter 9 examines the effects of co-operation between small companies of Eastern and Western Europe. Quite spontaneously since 1989 small companies have rediscovered the trade routes of the past. **Zagler** and **Ragacs** draw our attention on the role of these co-operations especially in the process of diffusion of innovation and demonstrate their positive effect on growth.

Chapter 10 focuses on the behaviour of multinational companies. Swedish MNCs were operating in the region before transition and old relationship helped developing new business. **Nordström, Vahlne** and **Torbacke** emphasise the sequential moves of five MNCs in the region and the differentiation of attitudes in term of risk taking. In most cases Eastern Europe strategies integrated into global corporate strategies.

Chapter 11 addresses the issue of EU enlargement. **Debié** outlines some of the difficulties of the enlargement process due to the of lack of political consensus in the West, ambivalent public support in CEE itself, lack of resources and absence of clear deadlines. Thus, companies operating in CEE still have to face the uncertainties of the agenda and maybe new internal regulatory barriers within CEE according to the status of the country regarding accession.

In spite of these limitations due to EU governance, the transition and enlargement process are offering an unusual window of opportunity for small and large firms, local and international companies doing business on a pan-European basis.

ABBREVIATIONS

ASEAN	Association of South East Asian Nations
CEE	Central and Eastern Europe
CEFTA	Central European Free Trade Agreement
CEMS	Community of European Management Schools
CIS	Commonwealth of Independent States
CMEA	Council for Mutual Economic Assistance
COMECON	See CMEA
CPE	Centrally Planned Economy
CR	Czech Republic
CZK	Czech Koruna
EBRD	European Bank for Reconstruction and Development
EFTA	European Free Trade Association
EU	European Union
FDI	Foreign Direct Investment
FPN	National Property Fund (Czech Republic)
GDP	Gross Domestic Product
GDR	German Democratic Republic
IMF	International Monetary Fund
IPFs	Investment Privatisation Funds (Czech Republic)
JV	Joint Venture
MBA	Master in Business Administration
MEBO	Management and Employee Buy Out
MNCs	Multinational Companies
NATO	North Atlantic Treaty Organisation
NIFs	National Investment Funds (Poland)

NIS	New Independent States: former republics of the Soviet Union, minus the Baltic States, and Mongolia
NGO	Non Governmental Organisation
OECD	Organisation for European Co-operation and Development
PAIZ	Polish Agency for Foreign Investment
Phare	A EU grant assistance programme for CEE
PLN	Polish Zloty
PSE	Prague Stock Exchange
SMEs	Small and Medium Size Enterprises
SOEs	State-Owned Enterprises
Tacis	EU grant assistance programme to twelve countries of the former Soviet Union and Mongolia
UN	United Nations
UNCTAD	United Nations Conference on Trade and Development
Visegrad Countries	Czech Republic, Hungary, Poland, Slovak Republic and Slovenia
WB	World Bank
WSE	Warsaw Stock Exchange

Chapter 1

Business strategies for economies in transition of Central and Eastern Europe

Jean-Paul Larçon
HEC School of Management, Paris

Abstract: Since the fall of the Berlin Wall in 1989, Central Europe has seen the radical political and economic status of 15 nations representing 135 million inhabitants moving away from authoritarian regimes and planned economy towards political democracy, market economy and integration into international trade. This new political and economic environment has been the theatre of new corporate strategies of both local companies and foreign corporations. The context and speed of transformation specifically gives to the first and fast movers the opportunity to increase significantly their competitive advantage.

1.   RETURN TO EUROPE

Immediately after the revolutions of 1989-1990, most new governments of Central Europe and public opinion favoured a «Return to Europe» policy which would be translated in political terms by joining the EU and NATO.

In terms of defence policy, the Warsaw Pact era (1955-1998) had been characterised by a high level of military threat from both sides but it was also a source of stability in the region. At that time the return to Europe could have created some instability and a return to nationalist conflicts of the past. The Baltic Republics were, for example, in a very difficult situation. Incorporated in the USSR since 1944, they had to resist the violent Russian interventions of 1991, to regain their independence and negotiate new political and economic relationships with their powerful neighbour and trade partner. The importance of Russian minorities, up to 40% in Latvia, and the problems linked to the territory of Kaliningrad are still a source of tension today. However all three states, at different paces and with different national styles, have already been able to achieve both political change towards democracy and economic transformation towards market economy.[1] Estonia, which made the most rapid progress in terms of market economy is on the short list of EU applicants.

Conflicting interests were also strong within the Czechoslovak Federation but in fact democracy and reason immediately prevailed: after the June 1992 Czech and Slovak Federated Republic elections, Czech and Slovak leaders decided to conclude a «velvet divorce» on 1 January 1993. The split had no negative influence on the rapid and successful political and economic transformation of the Czech Republic and Slovakia. Although coming from the smaller and poorer part of the Federation, Slovakia has since also achieved good economic results.

Local governments, EU and NATO have thus combined to resolve border disputes and ethnic minority issues in the regions peacefully and democratically. The Hungarian government worked through bilateral treaties to stabilise the situation of the Hungarian minorities abroad: the three million Hungarians living in neighbouring countries: two million in Transylvania (Romania) and six hundred thousand in Slovakia. This policy has been quite successful in Romania where the Democratic Federation of Hungarians in Romania represents ethnic Hungarians in the Bucharest parliament. The situation is more difficult in Slovakia under the authoritarian style of Slovak Vladimir Meciar's presidency. However, even in that case, the combined pressures of NATO and the EU whose association with Slovakia includes a clause protecting the rights of minorities and limiting potential conflicts.

Finally a new NATO and a new EU are emerging rapidly. NATO examined in 1995 the «why and how» of future admissions into the alliance with the «Study on the Nato enlargement» and at the Madrid summit of 1997 could invite the Czech Republic, Hungary and Poland to start negotiations with the Alliance. The door is still open to other candidates; Romania for example is considered to have made enough progress in its political reform efforts and in its treatment of ethnic minorities to be accepted as a NATO «candidate».

On the contrary, peaceful transition has not been achieved in the Balkans because of the relative political incapacity of the EU to exert a major structured influence in the area; this situation has also been exacerbated by the character of local nationalism. Out of the former Yugoslavia, only Slovenia, which expelled the Federal Army in 1991, has yet been able to establish firmly the basis of political democracy and a market economy.[2]

By contrast most of the energy of Croatia and the new Yugoslavia (Serbia and Montenegro) has been invested in the war effort since the disruption of the Federation in 1990 up to the implementation of the Dayton

Peace Accord in Bosnia in 1996. Thus the former Yugoslavia, apart from Slovenia and Albania, has been kept apart from the mainstream of the transition process that went on in the North and Centre of the region.

Applications for membership to the EU are good indicators of the major trends in the region and the speed of transition. Ten countries representing a population of one hundred and eight million inhabitants have applied to date for EU membership: the three Baltic Republics, Estonia, Latvia and Lithuania, Poland, Hungary, the Czech Republic, Slovakia, Romania, Bulgaria, and Slovenia.

The average purchasing power in these countries is 32% of the average of the fifteen member nations of the European Union. This ranges from the richest Slovenia and the Czech Republic, respectively 59% and 57% of EU average at PPP, to the poorest countries where the average lies between 18% and 24%: these are Romania, Bulgaria, Lithuania, Estonia and Latvia.[3]

Democracy and market economy are key criteria for EU admission. The «Copenhagen Criteria» defined in 1993 by the European Council seeks:
- stable institutions guaranteeing democracy, the rule of law, human rights and the protection of minorities;
- the existence of a functioning market economy as well as the capacity to cope with competitive pressure and market forces within the Union
- the ability to take on the obligations of membership including adherence to the aims of political, economic and monetary union.

In 1997 all the applicant countries had constitutions and institutional arrangements based on democratic principles, which are implemented in practice. Only Slovakia did not pass the test of the first political criterion because of the lack of stability of its institutions and the government's disregard for the rights of opposition and minorities.

From an economic standpoint, all countries have made good progress in their transition to a market economy but have to continue with their structural reforms especially in the banking, financial and the social security systems. Hungary and Poland come closest to meeting the economic conditions with the Czech Republic and Slovenia not far behind. Estonia has a market economy, but needs further efforts to meet competitive pressures.

This offers five countries, the Czech Republic, Estonia, Hungary, Poland and Slovenia, a market of sixty million people a potential green light for negotiations in 1998 and possible admission to the EU in 2002-2003. It does not mean rejecting those other candidates who are late comers in the transition process but share the common objectives. Romania, for example, the second-largest post-communist economy in the region with 22.7 million inhabitants, entered into the painful restructuring process and transfer of initiative to the private sector only after 1996.

Among leaders of the transition process Poland, with thirty nine million inhabitants is the largest economy of the region. Since 1990, the foundations for a new stable market economy have been laid. Poland liberalised prices, introduced convertibility of the Polish currency, and stabilised the exchange rate. Thanks to the shock therapy initiated by Leszek Balcerowicz, the downward trend in the economy was reversed rapidly and this industrialised and urban country was on the way to a successful transition. Poland, which after the Czech Republic became a member of the OECD in 1996, has entered the negotiation process to join the European Union and NATO in 1998. The political and economic environment in Poland, in addition to its growth potential, has created a positive climate for foreign investment.

The four other candidates for near-term EU entry, the Czech Republic, Estonia, Hungary and Slovenia, have also demonstrated their ability to manage the process of change so as to compete and co-operate effectively in an open economy.

2.   FROM PLAN TO MARKET: PRIVATISATION

For applicant countries and other states of the region the initiation, the development and the strengthening of the mechanisms of a functioning market economy have been a major challenge. The EU is officially neutral regarding the public and private sector. Article 22 of the Rome Treaty says that «in no way [should the EU] prejudice the rules in member states governing the system of property ownership».

But the tone has been set by international financial institutions such as the World Bank, the IMF and EBRD[4] bearing the principle that decentralised ownership was the best way to increase competition and improve performance. In 1997 the IMF, World Bank and EBRD reduced their former financial support to Romania by stopping public subsidies to companies, accelerating privatisation and closing or selling big loss-making industrial firms. Thus privatisation has been one of the key issues in Central Europe and, since 1989, the ten EU candidate countries have embarked on various privatisation schemes. This resulted in a massive transfer from public to private ownership so that the majority of Central European companies are now privately owned.

A new breed of entrepreneurs has been born. Eurostat, the Statistical Office of the European Community in Luxembourg, estimates that six years after the fall of the Berlin Wall 3.4 million enterprises were operating in market economy conditions in eleven Central and Eastern European countries. 68% of these companies are located in Poland, the Czech Republic and Hungary. Most of them were created from scratch and their average size was 7.4 employees. Most of these companies have difficulties today both in terms of production and sales; they suffer from both domestic competition and imports contributing to strong pressure on prices. This implies an incredible change of mentality, norms and values. Under the socialist system, appointment to a position in the Polish United Workers' Party was considered the greatest promotion for an executive; since 1990, the most desired type of promotion has been to become a successful entrepreneur, a member of the board or a top executive of a large corporation.

Poland's transformation has involved a very ambitious privatisation programme, first laid out in 1991, and finally implemented in 1995. The number of private firms in Poland has increased from 0.5 million in 1995 to more than 1.8 million in 1998. The main source of growth is in the private sector, and its dynamism is due to the establishment of new enterprises rather than the transformation of existing ones. In 1997 more than 65% of the work force was employed in the private sector and 100 firms were listed on the Warsaw Stock Exchange (WSE). In 1997, accelerating the pace of privatisation was and is still a priority for the country with a list of one hundred big companies remaining. The privatisation agenda included: TPSA, the Polish telecom monopoly, PEKAO, the biggest bank, and LOT the national airline.

In sectors like telecommunications and railways for example, some Central and Eastern Europe countries are now more advanced in deregulation than their western neighbours. In the field of energy, Hungary is progressing fast and is more advanced than France for electricity and gas liberalisation. In a sense some countries of Central Europe might even be able to go deeper in the privatisation process than some EU members: only 50 % of Austrian GDP is privately generated and Greece has also to increase its efforts on the road to privatisation. But, if completing privatisation per se is a good indicator of the success of transition, it is not the end of the process. There are other new priorities:

- Developing institutional frameworks for competition policy.
- Increasing the quality of management, of long term forecasting, of management systems in private companies and adapting corporate direction to the new competitive environment. Many local giants are still learning to dance, even if, according to the World Bank, the largest one hundred and fifty to two hundred companies in the Czech Republic, Hungary and Poland have reduced their workforce personnel by 32%, 47% and 33% respectively between 1989 and 1993.
- Increasing the quality and efficiency of the public sector: public administration, local government, health and education system
- Privatising and restructuring the banking and insurance sectors.

\-   Developing the new capital markets, which are still small, vulnerable and lacking in transparency. Newly created stock exchanges in CEE countries and investment funds have had a key role in terms of concentration of ownership in these early stages of development. In the Czech Republic 70% of the shares of the first wave of privatisation were controlled by fourteen private investment funds generally connected to leading local banks. Thus the narrow Prague stock exchange is still dominated by banks and funds and can be perceived as a private playground for privileged insiders.

3.   NEW ECONOMIC AND SOCIAL ENVIRONMENT

Globally, most countries of the region have recovered from the depression of the first years of transition and the region has managed to sustain a higher level of growth than that of its EU neighbours. In 1995, the growth rate in Central Europe was 5.2%, higher than the EU at 2.4% for the third year running. It is reasonable to expect a differential of that magnitude to continue in the medium term and, as such, Central Europe will be one of the fastest growing regions of Europe at a rate of between 4.5% to 5.5%.

The social and human cost of transition was very high during the years of recession followed by a more or less rapid recovery varying in extent, country by country. Both the Hungarian «gradualist» approach and the Polish «shock therapy» have produced good results. It is also clear that those countries that have not taken courageous decisions rapidly to reduce public deficits, master inflation and stabilise the currency, like Romania before 1997, have just lost time and made the task more difficult from a political and a social point of view.

Unemployment has developed in the region with peaks such as 14.9 % in Poland in 1995 yet very low current rates in the Czech Republic. These figures are not very different from those observed in Western Europe where the EU average was 10.5% in 1997, but there is a high probability that some of these low percentages are hiding cases of late restructuring of industry. Thus, even in situations of sustained economic growth, the transformation process may increase social differentiation and create large groups of worse-off people especially in those regions of Central Europe traditionally specialising in mature industries such as steel, textiles, and shipyards which face the highest restructuring challenges.[5]

Table 1 Unemployment

Unemployment	1994	1995	1996	1997
Bulgaria	14.5	12.5	11.1	15
Czech Republic	3.2	2.9	3.5	4.5
Poland	16	14.9	13.2	11.5
Hungary	10.4	10.4	10.5	10.4
Slovakia	14.5	13.1	12.8	13.1
Slovenia	14.4	12.5	11.1	15

Source: Eurostat

In 1997 inflation was curbed in most countries with the notable exceptions of Bulgaria and Romania.

Table 2 Inflation

inflation	1994	1995	1996	1997
Bulgaria	122	33	123	1250
Czech Republic	10.0	9.1	8.8	8.4
Hungary	18.8	28.2	23.6	18.3
Poland	32.2	27.8	19.9	15.0
Romania	136.8	32.3	8.2	52.9
Slovakia	13.4	9.9	5.8	6.3
Slovenia	2.0	13.4	9.9	8.4

Source: Eurostat

Considering the Czech Republic's remarkable macro-economic performance and its political stability, the crisis of the Czech Koruna in May 1997 was an unpleasant surprise for most analysts. The currency crisis resulted in a slowdown of the Czech economy in the short term, with annual growth limited to approximately 1.5% in 1997. Strong similarities can be observed with monetary crises in other emerging economies in Latin American and Asia and growth in Central Europe might face similar difficulties. However it could also - as in the Czech Republic in 1997/1998 - help to identify and correct quite quickly the weaknesses of the system: insufficient regulation, poor bank management and slow industrial restructuring.

Progressive monetary integration can be also foreseen: all candidate countries having to embrace the goal of EMU as part of the «acquis communautaire». Between 1990 and 1998 the majority of countries, except Romania, have gradually increased the links between their currency and the Deutsche Mark along with other European currencies and the US dollar.

This leads in the future to a strong monetary link with Euro countries and probably the use of the Euro as a secondary means of payment.

4.   FOREIGN   TRADE   AND   FOREIGN   DIRECT INVESTMENT

In 1989, the majority of trade was carried out within the region among eastern partners and since then foreign direct investment and international trade flows between Western and Eastern Europe have increased substantially.

The share of Polish exports to the former USSR and Eastern Europe dropped for example from 49.0% in 1985 to 23.2% in 1990 and 16.8% in 1995. On the contrary, the EU share increased from 22.5% to 44.3% in 1990 and 70.0% in 1995. In 1997, the six largest Central European economies considered together, Poland, the Czech Republic, Slovakia, Hungary, Bulgaria and Romania conducted 62% of their foreign trade with the European Union. Germany's share of this trade representing 31% of exports and 26% of imports (fig.1).

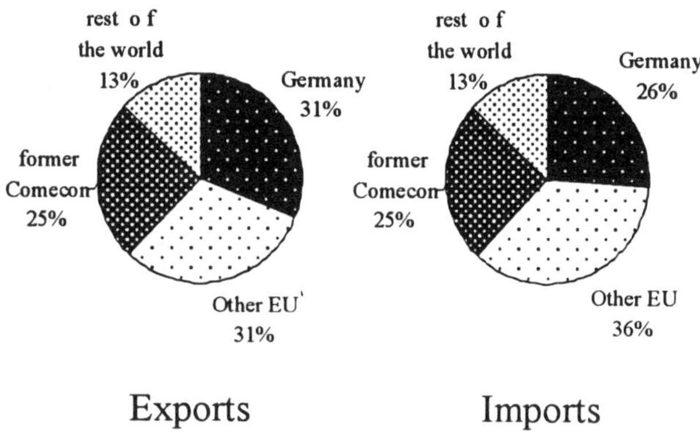

Figure 1. Trade Links of Bulgaria, Czech Republic,
Hungary, Poland, Romania in 1995
Source: Eurostat

German - Central European economic integration is a strong asset for the region. German trade with Central and Eastern Europe has grown continuously in recent years up to 9% of the total foreign trade volume in

1996. Trade opportunities in Central Europe will be supported in the short term by the reduction of internal barriers within the Central European Free Trade Agreement (CEFTA) which includes the Czech Republic, Hungary, Poland, Slovakia and Slovenia. Furthermore, the prospect of enlargement of the European Union should continue to provide opportunities in the medium term.

The flow of foreign direct investment in the region, which totalled $46 billion in the middle of 1996, ranks third after Asia and Latin America. However, investment is growing rapidly and the rate per capita is already higher than in Brazil or China.

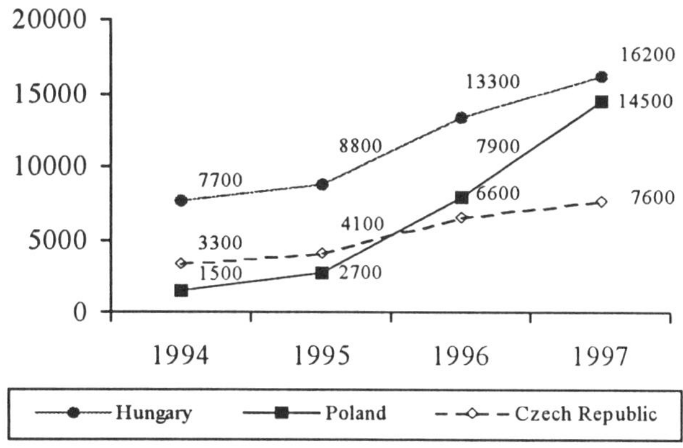

Figure 2. Cumulative FDI (US$ by end of 1997)

Source: EBRD

Hungary leads the way with $ 16.2 billion since the fall of communism, followed by Poland $14.5 billion and the Czech Republic $7.6 billion. Historically Hungary between 1989 and 1997 has attracted the largest amount of foreign direct investment in Central Europe as a result its early steps towards a market economy, its rapid privatisation policy, political stability and healthy business environment. Germany is the largest investor in the country, 28%, followed by the United States. One of the largest deals in Hungary was the acquisition in 1993 of 30% of the shares of Matav, the telephone company, for US $875 million by a consortium led by Deutsche Telekom and Ameritech. Foreign companies have entered all Hungarian economic sectors, including infrastructure, energy, consumer goods such as Ferruzi-Unilever, Electrolux, Sara Lee, pharmaceuticals, the take-over of Chinoin by Sanofi, automotive industry, General Motors and Ford. A company like Suzuki, which closed its Santana Motors car plant in Spain after twelve years of operation to start production in Hungary in 1992, reached the 60% target of local components and materials content by 1995. Two thirds of the output is already exported to EU markets, particularly Germany, Britain and the Netherlands. This large foreign presence in Hungary in turn creates favourable conditions for future growth and potentially large exports, especially in Europe.

Investment in Poland, the regional giant, is growing very rapidly. The inflow of foreign direct investment (FDI) more than doubled in 1996 which elevated Poland to the league of major recipients of FDI in per capita terms. Heavy investment continues despite the fact that foreign companies are still facing difficulties with the Polish legal and tax system. Germany ranks first in terms of invested capital, with 31%, while Asian companies arrived later but developed an active commercial and manufacturing presence. Japanese companies such as Matsushita, Mitsubishi and Sony, as well as South Korean chaebols, such as Samsung, Daewoo, Kia Motors and Hyundai have contributed to the Asian marketing presence. To date, foreign investors have focused primarily on industries such as automotive, tobacco, food, beverages, paper, cement, electro-engineering, and, more recently, distribution networks, supermarkets, banking and insurance. In 1997, Bank Handlowy became the largest privatisation of a financial institution in Central Europe.

In the Czech Republic between 1989 and 1997, political stability and good economic performance attracted investments of US$7.6 billion, with Germany being the leading foreign investor with 28.6%. The country has an active policy to attract foreign companies and among prime movers were Volkswagen, Philip Morris owning 70% of Tabak, Procter & Gamble, Coca-Cola, ABB, Unilever, and Nestlé, which along with Danone and EBRD, acquired 55% of Cokoladovny. The main target for new capital is the automotive sector, with car sales expected to double between 1994 and the year 2001. Since 1991, Volkswagen has invested US $2.5 billion in Skoda Automobilova, the largest Czech industrial enterprise. Another significant indicator is the decision by Matsushita, the world's largest producer of consumer electronics to establish a US $68 million Panasonic plant in Plzen, which will become part of Matsushita's global television set manufacturing network. Foreign companies produced about 11.2% of total output of the Czech economy in 1995.

FDI in the region has clearly accelerated since 1994 and is likely to grow in the future, with Poland as one of the largest targets. Thus the role of foreign enterprises in the privatisation and restructuring process is important quantitatively and qualitatively: it facilitates rapid change and forces local companies to improve their performance to meet these new competitors.

Host countries are competing actively to attract foreign investment, through active marketing abroad and incentive schemes in the longer term.[6]

The Czech Republic considers only very large investments for incentive schemes, for example, the Intel Corp. with $300-500 million for a computer chip plant and the $68 million Panasonic television plant in Plzen which have won both tax and tariff holidays; less advanced countries such as Romania will have to offer significant advantages to attract investment.

5.   STRATEGIES OF INTERNATIONAL COMPANIES

5.1   Goals

Economic theory suggests that FDI in Central Europe aims essentially at using lower factory costs to develop export-oriented manufacturing facilities. In 1996, the total labour cost in the Czech Republic was only US $4.00 per hour by comparison with US $30.00 in Germany. And, relative to other emerging countries, Central Europe has a higher level of education, a skilled labour force, a number of good, even excellent engineers and a strong technological and scientific tradition. So even if productivity could have been substantially lower than in the West at the beginning of the transition process, re-location could have been the primary motive in investment in Central Europe, as an alternative, for example, to investment in South East Asia.

Other characteristics of the region have, however, contributed to turn it into a strategic investment opportunity for foreign companies:
- Size of ill-exploited local markets
- Current or potential growth rates higher than in EU
- Less structured competition offering opportunity rapidly to build large local market shares
- Political and macro-economic stability
- Geographical and cultural proximity to EU
- Low tariffs or minimised trade barriers and future accession to EU
- Number and quality of opportunities of local sourcing, local manufacturing, sometimes local Research and Development.
- Low acquisition price of local companies.

Thus since 1990, many companies entered the region with dual ambitions: the first being dominance of the local and regional market, and the second being the development of an export platform for Western Europe and other international markets. The difference of living standards between the East and the West part of Europe was opening a space both for sales growth and cost reduction giving the opportunity for international companies to increase their competitive advantage throughout the region.

5.2   Process

Many companies have first focused on the opportunity of creating majority joint ventures through privatisation, and then have increased their presence with new acquisitions or building plants on greenfield sites.

Nestlé has developed its presence in CEE very systematically, starting with former East Germany, Hungary, the Czech Republic and then moving to Slovakia, Poland and Bulgaria. Presence in Poland started in 1994, via the purchase of a 47% stake in Gopland, which is now up to 93%. This chocolate factory of two thousand four hundred workers had a 15% local market share. Other acquisitions followed: mineral water, soups, sauces and deserts. Nestlé has modernised the plants, trained the personnel, built a logistic and distribution network, developed a marketing plan for both its global and local brands and finally, created a marketing and sales culture.

Local consumers' distinct characteristics in terms of taste or purchasing habits have led to the adaptation of brands, packaging, price, distribution and advertising strategies, but there is a strong mid-term convergence of Western and Central European consumer profile and marketing mix.[7]

In most cases local partners of foreign joint ventures have been minority partners and the joint venture a first step towards total control. One major reason for this scenario is that local partners have not, in the short term, the financial resources to match the growth of new private companies. The transfer of ownership has not generated cash in the privatised companies and new Central European capitalism has much less cash in hands than the family conglomerates of Asia or Latin America.

ABB has built a massive presence in Eastern Europe. Of its total of two hundred and fifteen thousand staff world-wide, the group employs twenty four thousand people in the former Eastern block. However, the risk for this company has to be carefully monitored. The total cumulated investment in the area, estimated at three hundred million US$ at the end of 1996, is in fact, relatively small thanks to the low price of the companies acquired; the investment is split between more than sixty joint ventures. Moreover, even if the company has had a small early presence in all countries, the de facto geographic focus shows a concentration of investment in the low risk heart of Central Europe: Poland, Hungary and the Czech Republic, representing two thirds of the total work force of ABB in the broad region: CEE and CIS (see table 4).

ABB Poland, the largest ABB business in the area involving a turnover of five hundred and seven million US$ in 1996 exports its gas turbines, low-pressure turbine rotors and generators all over the world. It is hard to determine the volume of the group's internal sales, but Polish subsidiarics are believed to export 20% of their production within the group which implies of course that local production achieves the world level in terms of quality standards. This also means that the group centralises its purchases and benefits from an estimated 40% difference between the cost of an ABB product manufactured in Poland and the cost of the same product manufactured in the EU by a Western competitor.

Table 4 ABB focus on Central Europe

Country	First Move	Number of Joint Ventures	Staff
Albania	1994	1	3
Bosnia-Herzegovina		1	2
Bulgaria	1996	3	495
Croatia	1996	2	535
Czech Republic	1991	9	6 719
Estonia	1991	4	154
Hungary	1990	7	2 156
Latvia	1992	2	309
Lithuania	1992	2	49
Macedonia	1994	1	2
Poland	1990	14	6 988
Romania	1992	4	1 420
Slovakia	1990	4	371
Slovenia	1992	1	7
Yugoslavia	1990	1	5
Total CEE			19235
Total CIS			4691
Total CEE and CIS			23 916

Source: ABB Annual report 1997

Percy Barnevik, the former chief executive of ABB, is a strong advocate at the EU level of a policy of division of labour based on manufacturing high technology products in the West and the more standard products in the emerging countries. In any case the changes currently taking place in Central Europe are not only creating market opportunities locally, but are also changing the competitive conditions throughout Europe and the rest of the world.

5.3   Vision

Multi-national corporations that have had the vision and capacity to build a profitable presence in the region in recent years are now reaping the benefits of prime movers:
- the best local companies acquired at low cost,
- large local market shares thanks to past presence, capacity, image or network of the local partner,
- increased experience in restructuring, transforming local units, recruiting and developing a local elite.

Local subsidiaries of multinational corporations in Central Europe pursue two long-term objectives: aggressive sales development in both the local and international markets and rapid integration within the global manufacturing and logistics networks of their parent companies. Their local presence can then be turned into a powerful weapon to compete globally with products and services of international standard at a lower cost.

In the automobile industry, Volkswagen's presence in the Czech Republic and in Slovakia, through its subsidiary Skoda, has three advantages. First, it increases Volkswagen's leadership in Europe through the conquest of local Central European markets. Second, it increases competitiveness through local manufacturing and purchasing; and third, it provides the possibility of using Skoda as an instrument for the Volkswagen Group's penetration into other emerging markets of Europe, Russia and Asia. For example, Skoda is currently discussing a project for a three hundred million $US plant in India. Of course, to exploit the advantages of its Central European presence, the Volkswagen Group has to manage the differentiation between its four brands, Volkswagen, Audi, Seat and Skoda, and simultaneously increase the synergies and mechanisms of co-ordination among them. This management implies a restructuring of the value chain at an international level, including the internationalisation and centralisation of purchases and relationships with suppliers.

Ferdinand Piech of Volkswagen describes the change as the lasting renovation in the structure of the value chain from the supplier to the consumer.

"Yesterday, the production site exported its product, today it's the purchase network that dictates its conditions. This trend brings the markets closer together, sections off exchange risk and provides an international cost advantage."[8]

But opportunities of transition are also fuelling the rivalry between global players and are frequently leading to hyper-competitive situations where speed, surprise, overbidding and government interventions play an increasing role. In the automotive industry all the global competitors are there, opening plants in Central Europe: Europeans, Americans, Japanese and Koreans.

Daewoo has been circling in on Europe from the East with greenfield projects and joint ventures in Poland, Hungary, Romania, Uzbekistan and the Ukraine. In Poland, where the car industry is booming, Daewoo acquired state auto-maker FSO by outbidding General Motors and promising the Polish government it would put $1.1 billion into FSO without reducing its twenty one thousand workforce for at least three years. This acquisition will allow Daewoo directly to challenge Fiat, the biggest single foreign investor in Poland with 51% of the market and the second top-selling carmaker in Central Europe after Volkswagen. Daewoo is also the largest investor in Romania with a major presence in the car industry, but also in consumer electronics and shipyards, and has been in a very good position to negotiate with local government the best administrative, tax and tariff conditions.

Thus Central European economies provide a unique window of opportunity for both global and regional players. German competitiveness will be boosted by Germany's strong presence in terms of trade and manufacturing, giving the opportunity for German companies to focus on higher value-added activities. Conversely, industrialists in Western Europe who have difficulties in implementing flexible production methods at home are facing a serious challenge: not only will they lose the opportunity, but tomorrow their domestic market will suffer.

5.4   Human Resources - Dilemmas of Transition

Quality control and human resource management are keys to successful business strategies in Central Europe. Quality is essential to meet the expectations of local and international clients, and local people are necessary to lead the business according to international standard practices.

Years of the planned economy in Central Europe did not cut ties with West-European culture nor with pre-war industrial and entrepreneurial traditions; Czech engineers, Polish trade companies, Hungarian bankers can build on both local roots and new opportunities for transition. However, an inefficient use of human resources was a major weakness during the years of the planned economy, and the opportunity for building on motivation, talent and responsibility is a major asset for newly privatised companies.

Individual evaluation, for example, is widely accepted in the CEE. However, the acquisition and development of managerial talent may take longer than the acquisition of scientific and technological skills. Basically in Central Europe, good managers and leaders are scarce because the situation requires more leadership and entrepreneurship than mere administrative skills. To establish a sustainable presence in Eastern Europe, international companies' primary responsibilities include not only a focused selection of geographical targets, a good timing of acquisitions or the development of greenfield projects but also the proper allocation and development of the human resources essential for leadership and profitable growth.

Successful presence in the CEE is thus widely linked to wide-scale training. Successfully to localise and integrate the seven thousand workers in its eleven Polish plants, ABB in 1993, set up an internal training programme centre in Warsaw. Its goal is to "facilitate the creation of modern companies, be competitive on the world market and offer the highest quality products and services." More specifically, this involves:

training managers and executives,

creating an ABB Poland network,

adapting Polish companies to the corporate group culture

Human Resource Management requires special attention in Central Europe. Nestlé appointed a Human Resources Co-ordinator for Central and Eastern Europe in 1996. Although based in Vevey, Switzerland, he spends more than half his time in the field, introducing Nestlé's methods so as to integrate employees as quickly as possible within the companies acquired in the area. Nestlé wants to replace its one hundred expatriates in Central and Eastern Europe as quickly as possible and Human Resources specialists have to identify the local managers with potential, recruit them, train and prepare them. Special training tools have been set up such as an Eastern European training programme for young marketing professionals with courses in logistics and sales.

Finally the local elite has to be integrated in the culture and the system of the Western company; close association and synergies between local national talents and corporate cultures of international corporations are the key to successful development in the region.

6.   CONCLUSIONS

Opportunities have already been great for international companies in CEE in these early years of transition and opportunities are still there in countries like Romania or Slovakia which have good potential but still have shortcomings within specific aspects of the transformation process. But independently of the immediate opportunities of transition the region may benefit from broader aspects of the economic integration of West and East. Signs are already there of an unusually attractive economic environment and business system:

- The CEE communist past has led to a lower state of public interventions than in the fifteen members of the European Union.
- Market growth is there and even if competition gets stronger, the situations of over-capacity that could be dangerous are limited such as in the car in industry in Poland.
- The required level of investment to enter emerging markets of the CEE is much smaller than the equivalent investment needed to create a market share in a developed region. Long-term presence is easiest to achieve for prime movers whatever position they have in their country of origin.
- The risk is limited because of the overall quality of institutional environment and the capacity of Western companies to choose their local partners.
- Social mutations, linked to privatisation and restructuring may lead to social conflict but employees of international companies or joint ventures are in a relatively favourable position.
- Restructuring local companies and re-organising the value chain on an international basis has been proved successful in most countries and industries.
- Western companies have been generally successful both in responding to the specific needs of local consumers, local employees and local environment and by incorporating their local subsidiaries in their global network and company culture.
- Human resources in terms of quality and quantity are available in the region as well as the desire to learn and the capacity to lead.

Thus, even if economic convergence between present EU members and newcomers in Central Europe does take time, a domestic market of five hundred million consumers has been born in Europe. From the point of view of rapidly developing economic maturity, the opportunities presented by an enlarged EU market together with the pressures of the disparate living standards between the two facets of Europe, West and East, Old and New are the driving forces of a virtuous circle of progress. Looking ahead, even if the perspectives in Russia and Ukraine are still difficult to predict, with the Federation of Russia, trade prospects are positive and foreign investment is growing rapidly. The EU is already Russia's biggest foreign market and a good relationship between an enlarged Europe and the Federation of Russia is a positive and exciting prospect for the future.

NOTES

1 see Hood, Kilis and Vahlne (1997)
2 see «Strategy for Economic Development of Slovenia», IMAD (Institute of Macroeconomic Analysis and Development), Ministry of Economic Relations and Development (Republic of Slovenia).
3 Eurostat Statistics in focus, Economy and Finance, n°29/97, overview of the Candidate countries'GDP.
4 EBRD since its creation has financed 647 projects for a total amount of ECU bn 47.6. 67% of the projects are private.
5 see Dauderstädt (1997)
6 three local invetsment agencies are especially active: CzechInvest (Czech Agency for Foreign Investment), ITD Hungary Hungarian Investment and Trade Development Agency and PAIZ Polish Agency for Foreign Investment.
7 see Nestorovic (1993)
8 Ferdinand Pïech in EIU Motor Business Europe, The Economist Intelligence Unit, 1st tr. 1997

REFERENCES

Balcerowicz, L., 1995, *Socialism, capitalism, transformation*, Central European Unversity Press, Budapest.
Bartlett Christopher A., Doz Yves L. et Hedlund G. (ed), 1990, *Managing the Global Firm*, Routledge, Londres et New York .
Bouteiller, E. and Larçon, J-P, 1996, *Stratégies d'entreprise dans les pays émergents*, Groupe HEC, Paris.
Csaba, L., 1995, *The Capitalist Revolution in Eastern Europe*, E. Elgar Publishing Co, Aldershot.
Dauderstädt, M., 1997, *Can the Young Democracies of East-Central Europe Cope with the Double impact of Transformation and Integration*, Friedrich-Ebert Stiftung, Bonn.
EBRD, 1997, *Transition Report 1997*, London: European Bank for Reconstruction and Development, London.
Estrin S., ed., 1994, *Privatization in Central & Eastern Europe*, Longman, London.
Hood, N., Kilis, R., Vahlne J-E (eds) 1997, *Transition in the Baltic States*, Macmillan Press Ltd, London.
Johnson, S., and Loveman, G.W., 1995, *Starting Over in Eastern Europe: Entrepreneurship and Economic Renewal*. Harvard Business School Press, Boston.
Kogut, Bruce, 1996, «Direct investment, experimentation, and corporate governance in transition economies» in Frydman, R., Gray, C.W. and Rapaczynski, A., 1996, eds., *Corporate Governance in Central Europe and Russia*, vol. 1, Central European University Press, pp 293-332., Budapest.
Meyer K. E., 1995, «Foreign direct investment in the early years of economic transition: a survey», in *Economics of Transition 3, n°.3, pp.* 301-320.

Mygind N., 1997, «Different paths of transition in the Baltics», working paper n°5 Center for East European Studies, Copenhagen Business School.
Nestorovic C., «Les balbutiements de Marketing à l'Est», *Courrier des pays de l'Est,* n°381 Août 1993, Paris.
OECD, 1997, *Towards a new global Age: Challenges and Opportunities*, Paris 1997.
World Bank, 1996, *World Development Report 1996: from Plan to Market*, Oxford University Press, New York.
Zecchini, S. Editor 1997, *Lessons from The Economic transition: Central and Eastern Europe in the 1990s*, Kluwer Academic Publishers, Dordrecht.

Chapter 2

Privatisation and Company Restructuring in Central and Eastern Europe: Issues and Progress

Saul Estrin
London Business School

Abstract: The efforts to privatise the state owned sector in central and eastern Europe are outlined and the implications for progress in transition analysed. The reasons for privatisation are summarised, focusing on both the need to raise corporate efficiency and the political pressures to embed capitalism. The need for rapid privatisation in the context of poorly developed capital markets has led to the widespread use of "mass privatisation" methods. The paper examines the merits and disadvantages of this approach, especially with respect to subsequent corporate governance. It argues that mass privatisation will not lead to ideal ownership structures for ensuing enterprise restructuring. The paper concludes by providing evidence on the forms of ownership that have emerged post-privatisation, notably the disproportionate amount of insider ownership, and discussing the evidence on the impact of privatisation to date, which appears to be modest.

In this paper, we outline the efforts to privatise the state owned firms of Central and Eastern Europe and consider the implications for evaluating progress in the region. It is hoped that privatisation will improve company performance and bring much-needed resources to the state coffers. The state owned sector produced more than 90% of total output, and virtually all of industrial production in the communist bloc as recently as 1989. This means that the shift back to private hands has to be more diverse in character than the privatisation in the West and represents an important indicator of performance in reform. The whole privatisation process has been much hampered by the lack of domestic savings, the deficiencies of the capital market and the profound scarcity of managerial know-how in the transitional economies.

While privatisation raises particular problems and dilemmas, it is merely one element, though an important one, in the process of transition from a socialist to capitalist economy. A considerable literature has emerged to define the principal economic reform tasks during transition, as well as to propose an appropriate sequence of changes. The major other components in a reform programme are macro-economic stabilisation following price liberalisation; opening the economy to foreign trade and competition; developing effective and liquid capital markets and institutional reform, including of the legal system and to the functioning of the state. The letter has often proved particularly difficult.

Privatisation is, however, pivotal to the success of market reforms. The reasons are partly ideological; the desire to rely on the free market because of previous economic failure. High on most lists of explanatory factors was the inefficiency of the state owned enterprise sector, which failed to invest or produce rationally, which squandered material inputs, labour and energy and which failed to innovate. It is inconceivable that the economies of the region can be turned around until new managers, and new systems to motivate both workers and managers, have been established.

In the following section, we consider how the privatisation debate has developed in transitional economies in recent years, with particular reference to the advantage and disadvantage of the most significant form of privatisation in the region: voucher privatisation. We then consider in detail the main options available to reforming governments, before concluding by summarising the various routes chosen and the likely outcome of these policy differences for the emerging market structures of different transitional economies.

1.   WHY PRIVATISE AT ALL?

Almost all observers take the need for privatisation, and indeed for rapid privatisation, for granted. Given that privatisation has in fact proved both difficult and slow, with progress limited in many countries, it is worth reminding ourselves of the reasoning behind this conclusion. We distinguish between economic and political arguments, the latter assuming considerable significance in the delicately balanced political situation of many transitional economies.

INCENTIVES AND EFFICIENCY

The primary argument for privatisation concerns incentives; in particular the potential dissonance between the task of restructuring socialist firms and the motivation of socialist managers. In all firms where owners do not directly control decision-making themselves, mechanisms of governance are required to ensure hired managers maximise profits. In the West, these problems are addressed (at least in Anglo-Saxon countries), by the disciplines of the capital market. The share price, which itself reflects a market based evaluation of the future profitability of the firm, is publicly available information upon which to evaluate the performance of one management team against another. Share prices can also form the basis for evaluation of managerial deficiencies leading to bankruptcy or associated financial restructuring. Perhaps most importantly the people monitoring the companies' performances are motivated to get it right by the prospect of their own financial gain if they can guess better than the market a firm's future prospects.

In contrast, state firms have no market based evaluation of their performance. Management is aware that governments are not particularly interested in profits, but in an variety of objectives, many political and social, and can exploit this lack of purpose to their own advantage, for example enjoying an "easy life" or failing to keep a tight grip on costs, especially labour costs.

Similar arguments apply in an extreme form in the transitional economies. The main task of management in the former, state enterprise is restructuring. One example is financial restructuring, including the stripping away of social assets such as housing, health clinics and crèches as well as the more conventional disposal of peripheral activities. There may be many of these because planning made firms wasteful of all resources, including plant and land. Another is reducing the labour force, estimated to be excessive by a factor of around 25% even before the recent recession. A third is developing new products and finding new markets, especially in West. The interests of the state as owner in these matters are mixed. Politicians may be under pressure to prevent restructuring to avoid unemployment.

In short, government in the transitional economies probably neither have the interest nor power to impose a profit orientation on managers. This will hinder effective change because the former socialist managers will still be in charge in most places, and their most likely interest in the face of all the changes to attempt to preserve the *status quo*, especially with respect to employment and the local community. Even if they had the appropriate skills and experience, managers do not have the incentive to restructure their organisations for competition on world markets. They will instead probably work in the interest of major stakeholders: the labour force as a whole (including management itself); the local community to which the firm may be a major supplier of public goods, services and housing as well as jobs; and perhaps even the networks of suppliers of intermediate inputs. There is no one in this list concerned to defend the return to capital, which can be assumed to take a relatively low priority.

There are occasions when state ownership and the absence of effective governance might have even more serious consequences for the transition process, namely when the players within the firm are motivated to play an endgame. For example, consider the situation in an enterprise which the reform process has left clearly non-viable; for example a supplier of defence components in the CMEA whose market has disappeared. Managers and workers may realise that once capital market forces are operating effectively, the company will be closed. In the interregnum, they have incentive to decapitalise the company, and to use its (possibly not insignificant) credit lines in effect to absorb assets from more productive uses to the decapitalisation process. It may be noted that negative net worth will be no constraint provided the firm has positive gross assets. One suspects that processes of this sort have become increasingly important in Russia in recent years, and underlines the widespread emergence of barter.

There is a further practical reason in support of privatisation prior to restructuring state owned firms, at least in the context of Central and Eastern Europe. Restructuring involves investment, and the governments of transitional economies have few resources to make available to the enterprise sector. Privatisation, at least in principle, holds out the promise of access to relatively cheap new funds from the new owners through the issuance of shares. Perhaps even more enticing is the hope that the new owners will be foreign firms, in part or in full, bringing simultaneously capital and access to Western design, technology, markets and managerial expertise.

IRREVERSIBILITY OF REFORM

The fundamental political reason for privatisation is to secure the irreversibility of the reform process. Particularly at the start of the transformation, political forces were in many countries quite evenly balanced.

Even in the countries where the communist path was firmly rejected at the start of the reforms, the enormous hardships suffered by the populations during reform revived the political fortunes of parties of the left. Probably the most important reason for the treacherous political waters in which reform politicians are swimming is that, at least at the outset, there is only a limited constituency of people who benefit from the transitional process. Reforms, it is true, bring in their train the eradication of shortage, the availability of goods, including Western goods, and the ability to travel. But they also bring lower real wages (sometimes markedly so), the destruction of savings through inflation, and the threat of unemployment. Most importantly, the benefits from reform are diffused around the population as a whole, but the costs are concentrated among a vocal group - workers and managers of large industrial firms - who have the power to slow the whole process.

It is the emergence of an entrepreneurial class upon which the economic, as and the political success of reform depends. A property-owning class committed from their own interests to the continuation of a market economy has to be created. The reformers can persuade workers and managers to support these changes by making them the owners of the firms in which they work.

2.   WHO WILL OWN THE FIRMS?

The reasons for privatisation are clear; as a symbol of reform and to address the manifest deficiencies of the enterprise sector. But the transitional economies are countries in which private domestic savings are scarce, capital market institutions are weak or non-existent and existing stakeholders in state owned firms are very powerful. Traditional modes of privatisation by the state divesting its assets through capital markets to individual and institutional private owners are very hard to implement. Much of the debate in the region has therefore revolved around alternative methods of privatisation.

Our discussion revolves around Table 1, which presents the main options available to reforming governments. The debate has focused around two closely related issues. The first is whether to attempt to sell state owned firms for something approaching their market price, or instead to distribute the ownership rights in the enterprise for free (or for nominal sums). The second issue is whether to seek owners from existing (or previous) stakeholders of from interested parties outside the firm, who must effect corporate governance through capital markets. Table 1 summarises the various options.

The arguments in favour of selling firms rather than giving them away seem in abstract convincing. Most importantly, the new owners are established via a process of financial exchange so that the people who obtain control are those who are willing to bid the most, presumably because they believe they can achieve the highest return from the assets. Selling also has the advantage of bringing badly needed revenues to the government coffers. Transition typically brings a budgetary crisis in its tail and the authorities would be foolish to forego a major source of revenue without good reason.

Table1: how to privatise and to whom

Privatisation To Whom

	Existing managers and workers	General Population	Previous Owners	Foreign and Domestic Private Firms
By Sale	Employee management buy-outs e.g. Hungary, Romania	Stock market floatation. few examples as yet.	-	Joint ventures, foreign direct investment, e.g. Hungary, East Germany
By Free Distribution	"Spontaneous privatisation", employee management take-overs of assets e.g. Russia	"Voucher privatisation" e.g. Poland, Czechoslovakia	Restitution e.g. Bulgaria, East Germany	

The efficiency arguments in favour of selling ownership rights to the highest bidder may be strong when capital markets function well, but transitional economies have poorly developed and illiquid capital markets. Hence the people best able to use the assets may not be able to enter the auction at all and selling may end up inefficient or infeasible. It will certainly be very slow. Even in the United Kingdom, with a technically competent and relatively honest civil service, sophisticated capital markets and where the privatisation revenues were only a modest proportion of domestic capital formation in any year, each privatisation project took several years to bring to fruition. Thus, in decade of frenetic privatisation activity in the United Kingdom, the volume of output that was transferred from the state to the private sector was only in the order of 7% of the industrial total. In contrast, the Czechoslovaks, Poles and Hungarians sought in their initial programmes to transfer ownership of around 50% of industrial output in the first three years of reform. Their civil services were not trained to make business plans or assess profitable opportunities, capital markets were at best fledgling and the required revenues exceeded domestic savings by a factor of 50 or more.

A major practical problem is valuation of companies. There is no good way to value firms in the former socialist economies. Most socialist enterprises did not keep the kind of accounting information necessary to establish a track record of profitability. Secondly, even if information about previous performance was available, its predictive power in the fundamentally different economic environment post-reform is highly questionable. Reform has meant major changes in input prices, especially for energy and material inputs, and for output prices as well as a collapse of old trading relations. These changes make estimates of future profitability highly speculative.

The idea of free distribution of the state's assets to outsiders provides an apparently simple and appealing solution to these problems. There is no need to find domestic buyers, nor to develop capital market institutions prior to privatisation. In principle there is no requirement to value the assets. Moreover free distribution schemes offer the potential of speed and could be highly egalitarian, or at least serve to reward key agents in the reform process. If, as we have argued above, the issue of speed is almost as important as the fact of privatisation itself, then the appeal of free distribution scheme is particularly strong to reforming governments bogged down in the detail of case by case privatisation.

One serious drawback however is that the government will fail to realise the value of its portfolio at a time when revenues are sorely needed. But the most serious danger from free distribution of shares is that it may not ensure adequate corporate governance for the newly privatised companies.. It is unclear whether free distribution to the population as a whole for example can ensure the emergence of real owners dedicated to the interest of profits. Free distribution may therefore lead to privatisation policies which affect the legal form of ownership rights while leaving the substance of managerial motivation and enterprise performance unchanged.

The impact of a free or virtually free distribution scheme on company performance depends on who are the beneficiaries. As can be seen in Table 1, there are two categories of people to whom the authorities could sell, or freely distribute, shares. The first are "insiders" to the firm; managers, workers and both. The second are members of the general population, either as a whole or those specifically discomforted by the previous nationalisation and who seek redress from the new regime.

One needs first to consider who make better owners of firms - outside capital holders exercising their influence through the stock exchange and financial institutions along Anglo-Saxon lines, or the existing stakeholders in the firm - managers; workers; and perhaps indirectly the debtholders who will predominantly be the commercial banks. The advantages of allocating dominant shareholdings to insiders are clear. The approach is very fast. Such a privatisation method is easy to administer, since the target group of buyers is already identified, and it could even raise some revenue, since managers and workers are often willing to make contribution towards the value of the assets that they are receiving. The insider approach also ensures that existing scarce managerial experience continues to be exploited.

However, there are three major problems with insider privatisation, whether free or at nominal prices. In the first place, employee-management ownership raises numerous questions of enterprise motivation and performance, especially if there are significant employee shareholdings. Many regard employee ownership as inextricably linked to the consumption of assets by workers in the form of higher wages. The danger from managerial ownership are less dramatic, but in the absence of a capital market allowing successful managers to withdraw their equity in the future, the motivational impact on company performance are not clearly as positive as one might hope. One could imagine management being forced to consume capital at the end of their life cycle in order to recoup previous investments. There is also the danger, if the government does press to sell the assets, that the fledgling private firms will carry excessive debt.

Managerial or employee-managerial ownership is also not the most suitable ownership form for enterprises about to embark on major restructuring. Decision-making authority is given to groups who might be removed, or at least find their position fundamentally altered, by more dispassionate analysts of restructuring needs. Thus workers in over manned plants will be loath to vote themselves out of job, while traditional socialist managers, now owners of the firm, will be unlikely to countenance choices that increase the importance of new colleagues in the hitherto insignificant finance, accounting and marketing divisions. Moreover, privatisation to insiders brings no direct new funds to the company, at a time when additional resources are the crucial ingredient for deep or "strategic" restructuring. The same criticism applies of course to other forms of voucher privatisation, with the important proviso that the new external owners have both the instruments and the control to bring in additional funds if they consider them to be required.

The final problem with distribution to existing stakeholders concerns the political legitimacy of the programme. The argument applies with particular force if managers and workers are simply given ownership rights in their firms. There are the political and social dangers in appeasing previous elites, a problem more marked in Central Europe than in the former Soviet Union. But the situation is hardly better if the state sells managers and workers their shares, because most observers realise that the insiders are likely to have a far better idea of the true value of the firm than the authorities, and are therefore likely to be able to obtain a very good price. Problems of this sort led to a public outcry against so-called spontaneous privatisation, even in highly pragmatic Hungary which quickly introduced fairly strict state supervision of the privatisation process. The political problems are hardly reduced if the privatisation to insiders includes widespread employee ownership. The reason is that the prospects of particular firms are very different, and there is no fair reason to justify the allocation of rights to highly unequal streams of income to the working population as a whole on the basis of where they happen to be employed at a particular moment.

The conventional western approach is to distribute shares to outsiders, and there two ways to do this in transition economies. One is to restore ownership rights to previous owners - restitution. The second is to distribute shares to the population as a whole - a voucher or certificate scheme. Both methods have the advantage of speed and in principle bringing external capital market pressures to bear on the restructuring process. Both also offer the possibility that additional external funding might be made available by new owners. This is because the creation of external ownership rights will typically be associated with the formation of capital market institutions that permit shareholders to withdraw their funds by selling their stake. However, in the short term the prospects here are not necessarily much better than with insider privatisation because in neither case do the new owners necessarily have recourse to significant funds. But outsider privatisations have the advantage that they can be constructed so as to be fair, and therefore to provide the political legitimacy so crucial in the early stages of reform.

The key problem with all these free distribution schemes is that they may fail to create effective forms of corporate governance. In the case of restitution, the problem may be that the individuals or families who have suddenly been given ownership rights neither understand, nor are interested to learn, the business which they have inherited. If there were perfect capital markets, they would simply sell the business to the highest bidder. However, this is not a likely outcome because the paucity of buyers and the asymmetries of information in the capital market are the reasons for following the policy of free distribution in the first place. The new owners may therefore have to take control themselves, and may well be far worse at management and restructuring than the existing managerial group. The alternative is that the newly restituted owners will leave decision-making authority in the hands of existing managers and workers. Restitution then leads *de facto* to the same outcome as free distribution of ownership rights to enterprise insiders.

The problem of corporate governance in the context of "mass" privatisation schemes has received much more attention. The difficulty here is that successful privatisation to the general public must imply that ownership rights are widely diffused among the population as a whole. But highly diffused ownership rights, and the absence of any dominant block of shares, means that control over managers will necessarily be weak. The distributional objective of voucher privatisation - to spread the new ownership rights as widely as possible among the new population - therefore conflicts with the aim of bringing effective external capital market pressures to bear on managerial decision-making. When ownership rights are widely diffused so that managers do not need to fear the dissatisfaction of a controlling block of shares acting in unanimity to remove them from their jobs or to enforce, for example, more radical restructuring policies, they may feel empowered to resist threatening changes.

The architects of voucher privatisation schemes have been very concerned to minimise such effects. They have sought to encourage the development of intermediate capital market institutions standing between the general public as shareholders and firms, concentrating ownership rights and able to exert effective corporate governance. The Polish scheme involves the construction of Investment Funds (which actually jointly own the former state owned enterprise sector) with free distribution of shares in these Funds to the population as a whole. In contrast, financial intermediaries were not an integral part of the Czechoslovak voucher scheme; instead Investment Funds sprang up on a competitive basis to exploit the profits available via economies of scale in information about firms and from concentrating ownership rights. In no country is it yet clear whether these groupings of ownership rights can actually offset the tremendous advantage in decision-making power offered to insiders from their superior access to information about the firm's production methods, markets, finance and prospects. We have also yet to see anywhere the emergence of a large scale secondary market in these externally held ownership rights, which would permit both a concentration of final ownership rights, rather than the rights of the intermediaries. The secondary market is also crucial in that, by giving investors the right to take their funds out when they wanted, it might encourage them to begin to put some additional funds into the enterprise sector, thereby facilitating the restructuring process.

3.   A TAXONOMY OF MASS PRIVATISATION

Most countries in transition have used some form of privatisation scheme. This section categorises mass privatisation schemes according to legal structures and privatisation methods. The material is summarised in table 2.

table 2. Mass Privatisation Programmes in Central and Eastern Europe and the Commonwealth of Independent States

country	Year voucher distribution began	All shares issued in waves or continuously?	Are vouchers bearer, tradeable, or nontradeable?	Is investment in funds allowed, encouraged or compulsory?
Albania	1995	Continuously	Bearer	Encouraged[1]
Armenia	1994	Continuously	Bearer	Allowed[2]
Belarus	1995	Continuously	Bearer	Encouraged[3]
Bulgaria	1995	Waves	Nontradeable	Encouraged
Czech Republic	1992	Waves	Nontradeable	Encouraged
Estonia	1993	Continuously	Tradeable[4]	Allowed[5]
Georgia	1995	Continuously	Tradeable	Allowed[2]
Kazakstan	1994	Waves	Nontradeable	Compulsory
Kyrgys Republic	1994	Continuously	Bearer	Allowed[6]
Latvia	1994	Continuously	Tradeable	Allowed[5]
Lithuania	1993	Continuously	Nontradeable	Allowed[5]
Moldavia	1994	Waves[7]	Nontradeable	Encouraged
Poland	1995	Waves	Tradeable	Compulsory
Romania[8]	1992	Continuously	Bearer	Compulsory[9]
Romania	1995	Waves	Nontradeable[10]	Allowed
Russia	1992	Continuously	Bearer	Encouraged
Slovak Republic	1992	Waves	Nontradeable	Encouraged
Slovenia	1994	Continuously	Nontradeable	Allowed
Ukraine	1995	Continuously	Nontreadable	Allowed

1 By July 1996 only one or two funds had applied to receive vouchers.

2 Although a legal entitlement exist to invest vouchers in funds, in practice this option was limited.

3 The results of the first voucher auction were cancelled in march 1995, and fund licences were suspended from then until August 1996.

4 Vouchers were nontradeable at the outset of the programme, but cash trading was legalised in the spring of 1994.

5 Citizens could also exchange vouchers for other things such as apartments or land.

6 Citizens could invest their vouchers in housing as well as hare. They can sell their vouchers to funds, but no formal mechanism exists for them to subscribe to funds..

7 Although the design of the Moldavian program was based on the offer of companies in waves, the waves were small in the early stages, and thus had many of the characteristics of a continuous issue.

8 In 1991 Romania introduced a scheme based on the distribution of certificates of ownership in five private ownership funds. In 1995 a supplementary mass privatisation programme was introduced involving the distribution of coupons that could be exchanged for company shares or fund shares, after which the funds are to be transformed into financial investment companies.

9 Under certain circumstances certificates of ownership in funds could be exchanged for company shares

10 Certificates of Ownership were bearer, coupons were registered and nontradeable.

Source: Estrin and Stone (1997)

The most conspicuous absentee is Hungary, but also none of the former Yugoslav economies have introduced mass privatisation except Slovenia. In the former Soviet Union, Azerbaijan, Turkmenistan and Uzbekistan have also not yet introduced a mass privatisation programme.

The table reports the year that voucher distribution began and provides information about three aspects of the design of such schemes:

(1)   The form in which the vouchers are issued. One issue concerns whether shares should be bearer or registered, and should they be tradeable? (Bearer shares are always tradeable). Behind this is the question of who receives the vouchers; the entire population, workers or managers. In some part of the former Soviet Union, questions of nationality, ethnicity, and seniority have also been relevant.

(2)   How should firms be sold? The shares could be brought to market continuously, as firms become ready, or in waves involving the simultaneous offer of 25% or more of companies eligible for privatisation. The latter approach allows buyers to compare alternative options but is administratively much more demanding. In the ambitious Czechoslovak scheme, shares in enterprises were transferred in waves comprising hundreds of firms simultaneously (Czechoslovakia did not break up until after the first wave of mass privatisation.) A computerised system was set up to mimic a general equilibrium market clearing process.

(3)   What kind of capital institutions should be built into the process? Mass privatisation transfers ownership rights but leaves the character of future capital markets open. As we have seen in some schemes, capital market intermediaries are an integral part of the programme while in others they are merely allowed or actively encouraged.

4.   OWNERSHIP STRUCTURE IN CENTRAL AND EASTERN EUROPE

This section examines the evidence on the ownership arrangements resulting from privatisation in Central and Eastern Europe. We focus on the share of the new private sector in output as well as the new owners of former state property.

The World Bank <u>Development Report</u> (1996) provides evidence on the extent of privatisation across all transitional economies. The shares of the private sector in GDP are reported for 26 countries. The share already exceeds 50% in ten countries and exceeds 33% in eighteen. The private sector share of GDP was highest in the Czech Republic (around 70%) and lowest in Belarus (around10%). Though it has proved harder than expected to privatise some large scale state enterprises, the pace of privatisation has been remarkable by Western standards.

We noted above that most transition countries have used a variety of privatisation methods. The situation is summarised for six leading transition countries in Table 3. Only in Estonia and Hungary have sales to outsider owners represented significant privatisation methods, and both of these countries have relied disproportionately on foreign direct investment to finance their privatisation strategies. Elsewhere, mass privatisation or subsidised buyouts by managers and workers have predominated.

Table 3: Methods of Privatisation of medium sized and large enterprises, by value to end 1995

	Sale to outsiders	Management-employee buyouts	"Equal Access" Vouchers	Restitution	Other	State owned
Czech Republic	5	-	50	2	3	40
Estonia	60	12	3	10	0	15
Hungary	40	2	0	4	12	42
Lithuania	<1	5	55	0	0	35
Poland (by number of firms)	3	14	6	0	23	54
Russia (by number of firms)	0	55	11	0	0	34

Source: World Bank Development Report, 1996

The relatively high share of output supplied by the private sector appears to be largely independent of the privatisation method adopted, or indeed of whether any sustained policy has been enacted at all. Thus, Poland, Hungary, the Czech Republic and Russia all have private sectors supplying more than 50% of output. However, Hungary did not have a mass privatisation policy; the Polish programme has been modest in comparison with other privatisation methods and the Russian and Czech schemes represent opposing modes of mass privatisation. An important reason is that most private sector growth everywhere has been through small scale privatisation of shops, farms and workshops, as well as through de novo growth of the small industrial enterprise sector. Some argue that the growth of the new private sector is at least as significant for the emerging market systems of Eastern Europe as the pace of privatisation of the large state owned industrial giants.   In summary one can classify the ownership arrangements resulting from privatisation as follows; firms can be owned or outsider owned, where "ownership is defined as a controlling interest in the firm.   Among insider owned firms, we can distinguish between manager owned and worker owned firms, while for outsider owned firms, we can highlight some key categories, notably foreign owned firms and firms owned by Investment Funds.

Earle and Estrin used data on five countries to categorise firms by dominant owner along these lines.   They found that a majority of private firms were insider owned in Poland, Romania and Russia, as well as a majority of domestically owned private firms in Hungary.   Only in the Czech Republic, of this sample, had mass privatisation created outsider ownership and even here the effectiveness of governance arrangements have been widely questioned..   A particularly interesting case is Russia where 83% of privatised firms were majority owned by insiders in 1994.   Of these, workers had a majority stake in 78%.   Insiders' average holding of shares was around 66%, as against 20% for outsiders and 14% for the state.   This had not changed greatly by 1996.

CONCLUSIONS

Privatisation in Central and Eastern Europe has complex and contradictory motives.   The two main reasons have been to improve corporate efficiency and to "depoliticise" the enterprise sector through the rapid transfer of control from the state to private hands.   This pressure for speed, combined with a shortage of domestic savings and an immature capital market, has led the transitional economies to innovate in methods of privatisation.   Thus a variety of mass privatisation methods have been developed.   These have contributed to a rapid growth in the share of private sector output and employment throughout the region, though progress has been slower among large firms in the industrial sector.

For most countries, there has been a clear trade-off between the speed and short-term effectiveness of privatisation, in terms of improved corporate governance.   Sales of firms to outsiders have been rare, and as a consequence, revenues from privatisation have been almost everywhere very small as a share of the government budget.   Privatisation strategies have tended to rely on manager-employee buyouts, mass privatisation schemes or both, and have resulted in the predominance of insider ownership.   At the same time, while capital market institutions are developing rapidly in many countries, the emergence of structures that could reliably enforce effective corporate governance has been slow.

It is much too early for a balanced judgement of the impact of privatisation on company performance in Central and Eastern Europe. Initial studies have found little evidence that privatised firms behave very differently from their state-owned counterparts, though in the more advanced countries some more robust findings about the effects of privatisation are emerging. Key issues for the future will be whether outsiders begin to purchase shares from managers and workers, allowing evolution to a more conventional system of capital market scrutiny, and whether the new private sector, whether by internal growth or acquisition of former state owned firms will eventually displace the privatised sector.

REFERENCES

"Ownership Structures, Patterns of Control and Enterprise Behavior in Russia", in Commander, S., Fan, Q and Schaffer, M., (with J. Earle and L. Leschenko), Enterprise Restructuring and Economic Policy in Russia, EDI and World Bank, 1997.

"The Provision of Social Benefits in State-Owned, Privatized and Private Firms in Poland", in Social Protection and the Enterprise in Transitional Economies, Martin Rein, Barry Friedman and Andreas Worgoetter (eds.), Cambridge University Press, 1997.

"A Taxonomy of Mass Privatization", in I.W. Liberman, R.M. Desai and S.S. Nestor (eds), Between State and Market Mass Privatization in Transition Economies, Washington DC, World Bank 1997.

"Privatization in Central and Eastern Europe", in R. Layard, P. Boone and S. Gomulka, (eds), Reform in Central and Eastern Europe, Cambridge, Mass., MIT Press, 1998.

"Privatization", forthcoming entry in New Palgrave Dictionary of Economics and Law, 1998.

"Privatization in Russia: the Consequences for Ownership Structure", in B. Granville and P. Oppenheimer (eds), The Russian Economy in the 1990s, Oxford University Press, forthcoming, 1998.

"State Enterprise Restructuring in Bulgaria Romania and Albania: Cross Country Studies", (with X. Richet and M. Dimitrov) in M. Dimitrov (ed), State Enterprise Restructuring in Bulgaria, Romania and Albania, Sofia, Gorex Press, 1997.

"The Legacies of Central Planning and the Problems of the Transition to a Market Economy in Ukraine", (with P. Hare and M. Ishaq) in T. Kuzio (ed), Independent Ukraine: Nation and State Building, Political and Economic Transition, M.E. Sharpe, forthcoming.

"The Effects of Output, Ownership and Legal form on Employment and Wages: Central European firms Before and during Transition", (with S. Svejnar), S. Commander (ed), Enterprise Restructuring and Unemployment in Models of Transition, forthcoming, MIT Press, 1998.

"State Ownership, Corporate Governance and Privatization" in S. Nestor, Corporate Governance and Privatization, OECD, forthcoming 1998.

Chapter 3

Lessons from Czech Privatisation

Ingeborg Nemcova
University of Economics, Prague

Abstract: Abstract: On the general assumption that private ownership would lead to better overall economic performance, the privatisation process has been the key to Czech transformation, Three types of privatisation have been implemented. The first type, «restitution» has almost been completed, even if some unsolved cases still limit the freedom of owners. The second type, «minor privatisation» is fully completed. The third type, «major privatisation» is going on, based on standard methods such as public tenders, auctions and capital market sales. The politically highly successful «voucher privatisation» has definitely been completed with 6.5 million individual shareholders, who exert a very weak control over the privatised companies. The «third wave» of voucher privatisation - a process of concentration of ownership - occurred in an unsophisticated market and, under the current legislation, damaged this market. The next step for government action is to seek strong foreign strategic partners for companies; foreign direct investors, who will introduce capital and, in the anticipated case of bank privatisation, they will also bring the necessary professional and managerial skills.

1.   PRIVATISATION AS A KEY TO TRANSFORMATION

1.1   The Essence of Economic Reform

The Czech Republic, formerly part of Czechoslovakia before the partition, decided to transform the Centrally Planned Economy (CPE) into a market-oriented economy after the Velvet Revolution in 1989. The final decision was prepared, step by step, through discussion and was passed by parliament in September 1990 in the form of a "Scenario for Economic Reform". The reform itself started on January 1, 1991. The underlying consent on the part of society was based on the desire to make the economic development of the country more efficient, since the CPE had failed in this regard as the history of previous attempts at reform had proved. The expectation of high economic efficiency was closely connected to the aspirations for an increasing standard of living for all classes and social groups in society. The main objective of the reform could be described as a real market implementation accompanied by a substantial change in the role of government in the economy. The term «real market« is understood to be, as far as possible, a free, non-regulated market. The question of necessary regulation was either discussed minimally or not at all.

Market implementation consisted of turning the existing markets, such as consumer markets or agricultural markets into competitive ones whilst removing the central pricing and regulation system: «liberalisation of prices« and abolition of state monopolies in the foreign trade markets was the declared aim. Markets had to be created in the areas where the CPE had used a heavy redistribution system of capital investments. In financial markets both the money and capital markets are the best examples of this new approach.

This reform made extensive use of the influence of foreign markets, and the opening of the economy for foreign trade and foreign capital was encouraged by currency convertibility and fewer restrictive controls on the movement of funds.

All reform was designed with great attention to macro-economic equilibrium: emphasis was given to minimising inflation by monetary and fiscal policies and by ensuring that levels of unemployment were socially acceptable. To maintain equilibrium these two measures were seen as the main contributors to the success of reforms.

Privatisation became a substantial issue of reform only after a serious discussion of the alternatives. The main argument for privatisation was the assumption that only a real sovereign owner would have a long-term incentive for accepting total responsibility concerning the efficient performance of his or her property. Only this type of owner would be interested in restructuring the former state-owned enterprises. Expectations were inspired by the theory of ownership rights. Restructuring was understood only very generally as a potential for a long-term rise of efficiency in companies.

The main alternative to privatisation was seen as renting state-owned property to individuals. The main argument against this was a firm requirement for tenants properly to maintain the property within strict time limits.

Another important part of the discussion concerned the future owners: who would get the right to privatise the property but under what conditions? A rejection of the so-called "third way" led to the refusal of privatisation to employees, including a reluctance to provide special, more advantageous credits to these groups or to co-operatives and to management buy-outs. There were some interesting consequences of these attitudes; Procter & Gamble, which bought a large detergent producer, Rakona Rakovnik, in 1991, were an exception as a result of having an ESOP (Employee Share Ownership Plan).

1.2   Initial Conditions

As an important aspect of transformation and privatisation, the initial conditions in 1990 and in subsequent years must be taken in account:

- To give some idea of the scale of the problem caused by the very limited supply of capital available in the economy, savings were only about 300 billion Czechoslovak Korunas (KCS) and the total value of fixed assets was only 2,605 billion KCS in the Czech Republic (CR).[1]
- The desire by a large part of the population to start their own private businesses. Entrepreneurial activities had been more restricted in the CPE of Czechoslovakia than in any other country of the former Soviet block.
- The indebtedness of a large number of State Owned Enterprises (SOEs). This originated partly from their poor performance in domestic or foreign markets largely because the government only accepted a very limited share of the country's risk in connection with state ordered deliveries. This was partly a result of the previous governmental policy in the late eighties. During this time companies had been forced to use bank credits extensively for their operations provided that the banking system (SBCS) had been involved in the decision-making process. This enforced participation was supposed to be an important element to increase performance of companies.
- Managers had almost no experience in managing market orientated companies. The potential behaviour of management or the managerial culture of the former Czechoslovakia had not in fact been mapped. Later analyses showed that the independent decision-making ability of the younger managerial generation in particular was not as poor as was expected after 40 years of a CPE system. Relatively high adaptability was observed. The practice of the CPE

had created a special way for managers to influence the decision-making processes in their companies. This system extensively involved the professional state administration apparatus, which has partly retained its mid-ranking influence since the reform. (See Machonin, P., Maly, M.) The government had expected so-called "privatisation agony": to manifest itself in very poor performance by state-owned companies where a decision on privatisation had been made but the implementation process was too slow. Large economic losses were expected and the only way to avoid them was seen to be high speed and massive privatisation. The pressures for speed had priority over clarity of the processes. Even the Courts of Justice did not have the right to check individual cases of privatisation which were based on governmental decisions.

- Sponsors of the transformation process preferred the de-regulatory, and to some extent de-monopolising, effects of privatisation rather than concern about over state budget revenues or income effects in general. Revenues from privatisation went into the National Property Fund (PNF), which had been strictly separated from the state budget. Later on this attitude changed.
- The state and government refused verbally to make any decisions on the future structure of the economy on the one hand, and, on the other hand, the government selected the winners of public tenders.
- Respect for the law is relatively low. There are a number of reasons for this. For example: the questionable quality of newly produced legislation requiring frequent amendments, flooding the Courts of Justice with a growing number of cases, cutting the size of state expenditure, and the scant respect for the law paid by politicians.

2.   PRIVATISATION FORMS AND METHODS

Privatisation might be understood in general as the rise of a private sector in the economy. But this is understood to be the result of two different processes and their combination:

- a legal process of transferring a state property to individuals or private companies
- the establishment of new private enterprises.

This chapter is mainly focused on the first or "transfer approach". At the beginning, let us distinguish between the form and the method of privatisation. The form is related to a legal Act or a group of Acts on privatisation. The term 'method' refers to the technical aspects of implementation such as auctions.

According to the legislation, there were three forms of privatisation. (See the list of related Acts in Appendix)

- restitution
- minor, small-scale privatisation
- major, large-scale privatisation

Each form has played a different role in the process, with very different consequences for the economy.

2.1   Restitution

- Restitution is the return of a property to its former owner, a private individual who had owned it before the communists came into power. Although the former Czechoslovakia, and later on the Czech Republic, had the largest scheme for restitution among the post-communist countries, not everything was returned and not everybody received back his or her property. There were very strict controls or limits, which have remained unchanged to this day.

These were:

- Limits concerning the person as the former or new owner: only naturalised persons, i.e. Czechoslovakian citizens, with a permanent address in the country, could claim back their property.
- Restrictions concerning the property that had only to be in the form of fixed assets, land, buildings or equipment.
- Time limit: the property had to have been nationalised, that is lost by the former owner after the date of the communist coup: February 25, 1948.

These conditions excluded relatively large groups of former private owners. Generally, these groups and cases were legally and historically very complicated, and the final solution had to be found step by step. The limits concerning people excluded, for example, all Czech emigrants from the past 40 years who could not resume their Czechoslovak citizenship under the previous regime. This fact was complicated by the initial requirement for a permanent address. After a finding by the Constitutional Court of Justice, this residential requirement was abolished and a new round of Restitution began.

The naturalisation requirement excluded even legal residents, business companies churches and Non Governmental Organisations (NGOs). But there were a few Acts, which returned certain property to churches and NGOs; these were mostly monasteries, convents and Roman Catholic

Church administration buildings. Cathedrals and churches were never nationalised. Only St Vitus Cathedral at Prague Castle became a legal case in the mid-90s, illustrating the very complex relationship between the Roman Catholic Church and the State.

NGO Sokol is a traditional sports association founded in the last century. Its property was in local gymnasia in cities and villages around the country. The majority of these gymnastic halls were returned to Sokol. The property of a similarly traditional association for tourism, Cesky Svaz Turistu, which owned a network of cheap hotels and shelters, has not been returned as the property has been used for business purposes.

The Roman Catholic Church emphasised the importance of Justice in the restitution, and together with its political representation, the Christian Political Party KDU-CSL, has started long-term negotiations with the government about restitution of land which was a property asset of the Church. These negotiations called "restitution full-stop" are still in progress. It is also necessary to note that the concept of justice was very important but was not the main aim of the process.

The combination of time and citizenship excluded from restitution the former Sudeten Germans who had been forced to leave Czechoslovakia in 1945-47 after World War II. After the Common Declaration of the Czech and German Parliaments, the German government did not support their claims.

The limit concerning the form of property even excluded restitution of "family joint-stock companies" when a family had owned 100% of the shares.

Looking at the implementation of restitution and its results, we can see that this has been the main form of privatisation in the sectors of agriculture and housing. Many small and medium sized companies also went through this form. The total amount of property, officially declared, varied from seventy to one hundred and twenty billion KCS. The bulk of this amount concerned ownership of agricultural land and property. There is little evidence of restitution of other property. Besides the "classic" restitution, there were two other processes, which had similar features:

- Transfer of a municipal property
- Transformation of co-operatives.

Legally, cities, towns and villages had never lost their property such as land, buildings, utility networks and small businesses but the property had been managed by the state. This transfer confirmed the ownership rights of municipalities and gave them a more independent position economically in relation to central government. Since that time, municipalities have issued municipal bonds and have taken bank credits mostly to support their development plans, even the City of Prague has obtained credit on

Euromarkets in London. About three hundred and thirty billion KCZ in property was transferred to municipalities under this Act.[2]

In the case of co-operatives and co-operative farms it was necessary to identify the co-operative member's property. In the late 80s, the members of co-operative farms were in a position very similar to that of employees: their incomes reflecting only the amount of work they did for the co-operative, even though they had contributed different property into the co-operative farm when they joined it in the 50s. All the co-operative members were given an opportunity to withdraw from the co-operative farm together with their previous property and to start private, independent farming. Another possibility was to stay in the co-operative that had to be re-financed, reflecting new principles of income distribution as well as the property value. This transformation of co-operatives concerned property totalling two hundred and twenty billion KCZ.

The institutional aspect of this form of restitution was relatively complicated. Execution was based on an agreement between the applicant submitting a claim and the "mandatory person" who owned the property. Courts of Justice decided on complex cases. Restitution has priority over all other forms of privatisation. In 1998 restitution is almost completed, although "restitution full-stop" negotiations have still not been finished. Unfinished restitution has been an economic problem and any property with an unresolved restitution claim is "frozen», and the handling and use of such a property is all but blocked.

2.2   Small-Scale Privatisation

Small-scale privatisation was small in the amount of property: property was worth 21 billion KCS as measured in prices offered at auction, and a little over 31 billion KCS was gained.[3]

This form was also "small-scale" since it privatised small and medium sized enterprises usually in trade and services. But this form was of great political importance. Many people at the beginning of the 90s had the desire to start their own business. This form gave them a legal opportunity to get a business space. The new owner bought just the assets at auction rather than the debts as in Major Privatisations. It was quite often the case that a large apartment building with some business space was involved in two different forms of privatisation: the whole building was an object for restitution and a 2-year rental of business space was sold in a small-scale privatisation auction. Two years later the contract had to be renewed as a voluntary agreement by both sides, but with a new private owner.

The whole process was organised by the Ministry for Privatisation, which appointed members of special "Privatisation Commissions". These local commissions were organised and were fully responsible in their districts. Very soon small-scale privatisation answered the needs of the public, proving that the great concerns by the government about privatisation were right and also bringing about the first results in the development of services. The process was fully completed in 1992/1993.

2.3 Large-Scale Privatisation

The government has been deciding, step by step, about the privatisation of different groups of companies or different industries. This has always been more or less a political decision. Three main groups were observed. The first and the second groups also used the voucher method and the third just the standardised method.

The prevailing method of Czech privatisation has been on a large-scale or «major privatisation». The form has used a number of different methods such as auctions, public tenders, selling shares of state-owned companies in the capital market or through direct sales. The most well known method, voucher privatisation, is a sort of Czechoslovak invention. What has been common and mandatory for all the methods employed has been a preparatory period in which all the state-owned companies which were about to be privatised have had to prepare a Privatisation Project. The companies' proposals were sent to the National Property Fund. In case of land property for agriculture to the Land Property Fund (Pozemkový Fond). A Privatisation Project suggests the most suitable method of privatisation, including the reasons in its favour as well as the financial aspects. The opinion of the antitrust authority is also taken into account. This authority is called The Department for Market Competition Protection and is now responsible to Parliament. During the peak of privatisation activity, the Department was turned into a Ministry directly responsible to the government. De-monopolisation has not, however, been a very significant factor in the process.

The project proposal is accompanied by a long-term business plan for the company being privatised and is the main information to assist the government in making a decision about the fate of the company. Everyone who is interested, including a foreigner, has the right to prepare and submit a Privatisation Project on any company which is offered for privatisation. In such a case, this person has the right to procure all relevant data about the company from its management.

Everyone has been allowed to participate, but the management of companies has been obliged to prepare a Privatisation Project on the company for which they have been responsible. This has ensured that there has been a minimum of one Privatisation Project for each company. Such

Privatisation Projects have usually been successful, since the management has the best knowledge of the industry, the market and the particular company during the period 1991-95. On average, there were four Privatisation Projects prepared for every company, but in fact the high interest of potential new owners was concentrated on a limited group of companies. After the Privatisation Projects were submitted to the government the Ministry for Privatisation organised the "red-tape aspects," the circulation of the projects through all the responsible ministries- and also recommended decisions about the companies. The whole government made the final decision, which was not allowed to be controlled, or revised- even by the Courts of Justice. The Ministry for Privatisation was abolished in 1996 and the remaining part of its work and responsibilities were passed to the Ministry of Finance and to the National Property Fund. This fund was established at the beginning of privatisation and its main role was administrating, or controlling the management, of the newly privatised companies. State-owned assets with a book value of nine hundred and thirty five billion KCZ has already passed through the FNP. This is over 80% of all the privatised assets in the Czech Republic.[4] The Fund was responsible to Parliament and was also used as a supplemental financial source for very different purposes.

2.3.1   Voucher Privatisation

The voucher method was suggested and used for the first time in Czechoslovakia in 1991-1993, the so-called first wave. After the split of the country it was used again only in the Czech Republic in 1993-94, the second wave. Slovakia, instead, offered its citizens very advantageous treasury-bills. This method was also used in the Baltic States and in Russia.

Let us imagine a simulation of a market to explain the method. On the supply side, a set of state-owned companies is offered. They were converted into a form of joint-stock companies where 100% of the shares were in the hands of the state. In the first wave, about eight hundred and eighty four companies were offered for sale and the starting price of shares was about two hundred and thirteen billion KCS on the Czech side of the country only. The second wave offered another eight hundred and sixty one companies of one hundred and fifty five billion KCZ. The prices were book values of the companies' assets.[5]

There were participants and their special "currency" was investment points, on the demand side. Only citizens over 18 years of age had the right to participate. They could buy a special Voucher Book worth one thousand investment points. Only one book was allowed per participant. They paid a little more than one thousand KCS (KCZ) for registration. So, for the majority of computations there was equality with 1 KCS equalling 1 investment point. The price was carefully set, the average salary in 1991 was three thousand three hundred KCS per month. The price seemed to be high enough to act as an incentive for participants but low enough not to be devastating. The number of participants in the future Czech Republic was 5.95 million in the first wave and 6.17 million in the second, out of the total 10.5 million inhabitants. This was almost the entire adult population. The estimated gains were thirty five thousand KCS in property in the first wave and twenty five thousand KCZ in the second wave per Voucher Book.

From the very beginning the government was not surprised that there were only few people interested in the scheme. The government prepared only 4 million voucher books for the total Czechoslovak population of 15.5 million. Additional books had to be printed and this caused a delay. The government forecasts started from a percentage of the population active in capital markets in the USA or in the UK. This percentage was transferred to the domestic population and a reserve was added. The idea of a direct relationship with a future capital market was very strong. But a massive interest appeared when an explanation was provided to the public by Viktor Kozeny -the founder of one group of Investment Privatisation Funds (IPF)- during a massive advertising campaign in autumn 1991. His offer was clear:

"Buy your Voucher Book, at One Thousand KCS and pass on to our IPF the right to allocate your points. We will do the work for you and you will become a shareholder of our funds with the right to receive dividends. Or, if you prefer cash, we will buy your shares for ten thousand KCS within one year after the end of the wave." He kept his word.

The technique of Voucher Privatisation consisted of a few rounds where participants allocated their points to buy shares of the companies. A special commission set a price in investment points for each company and round, according to a strategy of selling the maximum number of shares. The commission set the prices according to the following principles:

- When supply (S) and demand (D) in the case of one company was equal, the shares were sold out in the round.
- When S was higher than D in the next round the price would be lower; when D was higher the price would go up.

The method was computerised and used the postal network for submitting the participant's share orders. The method was very successful in selling out the shares of companies. The ownership of companies was distributed into a framework that had not been anticipated by the government. The majority of the property was gained by the IPFs, which were founded as a private business. A total of four hundred IPFs got 66% of property in the first wave and three hundred and fifty three IPFs got 55% of the property in the second wave.[6]

Individuals received a smaller part of the shares of companies and became shareholders of the IPFs. The most successful IPFs were established as "daughters" of the banks. The system was believed to be protected in a very smart and simple way against misuse. The Lizner lawsuit of insider trading and misuse by the former director of the Centre for Voucher Privatisation and Securities had raised very serious doubts. He was caught carrying over eight million KCZ in a bag. The public has never learned if this was corruption or a provocation or a premium for matching business partners. The fact is that Lizner was found guilty for misusing his position.

2.3.2   Results

Results of the Voucher Privatisation for the companies were:
- relatively weak control from the side of owners since ownership was rather dispersed. The number of shareholders in the biggest companies was in the tens of thousands,
- although IPFs were limited in their shares, their pressure for obtaining dividends was usually high. A good example of this was the truck producer TATRA, which was controlled by a number of IPFs,
- the IPFs had to resolve the ubiquitous dilemma of whether to concentrate their operation on raising income for their shareholders and to be a classic mutual fund, or to let the companies invest in the development of long term business objectives. Moreover, the government has been legally cutting the space for IPFs in companies, forcing them to follow mutual fund practices under relatively strong regulation. In the succeeding period, some of the IPFs were changed into holding companies, where regulation is minimal and control is in the hands of shareholders.
- the companies did not receive any new financial resources for modernisation and restructuring. Moreover, many of them had large debts from the previous period. The majority of companies have continued to make great use of bank credits. This, together with the fact that the largest and most influential IPFs were daughters of banks, has created a very interesting frame of relationships. The companies are owned partly or fully by the IPFs, which were daughters of banks. Usually the "mother" bank provided the majority of the credits. This led to interesting situations. A specific feature arises from the structure of Czech banking: four large banks dominate the sector: Komercni Bank, Ceska Sporitelna, CSOB, and Investicni a Postovni Banka with the State, represented by the National Property Fund, holding a control package.

- lack of available capital led the government to a decision to look for a strong foreign investor and, for this purpose, additional equity was raised in some companies without the agreement of shareholders. But finding a foreign investor was very difficult, since potential investors were wary of shares sold in voucher privatisation.
- in the summer of 1993 the shares of all the companies entered both capital markets: the Prague Stock Exchange and the computerised RM-System. The RM-System partly inherited the hardware and software of voucher privatisation that enabled an individual to carry out transactions directly without using broker services.
- They started at the price of one investment point equalling one KCZ, but within a few months their prices dropped to the level of 30-60%. A relatively large number of titles were traded only occasionally.
- All the participants were provided with very limited information on privatised companies during voucher privatisation. This led to two possible approaches: to take the voucher privatisation as a sort of entertaining game or to obtain or buy additional information. Everybody understands today that there is a price on information on the one hand, on the other hand, insider trading has been seen as an inevitable activity. Only recently has the proper regulation of capital markets been introduced.

2.3.3   The Third Wave of Voucher Privatisation – Revision of Results

At the end of 1995 the success of voucher privatisation was visible. Unfortunately, it was more in the field of policy than in the economy. The priority of high speed over clarity of the process and generally low respect for law in society caused problems. There was also an orientation of a large part of society towards short-term material gains and advantages that have created special circumstances for a revision of the results coming from voucher privatisation. This happened in 1996-97 and the process is called the «third wave» of voucher privatisation. But there was no other set of SOEs for privatisation and the state was passive on this point.

There were over six million inhabitants who owned various sorts of securities - shares of companies or IPFs at the beginning. In the end, there were only 2.5 million. The process took place in institutionalised capital markets and more often out of them. Small investors were individually addressed with offers to be bought out of their stock. Prices differed as did the conditions. This method was known as "vacuuming". The small Plzenska

Banka, under the control of the financial group Motoinvest played the most famous part. They invested in a large advertising campaign, addressing every household in the Czech Republic. The purpose was to concentrate the ownership of certain promising titles and to take them over.

The Government saw this process of concentration as very natural and anticipated an influx of owners who would restructure the companies. The position of government was very liberal: "the chances at the beginning were equal, only the stronger and smarter can win". In setting proper or internationally acceptable conditions for this competition the course of "learning from our (painful) mistakes" has been chosen.

Interesting on this point is a following commentary: «While foreign investors understand ownership as a means to do business, the prevailing motivation of Czech entrepreneurs for acquiring and concentrating ownership has been to increase power. It should be emphasised that there is a danger in acquiring ownership illegally or unethically as this may discredit the very concept of private ownership.»[7]

Certain frustration is visible: the number of inhabitants with a negative evaluation of voucher privatisation and its consequences has been growing in the last few years. According to the polls 69% had this attitude in March 1998 but only 54% in 1996. [8]

Moreover, the government was afraid of, and officially refused to provide any special advantages to an industry or group of companies. Unfortunately, the next steps following a take-over were not always about restructuring. Another Czech invention, "tunnelling", followed in a number of cases. Tunnelling is a term for the activity of owners or management when the assets of a company, factory, IPF, bank or hotel have been «taken out through a tunnel« - stolen in other words - but for the rest of the economy the company might be viable for an even longer time. Kreditni Banka Plzen was a very good illustration of tunnelling. The main problem in tunnelling is to distinguish between managerial failure and an intentional failure motivated usually by indirect gains. The economic results were the same: the social and political ones were not the same. Whatever these consequences were the concentration of ownership has been reached: the number of shareholders of any stock is, today, less than one third of the number in 1995. The coming period will show what the intentions of the new real owners are and how successful they may be in restructuring the companies.

2.4   Other Methods of Major Privatisation

Major Privatisation has been using a number of methods. Let us have a look at them from one point of view: what are the chances of restructuring the companies? The financial conditions for restructuring may be divided into three possible situations:

- A small percentage of a property has been transferred free of charge: for example when health care facilities are transferred to municipalities without charge.

The second and the third situations have the same feature: selling of the property. In one case the new owner is a domestic person naturalised or legal; in the second, a foreigner. These cases usually differ as regards price and financial resources available for the purchase.

The domestic investor usually uses credit for the purchase. The most frequent credit resources are the banks or the National Property Fund. Although the price is lower, the privatised company has to ensure the paying off the credit together with previous debts. This might seriously limit the financial resources for modernisation.

Foreign buyers can buy company shares as a portfolio investment in a capital market where the FNP sells them, or directly from the government. The FNP will prepare all aspects of the transaction but the government is responsible for the final decision. The direct foreign investor is usually asked to pay a higher price, which is set by giving advice to companies concerning the usual methods of evaluating assets, cash-flow etc. The price is also higher because of an ERDI (over 2.0) of the KCZ.

In the majority of cases the foreign buyer is also asked to invest in the company and insure these investments in some way. This does not necessarily mean that the company is not forced to generate money to repay the investment, but that the " insurance of investment" secures the chance for modernising and restructuring the company. There are a number of good examples such as Skoda Mlada Boleslav - Volkswagen (1991) or SPT Telecom - Telsource (1995).

A specific period for privatisation by foreign investors started approximately in the middle of 1996. At that time a decision was made about the privatisation of the first of the banks from among the "Big Four" - the Investicni a Postovni Banka IPB. In the event, the new owner of the control package is Nomura, but the government gained new experience resulting from its active role in the Czech management during the negotiation process. This forced the government to accept an even lower price and give up some revenues. On the other hand, the government again emphasised the priority for restructuring rather than budgetary considerations.

The "control" structure of the relationship between a company and a "bank family" in conjunction with the law on bankruptcy caused a situation where large insolvent companies were able to survive and the national interest in their bankruptcy was slight. The bankruptcy was not seen as a goal but as an instrument to release all resources blocked by an inefficient company. The remedy was seen as amending the legislation on bankruptcy and in the banks' change of approach. One problem is seen in the close relationship between banks and the IPFs in their families. Another problem is the behaviour of banks and one solution appears to rest in the suggestion that they should also be privatised.

The financial situation of the banks is a third problem. The problems of the economy have concentrated to some extent on the credit portfolio of the banks. After an audit in the middle of the 90s, the government started extensive activity in buying out dubious credits. This opened the door for the "Big Four" banks to get an international rating and to think about privatising with the assistance of a direct foreign investor. It was estimated that there was insufficient domestic capital in the Czech Republic and that a direct foreign investor would bring additional resources and specialist banking skills. But the privatisation of a bank is not a simple matter of privatisation since it has a significant impact upon the national financial ethos. The "Big Four" still control the majority of the economy.

Not only bank privatisation brought new experiences. There were other cases with similar results but slightly different reasons. Another example came from the mining industry where the state position was weakened because municipalities sold their shares to a private company in order to balance their budgets.

3.　　PRESENT DILEMMAS AND PERSPECTIVES

3.1　　Privatisation and Restructuring

Privatisation has comprehensively affected all aspects of Czech society and the economy:

- Politically: a promise of voucher privatisation proved to be a better pre-election promise than a tax reduction.
- Socially: social and income differentiation in society accelerated.
- Educationally: voucher privatisation was in fact a sort of capital market simulation. Was it really a learning by doing process? To some extent the answer is yes; insider trading is a good illustration.
- Ethical and credibility aspects emphasise the above effects.
- Relationship of economy and ecology has been opened in a very new way with the problem of responsibility for consequences of the ecological damage in the past.
- The State budgetary system both in terms of income and expenditure has been strongly affected by privatisation.

- Monetary consequences proved to be important, although voucher privatisation used the "artificial currency".
- Restructuring and economic growth had been expected. The economic growth with the exception of years 1994 and 1995 was very low. Although other reasons for that have to be recognised, expected results have not been observed.
- Efficiency of performance of the companies. The Czech Republic has been criticised that the transformation has not been yet carried out at the macro-economic level. This is connected to relatively weak budget constraints for both the banks and companies. It is also linked to company corporate governance.

3.2   Privatisation and Corporate Governance

Some authors suggest that a special Czech type of corporate governance has been formed.[9] But the question is about the precise character of this corporate governance style. A historical classification of different varieties of corporate governance offers three types:
- Anglo-American type using the capital market.
- German-Japanese, where a bank develops long term links with a relatively diversified group of businesses.
- Italian type, where the companies are governed by holdings, which might be used to exercise political interests.

The situation in the Czech Republic shows that the German-Japanese type might be quite widespread. The question remains about the consequences that may be expected from the reorganisation of the big banks. The Italian type could be seen in cases where former IPFs were changed into holding companies. How far this type could be connected with policy interests is questionable. The Anglo-American type was expected to be formed to some extent during voucher privatisation. The method partly failed in this area. The Czech capital market is not a place where a company will go to raise financial funds for development. But it is a market for purchasing power. Analyses showed the main transactions were carried out in dubious circumstances in the "third wave" of voucher privatisation.

Then we could consider the validity of the Czech approach in the context of a gradual movement towards a globalised economy? Since the very beginning of the transformation, the Czech Republic has been comparatively open to international economic relations, including privatisation using foreign investors. The second stage has begun: improving the business environment and especially the capital markets. It is evident that the Czech Republic cannot expect any higher growth unless significant foreign capital resources are forthcoming in a larger way. Therefore the business environment devotes its energies to attracting foreign investors and hopefully, the recent institutional changes will bring rapid improvements.

NOTES:

1 Statisticka rocenka CSFR 1990 (Statistical Yearbook), FSU Praha 1991, p.183, 193
2 The NPF data published in *Hospodarske noviny*, No 16, 23.1.199[1] 5, pp. 1-2; The KCS referred to currency in Czechoslovakia till 1992; for data starting in 1993, the KCZ is used.
3 The NPF data published in *Hospodarske noviny*, No 16, 23.1.1995, pp. 1-2
4 The NPF data published in *Hospodáøské* noviny, 1998, No 87 , 6.5.1998; The statistic data on privatisation differs very significantly because of different pricing.
5 Voucher Privatization in Facts and Figures, Centre for Voucher Privatization, Praha 1995, pp. 26-27
6 Voucher Privatization in Facts and Figures, Centre for Voucher Privatization, Praha 1995, pp. 26-27
7 Bohata, M.: Some Implications OF Voucher Privatisation for Corporate Governance, *Prague Economic Papers*, Vol. VII, 1998, No. 1,p.63
8 Sofres-factum data published in *Hospodarske noviny*, 1998, No 87, 6.5.1998, p. 4
9 For example: Bohata, M.: Some Implications OF Voucher Privatisation for Corporate Governance, *Prague Economic Papers*, Vol. VII, 1998, No. 1, pp. 59-66
10 Overview of Effective Legal Regulations, *The Czech Business and Trade* Vol. 1996, No 4, p.25

REFERENCES

Bohata, M.: Some Implications OF Voucher Privatisation for Corporate Governance, Prague Economic Papers, Vol. VII, 1998, No. 1, pp. 59-66
Egerer, R.: The influence of Privatisation Strategies and Corporate Governance Options on Development of Capital Markets in Central and Eastern Europe, Dissertation No 1806, Universitat St Gallen, Difo-Druck GmbH , Bamberg 1996
Estrin, S.: Privatization in Central and Eastern Europe, Longman, London-New York, 1994
Glatzova, Vl.: Co zajima zahranicni investory, Profit Vol.3, 1992, No 42, Appendix Radce
Hanke, S.H.: Privatization and Development, ICS Press, San Francisco, 1987
Hart, O.: Corporate Governance: Some Theory and Implications, The Economic Journal, Royal Economic Society, Vol. 105, May 1995, pp. 669-675
Havel, J.: Changes in Governance Structure od the Czech Enterprises: 1989-95, Prague Economic Papers, Vol V.,1996 No2, pp. 127-135
Havel, J.: Chování subjektù v transformaci, Studie 7/1997, Národohospodáøský ústav Josefa Hlávky, Praha 1997
Fogel, D.S. (edit.): Management in Emerging Markets, The Czechoslovak Case, Westview Press, Boulder, San Francisco, Oxford 1994
Frydman, R., Earle, J.S., Rapaczynski, A.: Small Privatization: the Transformation of Retail Trade and Consumer Services in the CR, Hungary and Poland, CEU Press, Budapest 1994
Frydman, R., Rapaczynski, A.: Privatization in Eastern Europe: is the state withering away?, CEU Press, Budapest 1994

Frydman, R., Gray, C.W., Rapaczynski, A.: Corporate Governance in Central Europe and Russia,I,II, CEU Press, Budapest 1996

Kasan, J. (ed.): Ceska ekonomika v 90. Letech (The Czech Economy in the 90s), FNH VSE Praha 1993, 1994, 1995

Kotrba, J.: Privatization and Restructuring - Friends or enemies?, WPS, Vol. 103, CERGE-EI Praha 1996

Lastovicka, R.: Privatization and Opening the Capital Markets in the Czech and Slovak Republics, WPS Vol. 54, CERGE-EI, Praha 1994

Machonin, P.: Social Transformation and Modernization, SLON Praha 1997

Matesova, J., Seda, R.: Financial Market in the CR as a means of Corporate Governance in Voucher Privatized Companies, WP 62? CERGE-EI, Praha 1994

Mejstrik, M.(ed.)« The Privatization Process in East-Central Europe, Evolutionary Process of Czech Privatizations, Kluwer Academic Publishers, Dordrecht-Boston-London, 1997

Mertlik, P.: Czech Privatization: From Public Ownership to Public Ownership in Five Years?, Prague Economic Papers, Vol.IV., 1995, No 4, pp. 321-337

Mlèoch, L.: Czech Privatization - penalties for the Speed (a criticism of the radical liberalism), Prague Economic Papers, Vol. VI. 1997, No 1, pp. 3-13

Mlèoch, L.: Privatizace jako problém institucionálního evolucionizmu, Finance a úvìr, Vol 45, 1995, No 4, pp.198-207

Molin, J.: Essays on Corporate Finance and Governance, Stockholm School of Economics, Stockholm 1996

Spevacek, V. (ed.): Ceska ekonomika v 90. Letech (The Czech Economy in the 90s), FNH VSE Praha 1996, 1997

Voucher privatization in Facts and Figures, Centre for Voucher Privatization, Praha 1995

Zemplinerova, A., Charap, J.: Restructuring in the Czech Economy, WP No 2, European Bank for Reconstruction and Development, London 1993.

APPENDIX - MAIN RELATED LEGISLATION

- Act No 427/1990 Coll. on transfer of state ownership of certain entities to other legal or natural persons (Small-Scale Privatisation Act) in amended version (10)
- Act of the Czech National Council No 500/1990 Coll. on the competency of bodies of the Czech Republic concerning transfers of state ownership of certain entities to other legal entities or physical persons, in amended versions
- Decree No 535/1990 Coll. on public auctions in the transfers of the state ownership of certain entities or natural persons and on the price of admission to the auctions
- Act No 92/1991 Coll. on conditions of the transfer of state-owned property to other persons (Large-Scale Privatisation Act) in amended versions
- Decree 98/1994 Coll. implementing the Act No 92/1991 Coll.
- Act of the Czech National Council No 171/1991 Coll. on the competency of bodies of the CR concerning the transfer of the state property to the other persons and also the National Property Fund of the CR, in amended versions
- Decree No 324/1991 Coll. specifying a binding structure for the preparation of a privatisation project in the version of Decree No 526/1991 Coll.
- Act No 248/1992 Coll. on investment companies and investment funds in amended versions
- Regulation of the Government No 222/1993 Coll. on the issue and application of investment vouchers
- Act No 403/1990 Coll. on mitigating the consequences of some property injuries (Restitution Act)
- Act No 87/1991 SB. on extra-judicial rehabilitations
- Act No 229/1991 Coll. on the arrangement of ownership relations to land and other agricultural property (full version Act No 195/1994 Coll. in the version of Constitutional Court Ruling No 131/1994 Coll.)
- Act of the Czech National Council No 243/1992 Coll. that governs some questions related to Act No 229/1991 Coll.
- Act of the Czech National Council No 221/1993 Coll. on land modifications and land offices
- Regulation of the Government of the CR No 504/1992 Coll. on the amount of cash indemnity granted according to Act No 229/1991 Coll.
- Regulation of the Government No 239/1993 Coll. specifying the methods of the announcement and execution of an auction of agricultural property.

Chapter 4

Development of Financial Markets: the Czech Case

Petr Musílek
University of Economics, Prague

Abstract: Many foreign investors have found the Czech Republic to be a strategically attractive investment location in Eastern Europe. However, investment activities in this country are associated with many hurdles and risks. Forty years of a planned economy have left their mark on financial life in general. Foreign investment companies do not always plan their investments sufficiently and thus make many mistakes when carrying them out. In this chapter we will outline the basic conditions for investment in the Czech Republic. It is intended to answer some of the broad and most important questions regarding portfolio investment opportunities in the Czech Republic.

1.   THE FINANCIAL MARKET REVIVAL

The financial markets in the Czech Republic are in the process of being re-established, having been in abeyance from the closure of the Stock Exchange in 1938 until the Velvet Revolution of 1989. The preconditions for its return have been created step by step since 1990, with the year 1993 being considered a milestone, a kind of Czech "big bang". In that year, a standard environment was created for the financial markets and they have now begun to function in a conventional manner.

This standard environment has come about through three circumstances, all of which are the fruits of private sector activities and of government initiatives in the period 1990-1993. Firstly, starting in 1993, legislation creating and regulating the scope of the financial markets was enacted, establishing the legal framework. Secondly, in 1993, two organised public markets came into being: the Prague Stock Exchange and the over-the-counter market called the RM-System. Finally, the most important factor was the entry in to the financial markets of products originating from the rapid and mass privatisation of state assets.

Many different methods of privatisation have been used in recent years by various countries, including public auction, direct sale, public tender or a combination thereof. The Czech Republic has enriched international experience with the phenomenon of voucher privatisation. Through this method, each adult citizen of the Czech Republic was given the opportunity, for a fee of CZK 1,000, to twice enter the process of a mass redistribution of the state-owned assets among small shareholders and thus acquire shares of companies being privatised directly or through newly established investment funds [1]

The first wave of the voucher privatisation ended in May 1993 and almost 1,000 joint stock companies were denationalised through this method which involved assets exceeding, in nominal value, CZK 200 billion (6.9 bil. US$). Seventy percent by value was acquired by investment privatisation funds through the voucher system. The remaining 30 percent were posted to holding accounts maintained by the Securities Centre for retail shareholders. More than 50 percent of the Czech economy was privatised in this wave.

The second wave of voucher privatisation took place in 1994-1995 and included more than 800 enterprises. Shares were again made available to Czech citizens and a majority took full advantage of their rights such that, after this wave, there were approximately 6 million shareholders in the Czech Republic holding securities of 1,700 privatised companies and investment funds.

The Czech voucher privatisation, an experiment hitherto unknown in the history of the world economy, ended in March 1995. Investment funds obtained approximately two thirds of the total shares privatised. Small investors received the remainder in return for voucher points. Until March 1993 the capital market consisted only of relatively small transactions in eight bonds traded on the preliminary "secondary market" which was organised by the Central Bank. Trading took place every fortnight starting in June 1991. This "preliminary" market ceased to exist in April 1993 when trading began on the Prague Stock Exchange.

In the period 1991-1993, basic changes in legal regulations were enacted which and broadened the scope of the financial markets. This was a period of permanent legislative change for markets and investors. In 1993 the situation could, however, be considered as having stabilised in the sense that all the major acts of investor legislation concerning investors had entered into force and any future changes will be in the form of corrections and amendments rather than of substantive change.

Czech financial market activities are directly regulated or influenced by the following Acts and legal regulations: Commercial Code[2], Securities Act[3], Stock Exchange Act[4] and Investment Fund Act[5].

Fundamental to the supervision of the capital markets was a division of the Ministry of Finance, which exercised the role of "the securities commission". It was responsible for dealing with the authorisation of Exchanges through the Commissioner for Stock Exchanges, Securities Dealers and Investment Funds and for setting appropriate listing and continuing reporting obligations for securities. In 1996-1997 amendments to the Securities Act, the Commercial Code and the Investment Funds Act were approved. The following year a new independent regulatory body - the Securities Commission – was created.

Foreign investments are protected in the Czech Republic not only by national law but also by bilateral agreements on the promotion and reciprocal protection of investments. Such agreements have been concluded with Finland, Austria, Sweden, Switzerland, France, Belgium, Luxembourg, Denmark, Germany, Canada, the Netherlands, Spain, Norway, Great Britain, China, Greece and the USA. The Czech Republic is also bound by the Convention on the Settlement of Investment Disputes between States and the Nationals of Other States.

International agreements on the limitation of double taxation also exist. Agreements have been signed with many countries including the Netherlands, France, Finland, Japan, Sri Lanka, Norway, Cyprus, Sweden, Spain, Denmark, Germany, Italy, Algeria, Belgium, India, China, Greece, Brazil, Nigeria, Tunisia, the United Kingdom, Luxembourg.

Czech law makes it possible for foreign entrepreneurs, both natural and legal persons, to carry out business activities under the same conditions as Czech entrepreneurs. Czech foreign exchange regulations and, agreements on investment promotion and protection guarantee repatriation of profits and capital. Upon request Czech banks are obliged to pay to a foreign investor the foreign currency equivalent of his return on invested capital in Czech currency. Return on invested capital is understood to include profits, interest, capital gains, return on securities and royalties derived from intellectual property. The Czech securities market is generally open to foreign investment.[6] The only restriction applies to: the first primary issue of government bonds, which was restricted from foreign investment; bank stocks, which require the prior approval of the Czech National Bank; and shares of industries of national importance such as defence which are prohibited to foreign investment.

2.   PUBLIC MARKETS

The Securities Commission regulates the organisation of the securities market, as well as of the activities of brokers. Brokers require a licence and must be physical persons performing a professional activity. At present, there are two organised markets: the Prague Stock Exchange and the over-the-counter market called RM-S.

2.1   The Prague Stock Exchange

2.1.1   History and Organisation of the Prague Stock Exchange (PSE)

The seeds of the first exchange in Prague were sown in the 1850's when mainly foreign exchange was traded. The exchange for securities and commodities trading was established in 1871 upon authorisation from the Austrian Ministry of Finance and Commerce. It was, however, closed during World War I and reopened only on February 3, 1919. The volume traded there fluctuated considerably until 1938 when trading was again suspended. After World War II the operations of the Prague Exchange were not restored and in 1952 the Exchange was officially abolished.

In 1990, after a hiatus of 50 years, the State Bank of Czechoslovakia put into effect an initiative aimed at reviving the Prague Stock Exchange as an inevitable step in the process of transformation to a market economy. Eight banks became members of the Preparatory Committee on Stock Exchange Foundation. In 1992 this institution transformed itself into a Stock Exchange. On 24 November 1992 a joint-stock company - Stock Exchange Prague a.s. - was registered in the Companies register. Prior to registration appropriate authorisation by the Ministry of Finance of the Czech Republic had been granted for conducting stock exchange operations. Twelve Czech and Slovak financial institutions and five brokerage companies became its founders and shareholders. In an unusually short period of time all preparatory work was completed, and the first trading session was held on its floor on April 6, 1993.

The organisational structure of the Exchange is formed by the Exchange and other related institutions. The Exchange itself is composed of three major bodies (table 1) and specialised committees.

Table 1.The Prague Stock Exchange organisation

<table>
<tr><td>

General Meeting of Shareholders:
1. electing and calling members of the Exchange Chamber and of its Supervisory Board and determining their remuneration and fees for their activities;
2. approving the exchange rules and regulation and any changes therein;
3. approving rules and procedures at the Court of Arbitration of the Exchange and the changes therein, including fee rates relating to the actions taken in the Court;
4. approving types of exchange fees and the guidelines for their determination.

</td></tr>
<tr><td>

Supervisory Board:
Composed of 6 members, it exercises control over the Prague Stock Exchange's activities and ensures that they are conducted in full compliance with the legal regulations, statutes and instructions issued by the General Meeting.

</td></tr>
<tr><td>

Stock Exchange Chamber :
statutory body directing the operation and acting on behalf of the Chamber.

</td></tr>
<tr><td>

Stock exchange committees:
1. Stock Exchange Committee on Membership,
2. Stock Exchange Committee on Listing of Securities,
3. Stock Exchange Committee on Dealing,
4. Stock Exchange Committee for the Preparation of Trading in Financial Derivatives (Financial Futures and Options).

</td></tr>
</table>

A similar position to that of the Stock Exchange is that of the Arbitration Court. To cover the liabilities of the Exchange and risks from Stock Exchange trades, members of the Stock Exchange pooled their resources to create the Guarantee Fund of the Stock Exchange. Furthermore, the Prague Stock Exchange created a subsidiary called UNIVYC for the settlement of Stock Exchange trades.

2.1.2   The Stock Exchange Membership

Membership of the Prague Stock Exchange is restricted to legal persons whose names are entered in the Commercial Register and who are authorised to trade in securities according to specific legal provisions (Securities Act or Banking Act) and who are shareholders of the Prague Stock Exchange, or persons (entities) who have obtained from the Exchange Chamber authorisation to trade in securities on the Prague Stock Exchange upon payment of the admission fee.

The Czech National Bank is also a member of the Exchange. Membership authorises members to buy and sell securities on the Prague Stock Exchange. Members always act in their own names. At the time of its inception, on November 24, 1992, the Prague Stock Exchange had 17 founding members. Its membership increased to 62 in 1993. It rose to 71 during the next 12 months, and the Prague Stock Exchange had 101 members at the end of 1995, of which 33 were banks and 68 brokers. The membership base further expanded moderately in 1996. The Exchange had 88 members in 1997.[7]

2.1.3   Listing Securities on the Exchange

At the beginning of 1995, securities were traded in two markets at the Prague Stock Exchange, namely the Listed Market and the Unlisted Market. The Listed Market traded those securities accepted by set rules. Issuers would file their applications for admission of their securities to the Listed Market with the Stock Exchange Listing Committee. The Unlisted Market traded only securities registered for trading on the basis of the application submitted by either the issuer or an Exchange member. The applications were subject to the decision of the General Secretary of the Exchange. Almost all the stocks from the process of voucher privatisation, with the exception of those few that were traded in the Listed Market, were traded on the Unlisted Market.

Effective September 1, 1995, the Prague Stock Exchange introduced new categories of markets after receiving a mandate to impose stricter rules. The market was gradually divided into three markets: Main, Parallel and Free.

The Main and Parallel markets are two segments of the former Listed Market. Inclusion of securities in these categories depends on the decisions of the Stock Exchange Securities Listing Committee which carefully weighs the overall financial condition of an issuer and rigorously assesses the quality of its securities. Issuers have an obligation to inform the Exchange of their business, financial results and its current financial position. For the Main Market, this obligation is to be met on a quarterly basis and for the Parallel Market semi-annually.

Securities which either have not met the requirements for admission to the two aforementioned markets trade in the Free Market, as do those whose issuers have not shown enough readiness to disclose information to the investment community. By this segmentation, the Exchange is logically highlighting and giving preference to securities which represent the majority of trading on the Exchange.

Of the over 1,700 stocks admitted to the Prague Stock Exchange after the completion of voucher privatisation, most no longer qualified for trading on the Exchange. In an effort to standardise trading and improve transparency on the Exchange 1,300 illiquid stocks were excluded from Free Market between December 1996 and September 1997.

2.1.4 Trading System on the Prague Stock Exchange

The Prague Stock Exchange uses an order-driven system based on centralisation and matching of bids and offers for securities at a specific moment in time. Thanks to its systems, the Prague Exchange has joined the group of computerised exchanges. Communication of member firms with the Exchange is provided through a direct terminal connection from the broker's office. Trading is based on electronic processing of orders. Five types of trading transactions are carried out on the Prague Stock Exchange (Table 2.).

Only prompt deals are concluded on the Prague Stock Exchange. Trading in financial derivatives (financial futures and options) will be launched in the second half of 1998.

Clearing and Settlement conform to G-30 recommendations with regards to delivery for payment and to settlement on a T+3 basis, i.e. payment for securities bought is against delivery the third day after the trade is concluded on the Prague Stock Exchange.

Settlement is carried out through the Clearing Centre of the Czech National Bank for the accounts of the Prague Stock Exchange members upon instructions from UNIVYC, the subsidiary of the Prague Stock Exchange responsible for the settlement of securities transactions, the maintenance of holding accounts for members, and record keeping of securities traded on the Exchange. At the same time as money settlement is taking place the transfer of securities is carried out at UNIVYC. Based on the instructions from UNIVYC, the Securities Center[8] transfers the securities to their new holder. Exchange members have established a mutual guarantee fund in case of any defaults. The Stock Exchange Guarantee Fund gives members of the Prague Stock Exchange the assurance that the liabilities resulting from exchange transactions will be met.

Basic statistics on stock exchange markets and their indicators are provided in Tables 3, 4 and 5.

Table 2 Transactions at the Prague Stock Exchange

Automated trading at a fixed price
This type of trade is based on electronic processing of orders for a purchase or sale of securities up to a set moment in time. The principle of time priority is not applied. Prices may vary from the preceding trade by 3 or 5 % depending on the trading group which the stock has been classified into.

Continuous trading at a fixed price
This type of trading is a direct follow up to trading at a fixed price. The purpose of entering additional orders in the trading system is to offset imbalances occurring at the time when the price is determined in the course of trading at a fixed price. Additional orders are satisfied according to time priority.

Continuous trading at a variable price
Under this trading method, trades are concluded on the basis of a continuous input of orders for both purchase and sale of stocks. Depending on the immediate status of supply of and demand for stocks, prices are set continuously, while the price priority and subsequently time priority principles are applied. The price fixed under automated trading at a fixed price represents the opening price for continuous trading. Continuous trading at a variable price started on March 15, 1996 in 5 stocks possessing the highest liquidity and 2 bond issues from the Main Market. At May 5, 1998 17 issues of shares were traded under this method.

Direct trades in blocks of securities
A direct trade is one concluded between two member firms of the Prague Stock Exchange and recorded within the trading system of the Exchange at an agreed price which is not related to that under fixed price or variable price trading. There is no limit to the volume of securities traded under this method. Direct trades can be settled from T+1 to T+15 and no guarantees of the Exchange Guarantee Fund apply to them.

Automated trades in blocks of securities
A block means one large order for a given security. The minimum value for a block has been set at CZK 500,000. Unlike direct trades, block trades are concluded anonymously on a time priority basis. As in the case of direct trades the price is not tied to any other trading price nor is it defined by a spread. Orders may be open and a minimum size may be specified.

2.2   RM-System

In many respects, the RM-System is a continuation of the voucher privatisation process. The network of computers and registration sites used in the first (and second) wave were taken over by the RM-S and turned into trading locations. The RM-S made its debut on May 24, 1993. The organiser of this market is the stock-holding company RM-System, in which PVT Ltd. and Investment and Postal Bank have decisive stakes. Trading on the RM-S is organised around 350 trading sites and orders are accepted from anyone fulfilling the very unrestrictive conditions of the "RM-S market order".

The key difference between the RM-S and the Prague Stock Exchange is that any physical or legal person who meets trading rules is permitted to trade on the RM-System, whereas only licensed traders and brokers have access to the Prague Stock Exchange. In the RM-S, securities may be bought or sold under various trade regimes. The customer may enter anonymous trading in the framework of a periodical auction (until 1995) or a current auction that enables more or less continuous trading.

Prior to an auction, the RM-S validates a sell order, blocking the shares in the owner's account with the Securities Centre while a buy order is validated by the buyer depositing sufficient cash in a special cash account at the Investment and Postal Bank. Deals concluded on the RM-S are settled at the Securities Centre and the Investment and Postal Bank. Most securities are traded in a dematerialised form and are booked.

The complete registration of issues is kept at the Securities Centre, which is a non-profit organisation directed by the Ministry of Finance. The RM-S was constructed on the premise that the Czech capital markets would likely require a system that went beyond a standard network of broker/dealers with access the market. Thus the RM-System was instrumental in playing a decisive role at the end of the first and second waves of voucher privatisation. During the four years of its existence, a significant change has occurred in the composition of the RM-S clients. A significant portion of retail clients still use the RM-S as a one-off platform via which they can sell shares acquired in voucher privatisation. However, a sizeable group of clients has emerged who give preference to the RM-S rather than going through a broker. This broadening of the client base has resulted in growth in the volume of trading. Whilst in 1993, when the market opened, volume was less than CZK 3 billion, in 1997 it exceeded CZK 100 billion.

Table 3. Basic data on the Prague Stock Exchange

	1993	1994	1995	1996	1997
Number of Members	62	71	101	106	88
Number of Issues	982	1,055	1,764	1,750	412
Total Trade Value (CZK billion)	9.0	62.0	195.4	393.2	697.5
Average Daily Trade Value (CZK billion)	0.220	0.385	0.835	1.579	2.718
Market Capitalisation - Stocks (CZK billion)	-	50.0	87.8	136.9	174.0
Number of Trading Sessions	41	161	234	249	250
Index PX-50	705.2	557.2	425.9	539.6	495.3

Source: The Prague Stock Exchange, February 1998, p.2

Table 4. Issues of shares with the highest total trade value

Ranking	Issuer	Value (CZK million)
1.	SPT Telecom	52,405.426
2.	Komercni Banka	40,570.956
3.	CEZ	32,877.001
4.	Vertex	7,143.220
5.	Skoda Plzn	6,554.105

Source: Fact Book 1997. The Prague Stock Exchange, 1998 , p.43.

Table 5: Companies with the highest market capitalisation at Dec.31, 1997

Ranking	Issuer	Market Capitalisation (CZK million)
1.	SPT Telecom	86,996.5
2.	CEZ	58,714.9
3.	Komercni banka	24,801.4
4.	Unipetrol	18,039.2
5.	Tabák	15,118.2

Source: Fact Book 1997, The Prague Stock Exchange, 1998, p.48

3.   CZECH STOCK PRICE BEHAVIOUR

Prices of stocks exhibited similar trends in both markets in 1993. After the opening of the markets in late spring/early summer a sharp drop was recorded. In September and October there was a sharp increase in a large group of shares after which prices gradually stabilised.

The Exchange's PX-50 index is the aggregate indicator which best reflects trends in the capital markets. It is based on the market capitalisation of the fifty most important issues traded on the automated trading system of the Prague Stock Exchange.

The sharp price rise at the beginning of the year 1994 continued to a lesser extent in February. The Prague Stock Exchange reached a March peak of 1,244.7, followed by a gradual three-month fall. At the beginning of June prices rose and then marked time during the summer months. A downward trend began in September, the market sank and the PX-50 Index closed the year down 26 %. The downward trend continued in 1995. After racing to an all-time high of 1,244.7 (March 1, 1994) the PX-50 Index turned south, closing on June 19, 1995 at 387.2. Many factors caused the "Crash" of the Czech Stock Market, including:

- The sell-off in emerging markets such as Mexico and Poland;
- overvaluation of stocks on the Prague Stock Exchange;
- the destabilising behaviour of hedge funds;
- the adverse impact of ongoing recapitalisation of major Czech
- banks;
- the impact of the second wave of voucher privatisation on   first-wave equities.

In 1996 the PX-50 rose 26.7 % to close at 539.6. Its low of 437.9 was recorded on the first trading session of the year on January 8, while the high of 582.0 points was reached on September 5. Although trading volume rose in 1997 the index fell over 8% to close at 495.3. The movement of stock prices is not only affected by changes in financial variables (profit, dividends, interest rates, money supply, inflation, exchange rates etc.), but also by psychological, legislative, technological, and other circumstances. However, the sensitivity of Czech stocks to changes in macroeconomic indicators is minimal. Over the period studied (30.9.1993 - 29.8.1997), the Czech stock market showed little correlation to the developed world's stock markets (see table 6).

The inter-dependence of individual national markets increases significantly during periods of world financial uncertainty. For example, the "Hong-Kong flu" (20.10 - 30.10.1997) infected nearly all world stock markets, including the Czech market. Our research shows that price movements on markets in the same time zones were particularly inter-related (see table 7).

Table 6. Correlation Matrix Stock Markets (30.9.1993-29.8. 1997)

	PX-50	DJIA	DAX	FTSE	CAC	Nikkei
PX-50	1	-0,29875	-0,12523	-0,20085	0,143754	0,247811
DJIA	-0,29875	1	0,93314	0,97847	0,746773	0,209906
DAX	-0,12523	0,93314	1	0,945793	0,898563	0,203441
FTSE	-0,20085	0,97847	0,945793	1	0,807563	0,192267
CAC	0,143754	0,746773	0,898563	0,807563	1	0,201509
Nikkei	0,247811	0,209906	0,203441	0,192267	0,201509	1

Source: Musílek, P.: Stock Price Behaviour. Dissertation Thesis, The University of Economics, Prague, 1997, p.82.

Table 7. Correlation Matrix Stock Markets: "Hong-Kong Flu"   (15.10. 1997-3.11.1997)

DJIA	DJIA	S+P	TSE	Nikk	HSI	FTS	DAX	CAC	ATX	SWI	PX	BUX	WIG	RTS
DJIA	1	0,934	0,972	0,695	0,718	0,873	0,821	0,869	0,802	0,854	0,751	0,633	0,801	0,774
S+P	0,934	1	0,915	0,508	0,521	0,700	0,689	0,712	0,662	0,726	0,599	0,521	0,634	0,636
TSE	0,972	0,915	1	0,709	0,703	0,838	0,836	0,862	0,815	0,863	0,660	0,690	0,795	0,791
Nikk	0,695	0,508	0,709	1	0,735	0,837	0,909	0,888	0,895	0,876	0,839	0,901	0,940	0,950
HSI	0,718	0,521	0,703	0,735	1	0,942	0,812	0,889	0,844	0,850	0,669	0,648	0,814	0,750
FTS	0,873	0,700	0,838	0,837	0,942	1	0,899	0,965	0,914	0,932	0,830	0,742	0,923	0,871
DAX	0,821	0,689	0,836	0,909	0,812	0,899	1	0,956	0,982	0,978	0,800	0,908	0,951	0,968
CAC	0,869	0,712	0,862	0,888	0,889	0,965	0,956	1	0.946	0,965	0,801	0,821	0,946	0,929
ATX	0,802	0,662	0,815	0,895	0,844	0,914	0,982	0,946	1	0,990	0,781	0,924	0,953	0,955
SWI	0,854	0,726	0,863	0,876	0,850	0,932	0,978	0,965	0,990	1	0,768	0,894	0,943	0,944
PX	0,751	0,599	0,660	0,839	0,669	0,830	0,800	0,801	0,781	0,768	1	0,697	0,886	0,844
BUX	0,633	0,521	0,690	0,901	0,648	0,742	0,908	0,821	0,924	0,894	0,697	1	0,911	0,951
WIG	0,801	0,634	0,795	0,940	0,814	0,923	0,951	0,946	0,953	0,943	0,886	0,911	1	0,984
RTS	0,774	0,636	0,791	0,950	0,750	0,871	0,968	0,929	0,955	0,944	0,844	0,951	0,984	1

DJIA-New York Stock Exchange, S+P (S+P 500)-New York Stock Exchange, TSE-Toronto, Nikk (Nikkei)-Tokyo, HSI (Hang Seng Index)-Hong Kong, FTS (FTSE-100)-London, DAX-Frankfurt, CAC-Paris, ATX-Vienna, SWI (SWISS-C)-Zurich, PX (PX-50)-Prague, BUX-Budapest, WIG-Warsaw, RTS-Moscow.

Source: Musílek, P.: Stock Price Behavior. The University of Economics, Prague, Dissertation Thesis, 1997, p.96

Prices of equity securities which are currently traded on the domestic and international markets move nearly identically. We determined a nearly perfect positive price correlation of stock instruments (ÈEZ I. and Èokoládovny) which are currently traded on the exchanges in Prague and Munich. Acquisitions are generally accompanied by abnormal price fluctuations. Stocks of companies that have been taken over are particularly likely to see a jump in price. The acquisition process in the mid-90´s on the newly emerging Czech stock market resulted not only in considerable fluctuations in the prices of equity securities as well as changes in ownership, but also in the development of illegal trading methods.

Today the Czech financial markets are going through a period when it is necessary to solve a series of questions arising from its unconventional origin, particularly compliance with ethical principles in securities trading, guarantees of conditions required for protection of investments, and unconditional respect for laws and rules determining the behaviour of individual participants in the securities markets. The main problems of the Czech financial market at present are:

- improving the current legislative framework (including implementing EU directives),
- strengthening the state regulatory role to ensure market integrity, fairness, and efficiency,
- small investor protection,
- increasing the public markets' attractiveness for investors.

CONCLUSION

The five years that have passed since trading started in the re-born Czech financial markets have been stigmatised by a rapid development. While the method and speedy pace of the mass privatisation carried out in the Czech Republic have evoked respect in the world of finance, insufficient attention has been paid to regulation. The Czech financial markets are still functioning as an instrument designed primarily for privatisation rather than as a source of capital for companies.

NOTES

1 262 funds participated in the first wave of the voucher privatisation and 195 in the second, while some funds from the first wave also took part in the second. Of this number, 114 funds were converted into holding companies during 1995-1996.

2 Establishment of companies, rights and obligations of partners, shareholders, conditions for and methods of issuing shares, and operation of trade companies.

3 Regulates in the broadest sense, issuance, trading and organising of the market in securities. Sets out the basic legal position of securities in the Czech Republic

4 Allowing the authorisation of the Stock Exchange by the Securities Commission.

5 Sets out the legal and supervisory arrangements relating to Investment Funds, particularly those involved in the voucher privatisation process.

6 The Czech capital markets have now reached some parameters that are fully comparable with other European markets. But despite their dynamic development, the main source of financing in the Czech economy remains debt.

7 The most important bank members are Komercni banka, Investicni a Postovni banka, Ceska sporitelna, Ceskoslovenska obchodni banka. The largest broker members are Patria Finance, Expandia Finance, Prague International Securities, Wood and Company.

8 A Czech national securities depository, organised by the state. The Centre keeps records of securities in a separate account for each owner and in a register for securities issuers.

9 Total trade volume transacted through the Prague Stock Exchange reached almost CZK 700 billion, which represented about a two-fold increment over 1996.

REFERENCES

Annual Reports. The Prague Stock Exchange, Prague, 1994, 1995, 1996, 1997.

Annual Reports. Czech National Bank, Prague, 1994, 1995, 1996, 1997.

Fact Books. The Prague Stock Exchange, Prague, 1995, 1996, 1997.

Musílek, P.: The Investment Opportunities for Foreign Investors in the Czech Republic: Stock Investment and Real Estate Investment. Dissertation Report. Leeds Metropolitan University, 1996.

Musílek, P.: Stock Price Behavior. Dissertation Thesis. The University of Economics, Prague, 1997.

The Czech Capital Market: Organisers and Participants. The Prague Stock Exchange and Agentura Prestige, Prague, 1997.

The Prague Stock Exchange. Basic Information, Prague, 1997.

Chapter 5

Competitiveness and Industry Restructuring: the Case of Hungary

Attila Chikán and Erzsébet Czakó

Budapest University of Economic Sciences

Abstract   This paper concentrates primarily on the undiscovered side of competitiveness and industrial restructuring of the Hungarian economy, these include micro and sub-micro factors that influence the competitiveness of companies. Papers on transition are rich and valuable in the description of macro issues on the economic transition process, but they usually ignore other factors like general macro economic policy and its measurable results. In this paper, we provide a picture of the factors that enhance or prevent Hungarian enterprises from being more competitive in changing macroeconomic and international circumstances.

1.   INTRODUCTION

The Hungarian version of this paper was published in November 1997 as the final report of a two-year research program entitled, «In Global Competition - Microeconomic Factors of Competitiveness of the Hungarian Economy». The English version, on which this paper is based, was completed in March 1998 (see Chikán, 1998). This paper summarises the results of the analysis based on the work of approximately 200 researchers and practitioners in the program. Its aim is to give an overview of conclusions which we consider most important for the practice of business and governmental economic policy.

First, we present findings on the factors of competitiveness, which were organised into four sub-chapters. This approach emphasises key areas that has influenced competitiveness: changes of the economic mechanism from shortage economy into a market one, the social acceptance of the changes, the characteristics of economic policy and, finally, we describe the operations of enterprises. The last chapter is about the most important factors that have played a key role in enhancing the competitiveness of the Hungarian microsphere.

The paper is descriptive character: we did not try to make explicit suggestions here. Our objective was to publish an analysis of the current situation that is based on characteristic statements, clearly observable value, but free from any influence of everyday politics.

We have a differentiated picture of the competitiveness of the Hungarian enterprise sector, in that we found both positive and negative characteristics. In general, our enterprise sector has definite chances in the global competition, in the shadow of multinational giants (in some cases in their side-current). However, for their success difficult and comprehensive social, political and economic changes are necessary which would include such remote topics as social security, economic values and managerial methodology.

2.   MICROECONOMIC FACTORS OF COMPETITIVENESS: CONCLUSIONS OF THE PROGRAM

In this section the conclusions of the program will be described. First, the situation of the enterprise sphere in Hungary will be characterised, then the general analysis of its competitiveness will be discussed in three sections. The first deals with the social background, the second, with economic policy impacts, and the third, examines the operation of enterprises.

2.1   Over the shortage economy

> The operations of Hungarian companies show the characteristics of a market economy.

(1)   The analysis of enterprise behaviour shows that the activity of Hungarian enterprises can already be described with the characteristics of a market economy. In this sphere the transition has been completed. This, of course, does not mean that there will not be further changes (or that there is no need for further changes).

However, these changes will go on within the framework of a market economy. It would lead to serious mistakes both in economic policy and in enterprise strategy if we did not realise that the challenges we face now are not consequences of the transition (and therefore will not disappear «when the transition is completed») but that they have a root (perhaps going back centuries of history) in the Hungarian reality. We must see that this is «our» market economy, hich has to be operated as effectively as possible. Many changes are necessary but these, if carried out, will happen within the market system.

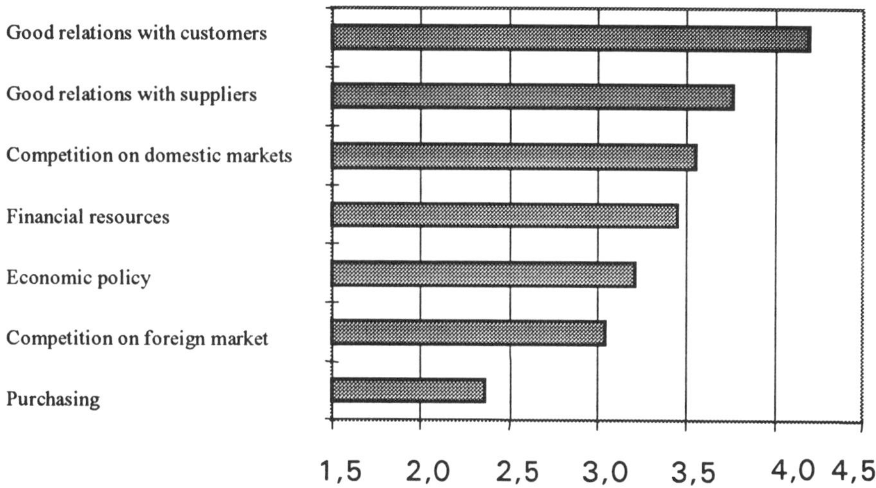

Figure 1. The ranking of the main environmental factors influencing operations shows an almost completely opposite order compared to the ranking in a shortage economy

Averages of weights given by 325 respondents (1-5)

The social transition is a long lasting process.

(2) The dominance of the market economy's characteristics in the enterprise sphere does not mean that the transition of the Hungarian society has been completed. From among all spheres of the Hungarian society the enterprise sphere has reacted fastest to the changing requirements - primarily and naturally because, naturally, this is the sphere where the interest structure characteristic to the «new» system has had the most direct effects.

> Companies' performance has improved but improvement is slower than
> in the most developed countries.

(2)   The market characteristics have fundamentally changed, from the sellers' market to the buyers' market. The greatly increased customer orientation is the main reason behind the substantially increased market performance of companies. Cost and price sensitivity have increased and the extension of production is no longer constrained by the availability of resources but by the limits set by customer demand. Power relations on the market have changed in favour of customers. The general over demand resembles the characteristics of market economies.

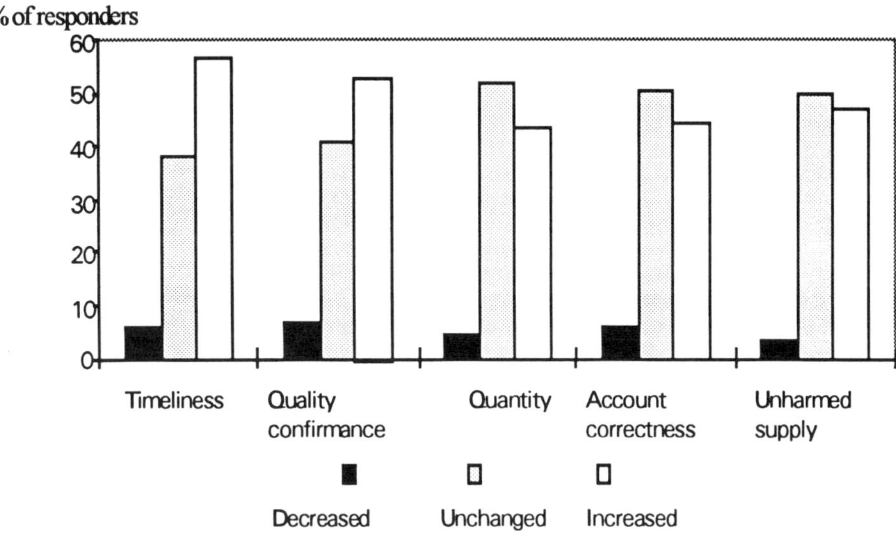

Figure 2. Customer service has substantially improved since 1992 (in % of 325 companies responding

(3) The improved performance is honoured by the market and since improvement is not equal at all companies, an increasing differentiation among companies is seen. Companies had rather different initial conditions at the beginning of the transition; however, today the differentiating factors have become independent of those conditions. The main success criteria are customer service, flexibility, reliability and quality. The chances of making extraordinary profit because of the transition conditions are over, both in the legal and (fortunately) in the illegal spheres.

(4) Despite substantial development, the rate of improvement of Hungarian companies is lagging behind that of the companies in the leading economies. This means that only those Hungarian companies which perform well above the average Hungarian level can be successful in global competition.

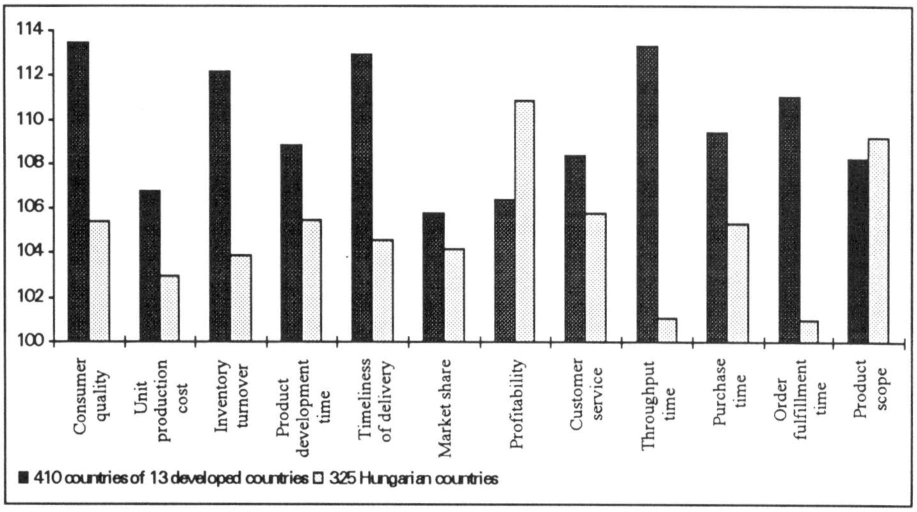

Figure 3. Production and logistics performance of companies in the most developed countries has improved faster than in Hungary

2.2   Social environment

(1) On the eve of transition major public opinion considered the transformation to a market economy very desirable: the liberalisation of the market was supported, and there was a consensus in stopping uneconomical production and closing non profitable factories; the inflow of foreign capital was welcome etc. This situation has gradually changed, for today the general attitude favours the limitation of market.

> The social acceptance of the market economy has been seriously deteriorating since the beginning of the transition.

While market-oriented operations had public support at least at the beginning of the transition, the attitude towards privatisation was ambivalent from the very beginning. Small property holdings were accepted, but there was a strong negative attitude against the private ownership of large companies. From among the forms of privatisation employee ownership programs were followed with sympathy, but auction-type privatisation, when the property was sold for those who promised more, was opposed. The support of inflow of foreign capital has gradually deteriorated.

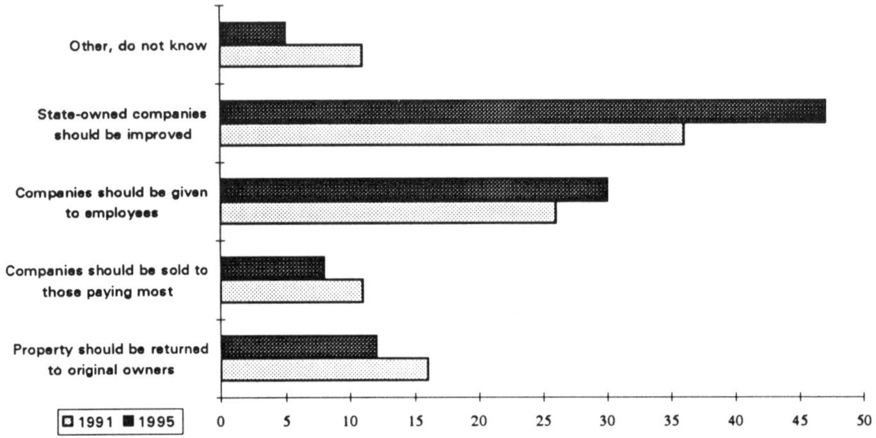

Figure 4. The social support of privatisation is rather low (Tárki survey)

(2) The idea of maintaining (or, better to say, restating) social security is very attractive for most of the population, while the increase of income differentiation is followed with very negative feeling. Even those who support the market economy in general still expect the government to take responsibility to diminish social differences.

(3) Research studies, of course, do not find the Hungarian society homogeneous. It seems that five main types of attitudes towards the market economy can be revealed: About one seventh of the population can be considered core supporters of the market economy and about 40% are definitely anti-capitalist, against the spread of private property. Accordingly, close to half of the population has double feelings towards the transition.

The low level of social acceptance of the market economy has a strong negative impact on competitiveness.

(4) Based on the above it is clear that the legitimacy of economic and social transition of the country is at a low level. This attitude slows down the development of competitiveness. We believe that there is no mystery behind this phenomenon: the reasons for that attitude can we found partly in historical experiences and traditions, partly in the developments during the transition. The latter group of reasons resulted came partly as an objective consequence of the transition (the increase of social uncertainties was unavoidable, perhaps the extent can be questioned), and as result of partly followed political mistakes and scandals which deteriorated public atmosphere.

(5) The low level of legitimacy of the market economy leads directly to the acceptance or at least «understanding» of features like black economy, low tax-paying morale and pessimism of the population which in turn deteriorates legitimacy. This vicious circle is, according to us, one of the most important problems hindering competitiveness and integration of the Hungarian economy.

> There is a mixed picture of business ethics.

(6) In direct connection with the above phenomena the view of business ethics and corporate culture is mixed. Institutions supporting ethical business behaviour at the company level are in formation, about 10% of the companies have their own ethical codes. Those companies which operate on the markets of the most developed countries consider ethical behaviour more important. At the same time our research does not suggest that foreign companies operating on the Hungarian market would be at a higher ethical level than the average Hungarian companies. Environmental friendliness, mostly because of the relatively low environmental consciousness of the population, still does not provide a competitive edge, though it is an accepted norm by Hungarian companies on the international markets.

> Regional differentiation in the country is reflected also in competitiveness.

(7) We analysed the regional aspects of competitiveness based on extensive surveys. The importance of regional aspects is increasing in competitiveness. In many respects international competition goes on between regions rather than countries, especially within the European Union. Regional analyses give much the same results in each field: Budapest and its agglomeration plus the (mostly North-) Western part of the country are in better shape and position. It is important to note that those companies which

produce mostly for domestic markets are concentrated in the less developed area, so the various regions take part in international competition to a very different extent. There are good possibilities, according to our data, that the South-Transdanubian and the South-Eastern region; as it is known will catch-up, but the North-Eastern region is in the most difficult situation.

(8) The shortcomings of the Hungarian economic information system became very apparent during the transition. This is partly the objective consequence of rapid change and the result of subjective based reasons. There are no credible data regarding most microeconomic processes. This increases the risk of economic activity, and makes handling uncertainties more expensive, which substantially decreases competitiveness. Since the maintenance of information shortage is a source of profit for many, there is a conflict of interests here, so a fast change in the situation cannot be expected.

(9) An important aspect of social embededness of companies is their relation to local governments. Extended research in that area revealed that local governments, as a rule, have appropriate means of influencing local business and development, including their relationship with companies operating in their territory. Local governments maintain important servicing and organising functions besides their role of public policy. Their competition for private investments is an important factor in forming favourable general conditions for investments in the country.

> Orientation given by the education system is not favourable for becoming a successful economic actor.

(10) The orientation of the Hungarian public education system is not favourable for competitiveness. Our education is based on the transfer of cognitive knowledge. Factors developing successful business sense: success orientation, entrepreneurship, judgement of risk (effects of failure), compromise-seeking, conflict-handling, empathy, self-reliance etc.- are deficient in Hungarian socialisation.

> Investments in education are at a low level.

The general lack of resources experienced in the Hungarian education system, reinforced by governmental policy, is a great obstacle to the development of the country.

## 2.3	Economic policy

> We still lack a clear economic policy concept for the long-term
> development of the market economy.

(1) Our research indicates that the completion of the transition and the relatively good performance of the Hungarian economy should be attributed more to the strength of the mechanisms of the market economy than to the active contribution of economic policy. Since the beginning of the transition we had two coalitions in government. Each had measures and steps both for and against competitiveness. According to the opinion of executives, economic policy (and its institutions) has had more negative than positive effects on competitiveness.

> Privatisation, with all the problems it had, has contributed positively to
> the development of competitiveness.

(2) If we consider those areas of economic policy which are in closest connection with competitiveness, we have to mention privatisation, as a core area of the transition. It is also an economic success story: it is clear that in the process of privatisation, which resulted in «real owners», the foundations of the long-term structural changes have been laid. From here, ownership structure can change in a generic manner. This is true despite the faults, losses and ethical problems which occurred along the way. Privatisation (due to a great extent, but not exclusively to the inflow of foreign capital) had a very positive effect on competitiveness.

(3) The stability of macroeconomic processes is another important factor of competitiveness. The government's role in stabilisation has been successful since the Bokros-package (named after the then Minister of Finance in 1995) and it has improved competitiveness of Hungarian companies.

> The high rate of redistribution of GDP is not sustainable.

(4) The taxation system, the high rate and changing nature of the redistribution of incomes, has a grave negative effect on competitiveness. We did not study the reasons behind the application of this systems in the framework of this project, but it is at least questionable whether it is necessary to maintain such a high level of redistribution. We accept that there is a politically rational basis for the high level of centralisation of

incomes (especially considering the findings about the social acceptance of the market economy), we still believe that here the appropriate proportions are not kept.

(5) As for the competition policy, it corresponds to the expectations towards an efficiency-oriented competition policy and as such, it helps competitiveness. The handling of natural monopolies and the effectiveness of their regulation is questionable.

> Joining the EU involves rather specific requirements about competitiveness. Most of them are already clear.

(6) The main task of the Hungarian economic policy in the next few years will be the preparation of the country to join the EU. In this course we have to make steps forward regarding growth, inflation and budget balance. Further, we have to respond to several (explicit and latent) expectations about competitiveness of our enterprise sphere as well. The general effectiveness of our economy has increased substantially in the last few years, however, it is still much lower than that of the developed countries. It is highly doubtful whether the low rate of wages really means a competitive edge in the long run. The role of agriculture and its place in economic policy is also questionable.

> The government's economic policy is greatly responsible for the problems in innovation and education.

(7) Having analysed the results of our research, we consider the government's policy towards innovation and education as most inappropriate. While all international experience shows that already in the medium term (in connection with Hungary's plan to join the European Union) these are the two most important factors of competitiveness, both seem to be disfavoured from the point of view of government support. It is worth noting that the World Competitiveness Yearbook of 1996, which has a substantial influence on the international professional judgement of the various countries, reports that the situation in these two spheres is becoming dramatic (though the report can be criticised, its influence is indisputable). Investments and budgets are low in both spheres, salaries are insufficient, and there is a danger of exodus of the most qualified intelligence from the country. If we had to assess Hungarian development based on these two spheres, the result would be disastrous.

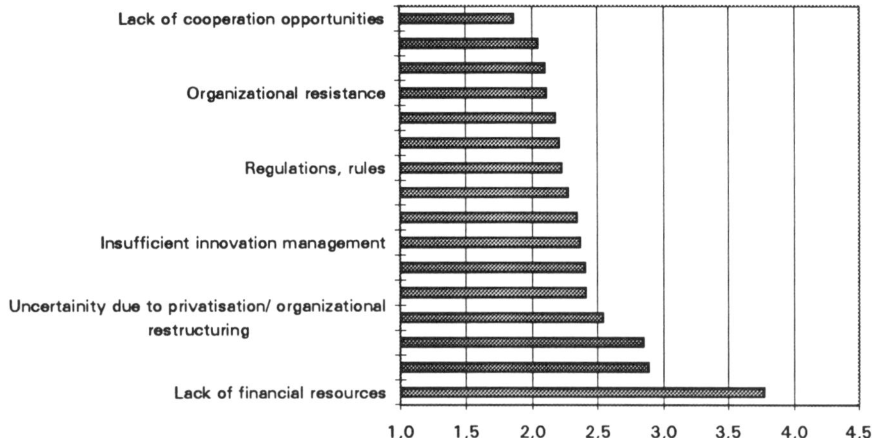

Figure 5. The most fundamental reasons obstructing innovation: lack of financial resources and high taxes

(8) In the last few years there were a lot of words (mostly complaints) about import liberalisation, the actual extent of which according to many sources substantially reduced the competitiveness of Hungarian companies. It is difficult to give an unbiased opinion on this issue. We believe that the wide-range liberalisation has helped more than it has harmed. In some cases perhaps the government could have been more determined about specific market protection measures, but the maintenance of liberalised import has a positive effect on competitiveness.

> Foreign direct investments had a substantial positive effect on the international integration and competitiveness of the economy.

(9) Foreign Direct Investment is one of the success stories of the Hungarian economy. Under the conditions of very scarce investable capital and a privatisation policy which was looking for »real» owners, FDI necessarily played a crucial role in privatisation. The overall evaluation of this role is unanimously positive, despite several problems in the process. From the point of view of competitiveness, the current ownership structure has a lot of advantages. Some of the effects are direct: the presence of large multinationals and the smaller joint ventures helps our integration, and

contributes to our preparedness in technology and management. Also, the multiplier effects are important: they force the partner's improvement of performance, provide example (even though not to the extent sometimes believed), and transfer specific know-how to domestic companies.

Altogether led to the fundamental importance of FDI in competitiveness even on the long run (just like in other, more developed countries). No doubt, there are also risk factors, and not all foreign investor/partners live up to the expectations, but this does not alter the overall picture.

2.4 Strategy, management, operations

2.4.1 Strategic management

Active, dynamic company strategies gain ground.

(1) There were very basic changes in the strategy and strategic behaviour of Hungarian companies in the last few years and these changes were mostly favourable from the point of view of competitiveness. There was a substantial increase in the proportion of those companies which followed an active (offensive or growth-oriented) strategy against those with a passive (defensive or withdrawing) strategy.

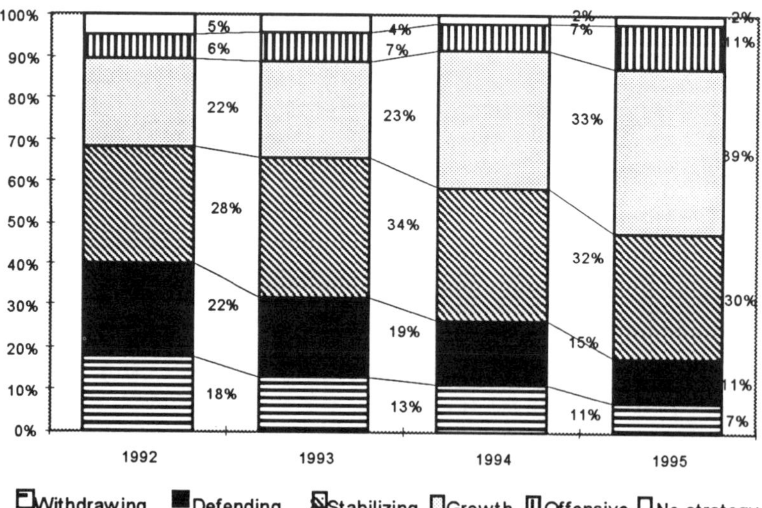

Figure 6. Company strategies became more active between 1992 and 1995

However, conscious strategic behaviour has not become general yet. More and more Hungarian managers, having gone through privatisation and the bumps of transition, feel the necessity of formalising their mission and strategy; however many of them do not yet see a close connection between following a meaningful strategy and competitiveness. Lobbying the government still plays a greater role than in the developed countries. It is interesting to see that foreign companies are no exception in this behaviour.

The new management elite is very much structured, mostly by attitude to political activity and by methodological skills.

It is a favourable development that there is a sharp upswing in the variety of strategies, and in connection with that, the variety of organisational forms. True, however, that according to our research, organisational development depends in many cases on subjective factors rather than on planned organisation design.

(2) As for management, it is of critical importance that rather early in the transition a sufficiently large group of managers have developed, the elite of which was not only able to adapt to the new requirements, but became the engine of economic restructuring, and even further, of the development of civil society. This group is very much structured, mainly along two dimensions: the attitude towards the roles in politics and professional qualifications. The internal structuring of the managers' group had, for some time, a negative effect on close inter-company co-operation and integrated relations, but this is no longer the case.

(3) As for management approaches to methodologies, two developments must be mentioned. First, the rapid spread of the controlling function, which now operates well and is of key importance at most companies (even if in many cases with some methodological problems - but certainly building on international standards). As for management decision techniques, most companies are several years behind their Western European colleagues; and the role of personality of the decision-maker is too large.

The prestige of methodological education is rather low.

(4) The picture is mixed about the use of up-to-date management skills and knowledge. Foreign investors usually brought along management culture and methods, and their companies in Hungary had to follow this imported approach (for better or worse). At these companies, the learning process was fast but one-sided. At domestic companies the situation is very diverse: from world-class to very under-informed management, can be observed. In general, we believe that a substantial proportion of the managers still do not understand the real importance of continuous education and re-education.

We forecast that the professional level of management will be one of the most important differentiating factors among companies in the next decade.

2.4.2   Inter-company relations, sectorial characteristics

(5) The analysis of the relationship structure among companies shows that the organising forces of the Hungarian economy are those characteristic of market economies. Our analysis does not support the view that in the cross-ownership of companies the pre-transition relations would survive. In the owner and capital searching strategy of companies there is a great variety, which reflects adaptability of companies.

> Foreign investments of Hungarian companies are becoming more and more substantial.

(6) External investments (in other companies) have a modest effect on strengthening inter-company relations. However, in the coming years we may expect a fast increase of these investments. The barriers that prevented companies in making such investments have been mostly removed. A special and relatively new feature is the increase of investments of Hungarian companies in foreign markets, in many cases Eastern European. The weight of this latter investment relationships is still modest, but is an important direction of future development. In the Eastern markets the relatively larger experience of Hungarian companies can be utilised. However, these markets are still rather risky.

> The strength of the inter-company net is less than in most developed countries.

(7) As for long-term co-operation and strategic alliances, we have found that they can be observed only at a relatively small number of companies, but their spreading is fast. Interestingly, strategic alliances are mostly established among companies which would have been strong even without these alliances. Therefore, it cannot be said whether the performance indices of companies in strategic alliances are better because of their own strength or because of their participation in the strategic alliance.

(8) In the developed countries, chambers of commerce, professional and sectorial associations play a key role in strengthening inter-company networks. We have found that even though these organisations have developed a lot since the beginning of the transition, their role in increasing competitiveness is still not substantial.

The majority of sectors in the Hungarian economy are becoming
international on the grounds of resource - based competitiveness.

(9) We have completed structured studies in ten industries: pharmaceuticals, plastics, aluminium, iron and steel, poultry, milk, fruit and vegetable, motor vehicles, tourism and textile. From among these the pharmaceutical industry is the only one which has globalised itself as an «innovation-based» sector (as defined in the introduction). It has adapted very successfully, increasing its competitiveness. Vehicle assembling and parts production has also developed very quickly, mainly in an investment-based manner, following large investments by multinationals. This industry, as can be expected, has had a very positive effect on the economy as a whole, but it is still a question as to how far this effect will spread and whether this sector will not form an isolated circle. Iron and steel, aluminium, plastics and textile are trading internationally on a «resource based» level. The integration of these sectors into the global economy is a fact, but this does not mean they are stable. The fruit and vegetable and the poultry industry are strongly export-oriented, but we cannot discuss about their globalisation. The milk industry has shown dynamic growth, but it is not export-oriented. The only service industry examined, tourism, has a good perspective, however with a lot of uncertainties.

The details of the sector studies cannot be discussed here. The general picture is that the international integration of the sectors analysed has developed substantially, on the basis of which we forecast that there will be no further cataclysms in the sectorial structure in Hungary, even in the case of our joining the EU. Obviously, this does not mean that there is no need for important adaptive steps, but we may say that the sectorial framework of the operation of Hungarian companies is as stable as such things can be, and that Hungarian companies must find their competitive advantage under these conditions.

No further cataclysms should be expected in the changes of sectoral
structure.

(10) A special project dealt with the operation and competitiveness of the banking sector. The institutional changes at the end of the eighties were followed by an increased market competition, which has rocked the bank system. After the low point in 1993 recovery has begun: under the conditions of sharp competition and strict government monetary policy our banks have increased their efficiency and effectiveness and in the gradually improving macroeconomic environment they have also started to reduce interest rate.

During the restructuring the Hungarian banking system has adapted to the competitive environment, even though at the price of severe losses.

2.4.3   Business activity, enterprise operation

(11) As it has already been discussed, the operation of Hungarian companies can already be described by the characteristics of a market economy. At the vast majority of companies business activity has been reorganised according to a market-oriented logic, which moved to the improvement of market performance. It is worth mentioning that, according to our investigations, foreign and jointly owned companies do not show an overall better performance, only leading companies. The favourable picture regarding foreign companies and their outstanding performance has been formed on the basis of a few well-known (mostly multinational) companies. It is a matter of fact, however, that these leading companies have caused an important pulling effect on the performance of a number of Hungarian companies (both partners and competitors).

The internal integration of operational functions is rather low.

(12) The various functional areas within the company (marketing, finance, production etc.) have developed unequally - this is a key reason why those strategies and methodologies which build on the integration of these functions could not be implemented on a wide range of companies. Also, the level of integration of information systems is low at most companies. As a positive development we experienced that the occurrence of sophisticated managerial information systems is relatively frequent.

(13) The functions most effectively supporting competitiveness (according to the view of Hungarian managers) are human resource management, controlling, information management, quality management and logistics - which means that Hungarian managers see the connection between integrated operation and competitiveness (since these functions play key role in integration), even though they, as described in (12), still do not operate that way. This is promising for the future.

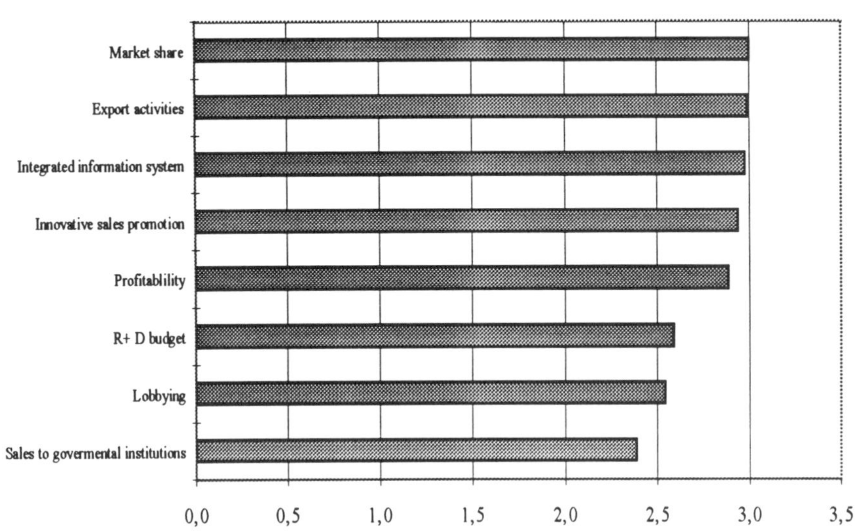

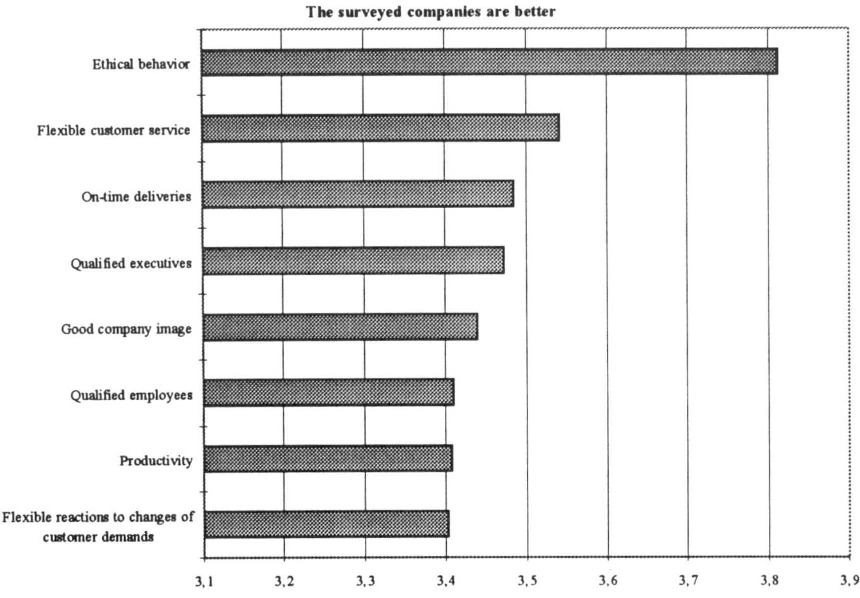

Figure7 . Performance compared to main competitors

> The backwardness of innovation is partly a consequence of managerial attitude.

(14) All analyses consider innovation as a main carrier of competitiveness, so it is quite disappointing that R&D activity is rather underdeveloped in most Hungarian companies, concerning both R&D spending and organisational background. This is the functional area where Hungarian companies feel most handicapped compared to their competitors. Unfortunately, not all managers weigh innovation properly from the point of view of competitiveness - these people do a lot of harm to their companies by muddling through day by day, trying to ensure survival this way. Naturally, this is not only a question of views - scarce financial resources are a key issue. However, the majority of managers fully understand that no strategy without proper innovation can lead to sustainable market competitiveness.

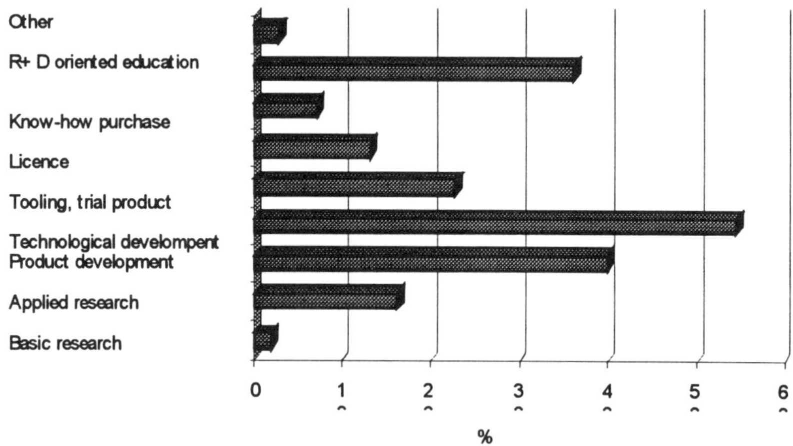

Figure 8. Various R&D activities are performed only by a small percentage of the responding companies

The methodology of decision and functional policy making should be
substantially improved.

(15) As for the methodology of operations, recent developments led to a situation in which our companies are not only behind the world's leading companies, but the distance is increasing - while at the same time current trends in Hungary compare favourably not only with the ex-socialist countries but with the less developed Western European countries as well. The deciding factors here are exactly innovation and education. Their development will determine whether we can integrate into the global economy at a favourable level.

(16) Generally speaking, competitiveness of Hungarian companies has been positively influenced by the development of the use of computers in business. There was a fast improvement in the country-wide information networks. They are now available for anyone and their actual utilisation is also increasing, though not at a revolutionary pace. Besides further financial investments in the area, further education and training efforts would be necessary.

3.   SEVEN MAIN THESES ON COMPETITIVENESS

In this chapter a brief summary of the main conclusions is given. A detailed description of the conclusions is provided in the previous chapters, while the empirical background and the arguments behind the conclusions are included in the papers prepared during the program. Main conclusions are forthcoming in the Society and Economy, the English language periodical of the Budapest University of Economic Sciences.

The transition of the business sphere has been completed.

1. The transition of the Hungarian enterprise sector has been basically completed; the behaviour of enterprises shows the characteristics of a market economy. Obviously, this does not mean that there will still not be very important changes in the Hungarian economy, but the characteristics and operation of our economy cannot be explained referring to the transition any more. This is «our» market economy; further changes will go on in this framework.

The performance of companies has improved substantially.

2. The performance of the now predominantly market-oriented enterprise sphere has significantly improved. However, the speed of performance improvement is still lower than that of most developed countries, so our handicap is increasing. At the same time, the distance from the countries that lag further behind is also increasing.

The social legitimacy of the market economy is low.

3. The legitimacy of the market economy is rather low. This leads to consequences which generally and to a great extent hinder the competitiveness of our economy. The black economy, the low tax paying morality, and the low level of business ethics increase the cost of the operation of the economy and increase the friction and disturbances in economic processes. The negative social phenomena and the lack of legitimacy mutually reinforce each other. Improved performance is the consequence of the effects of market forces. Governmental economic policy was not very supportive.

The improved performance is the consequence of the effects of market forces. Governmental economic policy was not very supportive.

4. The evaluation of economic policy of both governing party coalitions since the beginning of the transition gives a mixed picture: there were measures, which helped, and others which decreased competitiveness. According to the views expressed by company executives, economic policy had a mostly unfavourable effect on competitiveness. The improved performance of the microsphere is a result of the strength of the organising power of the market and not a consequence of economic policy. Macroeconomic stability experienced in the last two years has been achieved at the expense of harder operating conditions of companies (which, on the other hand, helps improving competitiveness on the long run). Both governments share the responsibility for the low level of legitimacy of the market economy. On the other hand, the Hungarian way of privatisation has had a rather strong positive effect on competitiveness.

The main obstacles for improving competitiveness are the weaknesses in innovation and education.

5. The two outstanding direct obstacles to improvement of competitiveness are the weaknesses of the innovation and education systems. In both fields, much larger direct and indirect governmental assistance would be necessary, but it has to be stated that the attitude of executives is not always appropriate either.

> Sectorial restructuring of the economy has been basically completed.

6. The structure of the Hungarian economy has fundamentally changed in the last few years, according to the needs of transformation to a market economy. The further development of the sectorial structure of the economy from now on will go on in an organic manner, within the frame of the market economy. No major structural shocks can be expected in the future, even if Hungary joins the EU - the sectorial structure of the economy puts no problems on competitiveness.

> Methodological knowledge and skills are very important differentiating factors among companies and their managers.

7. Today rather large differences can already be observed between companies and between executives and managers regarding managerial skills and professional competence. These differences, considering that the mobility of managers has also greatly increased, will be key factors in differentiating competitiveness among companies.

4.   CONCLUSIONS

The theses described in our paper illustrates why we formulated the opinion about the competitiveness of the Hungarian enterprise sphere in the introduction: we have a good chance, but very important changes are necessary for lasting success.

At the end of the research program, however, we have more questions about the competitiveness of our companies than at the beginning. Most of these questions cannot be answered within the chosen boundaries of this research. Who knows what the meaning of the word ''competitiveness'' will be in a decade or two, in the world of global corporations, of integration embracing whole continents, of micro-regions with very effective representations of their interests, and of the networks of information superhighways? Difficult to answer. However, to have a chance, we at least must have a clear view about our potential: we wish to contribute to this self-discovery with our research program and this paper.

REFERENCES

Ábel, István - Polivka, Gábor (1998) Competition in Banking, Hungary, 1990-1995, forthcoming, Economy and Society, vol.3.

Bartók, István (1998) Economic Policy Impacts and Competitiveness of the Hungarian Economy, forthcoming, Economy and Society, vol.3.

Chikán, Attila (1998) Report on Competitiveness of the Hungarian Enterprise Sphere. Final Report of the Research Program «In Global Competition - Microeconomic Factors of Competitiveness of the Hungarian Economy, Budapest University of Economic Sciences, March

Chikán, Attila (1998) Firm Networks in the Hungarian Economy, forthcoming, Economy and Society, vol.3.

Chikán, Attila - Czakó, Erzsébet - Demeter, Krisztina (1997) Companies in Forced March, In Global Competition Research Program, BUES Dept. of Business Economics, May

Czakó, Erzsébet (1998) Competitiveness of Selected Hungarian Industries, forthcoming, Economy and Society, vol.3.

Csányi, Tamás (1998)The Integration Role of the Information, forthcoming, Economy and Society, vol.3.

Demeter, Krisztina (1998) Business Processes Management and Competitiveness, forthcoming, Economy and Society, vol.3.

Dertouzos, Michael L. - Lester, Richard K. - Solow, Rober M. (1990) Made in America. Regaining the Productive Edge, Harper Perennial edition

Dobák, Miklós et. al. (1998) Managerial and Organization Constituents of Competitiveness, forthcoming, Economy and Society, vol.3.

OECD (1996) Industrial Competitiveness, OECD, Paris

Porter, Michael E. (1990) The Competitive Advantage of Nations, The Free Press, New York

Zsolnai, László (1998) Social Aspects of Competitiveness of the Hungarian Economy, forthcoming, Economy and Society, vol.3.

Chapter 6

The Ethical Fabric of a Transforming Economy: the Case of Hungary

Laszlo Zsolnai
Budapest University of Economic Sciences

Abstract: The paper studies the ethical fabric of the Hungarian economy during the transformation process. Basic facts of economic transformation are analysed from an ethical perspective. The dominant opinion climate of the Hungarian society is reported. The ethical attitudes of Hungarian managers are presented in comparison to Austrian managers. Different patterns of ethicality of companies are identified and explained. Future prospects are emphasised in the light of the integration of Hungary in the European Union.

In the late 1990s in the Hungarian economy the most important ethical problems are the general *erosion* of *ethical norms* and the growing *social irresponsiveness*, or even negative empathy among the economic actors. These very unfortunate characteristics are virulent partly because of the detrimental socio-cultural heritage of *state-socialism*, partly because of the *transition process* itself.

The *Communist Party* often used ethical arguments against the marketisation process and the market ideology during the 70s and early 80s. In the name of the so-called "socialist ethics" party officials made regular attacks on the entrepreneurs and entrepreneurial activities.

The role of the *Churches* was another problem. The leader of the Christian Churches, and especially the Catholic Church, collaborated with the Communist Party and excommunicated their priests, monks, and believers who represented genuine Christian morality in public and political life. So, most of the Hungarian Churches lost their moral authority in the eyes of people.

The crux of the matter is that the whole political-economic system was more or less *illegitimate* for the people. For this reason they thought that almost any form of *unethical behaviour was permissible* against the Party-State. Cheating, theft, lying, and free riding were considered as normal or at least tolerable in the state or state related sectors of the economy.

It is not an exaggeration to say that the Communist heritage is really detrimental for the revival of economic and social morality in Hungary.

The transition process itself produces additional obstacles to the development of ethicality in general and that of business ethics in particular. There are powerful factors that force people and managers not to behave ethically in the economic life. The most important factors are *uncertainty, time pressure, high stakes* and *low standard of living*.

Business life is rather uncertain in Hungary. Property rights are not well defined in many cases. The legal system is not fully developed and its functioning is far from perfect. Changes in the governing parties, the rise and fall of the political powers present high and unknown risk for managers.

There is a general feeling among Hungarians that these years will finally determine who will be rich and who will be poor, once and for all. People act under continuous time pressure. And stakes are really high. The privatisation process provides enormous profit opportunities for well-informed managers.

Finally, the standard of living considerably decreased at least for 60-70 % of people. The most important business of the average Hungarian is to survive even at any price. (Zsolnai, L. 1998)

1.   THE SOCIAL RECEPTION OF MARKET ECONOMY

The enormous *social cost* of economic transformation is reflected by the climate of opinion of Hungarian society. In their recent study *Robert Angelusz* and *Robert Tardos*[1] describe the most important changes in the reception of market economy in Hungary. (Angelusz, R. & Tardos, R. 1996, 1997-1998)

The dominant *climate of opinion* having evolved by the eve of the system change in Hungary, unanimously stood for market liberalisation and rejected the maintenance of market barriers. Nevertheless, this condition has later underwent a gradual shift, first with pro and contra attitudes coming to a balance, then pro-restriction arguments gaining predominance.

While in the initial period of the system change, the introduction of market economy was received basically favourable expectations, public thinking on property issues was characterised by a sort of conservatism and at least some ambivalence. This has revealed itself in several aspects. While more people agree than disagree with "grounding economic development on public firms", with regard to the largest plants but it is the minority accept the dominance of private property. Similarly, according to repeated research evidence, public opinion is more favourable toward small ownership than large-scale private property.

Out of various forms of privatisation the version of selling state enterprises for those paying most (based on tenders or auctions) attracted special aversion, but re-privatisation (returning goods to the original owners) was also favoured by only a small minority. More people agreed with the idea of workers' ownership. But the most popular alternative throughout the period, even growing in preference, was the suggestion of modernised state ownership with competent managers.

A clear picture of the social basis of various forms of privatisation is outlined by the survey findings. One can observe a totally different social background on the part of the re-privatisation and the auction/tender solution. The main protagonists of re-privatisation belong to the social circles of the Smallholders' Party, old, poorly-education people, and once small landowners. The option of selling for cash, in turn, attracts members of groups high in the social hierarchy: those with high education, above-average income, living in the capital, with a good starting position in the competition for capital goods. The idea of workers' ownership is mainly popular with employees of state institutions and enterprises, affiliated to the trade unions, with somewhat above average education. The version of modernised state ownership was preferred first of all by low-education respondents, once affiliated with the former Socialist Party.

As to the dynamics of attitudes on property issues during the recent years, one can observe an unusual pattern, suggesting a kind of schizophrenic state of public consciousness: despite the fact that the centrally situated, opinion-leading groups are inclined toward the extension of private property, it is more and more the opposite standpoint that tends to dominate mainstream thinking.

By 1993 data, 17 % of the adult population became involved in introducing some of the new forms of private enterprise in Hungary. Taking account also of further plans of enterprise or buying some capital goods, the proportion of those personally affected, to some degree, by some form of privatisation amounted to 28%. According to the revealed relationships, privatisation involvement had a large impact on the formation of property attitudes. It is those who have been active in this process in some way who tend to have a more positive expectation of private property gaining ground in the economy.

Background of political socialisation and present political-ideological orientation is a further important factor. Those with a left-wing identification proved to be a lot more ambivalent about property issues.

According to the findings, opinions on the role of foreign capital are one of the most important background factors of property attitudes. Immediately after the change of system, great expectations were attached to the rapid and massive influx of foreign capital. Similarly in the context of the change in attitudes toward market economy, the period between 1991 and 1993 saw a diminution in the proportion of those favouring foreign capital without doubts and by 1995 the camps of pro and contra arguments became practically even.

At the beginning of the privatisation process the encouragement of capital influx and the facilitation of domestic capital acquisition were regarded by public opinion as two reconcilable objectives. Data suggests that as years passed the joint realisation of these goals became more and more contradictory in public thought. Dwindling enthusiasm toward foreign capital did, however, not shift to general hostility with the claim of "crowding foreign capital out of the economy".

Growing sensitivity concerning social security has exerted another curbing effect on the spread of popular support for market economy and privatisation. Traditional aversion toward income differentiation partially originating from ideological sources has been even made reinforced by recent trends of polarisation. Those finding income differences as exaggerated are less inclined to favour economic development based on private firms, private ownership of large industrial enterprises and the closing of unprofitable plants.

In the public agenda social security issues rank high whether with regard to the extent of income differences, or to unemployment and poverty and this priority has even increased after the change of system. Government's responsibility for the attenuation of social differences is emphasised even among most supporters of market economy, and this general acceptance can serve as a basis of argument for representatives of the camp of social security.

Survey data had made it possible to elaborate an empirical typology of global attitudes on the transition to market economy. The five types revealed by the analyses can be grouped into three larger categories on the basis of their main orientations. Approximately one seventh of the population can be taken account of as part of the liberal field: "pro domestic capital" and "socio-liberal" groups. They constitute the core of social support for market economy. Two further types, the "social anti-capitalist" and the "anti-capitalist" amounting together to about two fifths of the population have a tendency of anti-capitalism and aversion toward the extension of market economy. The largest part of the population with almost 50% belongs to the "inconsistent" type, which is characterised by certain ambivalence. People in this category accept and support the dominant role of private property. They would restrict, however, market competition and display special attention to problems of unemployment.

Table 1 Attitudes of Hungarians to market economy transition in the mid 1990s

Attitude categories	Representation of population
"liberals"	14%
"anti-capitalists"	38%
"ambivalents"	48%

Research findings have repeatedly referred to the relationship between general economic climate, state of living conditions among the population on the one hand and attitudes toward the transformation of economic institutions on the other. Lack of economic growth, frustration of wide strata, declining conditions of the middle class all contribute to weakening the faith in the performance of new institutions. Amidst permanent stagnation a level of public trust is unlikely to emerge that could make even those still lagging behind believe that their turn will come in the foreseeable future.

Not unrelated to those above, identification with the new conditions depends a lot on the existence (or lack) of positive examples that would present the ascent of certain persons or groups as a legitimate success built on some generally acknowledged achievement. These positive stories of becoming rich may be the more mobilising the more frequently they have to do with real 'self-made-men' coming from below and suggesting the availability of opportunities for a variety of people. The social climate around market economy is certainly greatly influenced by the fulfilment of consumers' market expectations. Burdens caused by inflation and unemployment may be much compensated by an improvement in the supply and quality of goods, market fairness and consumer sovereignty. In this way the most obvious advantages of demand-constrained economy rise clearly to the surface. One of the most remarkable lessons to be drawn from the global analysis of attitude types concerns the fact that the most frequent category embracing almost half of the population, displays an inconsistent attitude toward market economy, with a general acceptance of the principles but accompanied by reservations due to unfavourable consequences. The standpoints of this important group, still not firm and modifiable in various directions, will certainly be much affected by their everyday experiences.

Making them interested and winning their support may be decisive with regard to future opinion climate surrounding the transformation process.

Among further factors in the background of unfavourable judgements and ambivalent attitudes, the socialisation inheritance of past ideology certainly plays a role in having elevated the value of equality above that of freedom and achievement in earlier decades. This value as a principal basis of legitimating for egalitarian tendencies has a restrictive role particularly under stagnant conditions and growing social polarisation. Nevertheless, it embodies certain a state of mind, a kind of social awareness that would be wrong to ignore when laying down the foundations of a new society based on competition.

2. ETHICAL ATTITUDES OF HUNGARIAN MANAGERS

In 1995-1996 we conducted a comparative research in collaboration with the *Vienna University of Economics* focusing on the ethical attitudes of Hungarian and Austrian managers and economics students. We used a questionnaire developed by our collaborative partner *Franz R. Hrubi.*

The questionnaire contains open questions such as "What are the main advantages of the market economy?, "What are the most important functions of the company?", "What are the typical characteristics of a successful manager?" and "To whom are the managers of the company responsible?". In addition respondents were asked to express their agreement or disagreement on a Lickert-type scale concerning about sixty ethically relevant statements.

In each category group questioned we had seventy two to one hundred and eighty respondents with the help of the members of the Austrian Managerial Association WdF, the members of the National Association of Hungarian Managers, the students of the Budapest University of Economic Sciences and the students of the Vienna Economics University.[4]

The dominant ethical attitudes of the Hungarian managers are rather different from those of the Austrian managers. While social and ethical considerations play a major role in the attitudes of Austrian managers concerning their company-level decisions and policies, Hungarian managers are much more hard-line in their practices. However, Austrian managers seem to actively deny the "social role of the government" and are against governmental interventions in economic life. Hungarian managers accept the role of the government as a major provider of social security and justice.

As a general conclusion, we can state that typical *ethical attitude* of *Hungarian* and *Austrian managers* reflect rather different ways of thinking.

Hungarian managers seem to believe in a *"pure capitalist"*, ownership-oriented *corporate practice* and at the same time they opt for a *paternalistic state* that provides public goods and services for the people. In sharp contrast to this Austrian managers represent a *socially responsible corporate philosophy* and at the same time they prefer a *liberal*, less interventionist *economic policy.*

Interestingly enough the ethical attitudes of *Hungarian* and *Austrian economics students* are very *similar.* Young economist groups in both countries prefer a *social market economy* in which *environmental values* are highly protected. Both Hungarian and Austrian students typically envision the *socially responsible company* in which interests and needs of various stakeholder groups are harmonised with the profit motive of the owners of the company.

I think the fact that Hungarian young economists represent a very European pattern of ethical attitudes is a *promising sign* for the future development of the Hungarian economy. However it remains questionable whether such ethical attitudes can survive in the present context of the economic transformation.

3. ETHICALITY OF COMPANIES

In 1996-1997 we conducted an empirical research into the ethicality of companies in Hungary.[2] (Zsolnai, L. 1997)

Our research was based on data gathered from questionnaires collected from *325 companies* balanced by company size, ownership structure, industry category, and geographical location. The questionnaire asked top managers of the companies about the *ethical institutions*, the *stakeholder policy, customer orientation*, and *charity* of their companies.

Ethicality was defined as a capability of companies to make steps toward developing their "corporate social policy process" which is characterised by *Edwin M. Epstein* as individual and collective examination of the ethical meaning and consequences of corporate actions on the affected parties and the management of stakeholders concerning the product of organisational policies and behaviour. (Epstein, E. M. 1987)

In our study the existence or lack of ethical institutions, stakeholder policy and charity was used as an indicator of ethicality of companies. We also included consumer orientation as an indicator, since in the context of economic transformation, the attention to the needs and voices of consumers is not merely marketing but has ethical significance too.

We conducted a cluster analysis in order to classify the companies in our sample by the above mentioned dimensions.[3] As a result we got *five clusters* as follows:

(1) *"Eminent"* In this cluster those companies can be found which have the highest ranking in every dimension. Eminent companies have institutionalised ethics and stakeholder policy. They are the most customer-oriented and donate the highest amount to charity. The *largest companies* (above 1 000 M HUF turnover) are highly over-represented in this cluster. Surprisingly, there is *no* significant *difference* by means of *ownership*.

(2) *"Non-formalised"* In this cluster companies are very conscious toward their customers and allocate a lot to charity. However, ethical institutions and stakeholder policy are virtually non-existent in these companies. There is no significant difference by size. *State-owned companies* are *underrepresented* and *Hungarian private companies* are *over-represented* in this cluster.

(3) *"Stingy"* Companies in this cluster are very similar to the eminent companies but they score near zero in charity. *Foreign companies* are highly *over-represented* in this cluster. There is *no* significant *difference* by *size*.

(4) *"Satisficer"* In this cluster companies scored near the average in almost every dimension except in stakeholder policy where they have fairly high ranking. There is *no* significant *difference* by *size*. *State owned companies* are *over-represented* while *Hungarian private companies* are *underrepresented* in this cluster.

(5) *"Underdogs"* Companies in this cluster perform worst in every dimension. *Small* and *medium size* companies with *Hungarian ownership* are *over-represented* in this cluster.

We were interested in the underlying factors that can explain the differences in ethicality of the companies. Using data about different aspects of corporate strategy we formed other clusters reflecting the *strategic orientation* and the *strategic constraints* of the companies.

We identified the following strategic clusters of the companies under study.

(α) *"Strongly export-oriented"* Good organisational and financial capabilities and strong export orientation characterise the companies in this cluster.

(β) *"Struggling export-oriented"* Companies in this cluster have a strong customer-orientation and export-orientation but their financial capabilities are rather limited.

(γ) *"Domestic market oriented"* Customers in the domestic market are of high concern for companies in this cluster but they have strong financial constraints.

(δ) *"Big domestic monopolist"* There are no organisational or financial constraints for companies in this cluster but they lack market orientation.

(ε) *"Non-competitive"* The financial constraints are not significant for companies in this cluster and there is an almost total *lack* of *market orientation*. Customers are not a strategic focus for these companies.

We analysed the *fit* of the *ethicality clusters* and the *strategic clusters* of the companies. *Table 2* shows the most important relationships between these groups of clusters. Signs "+" and "+ +" indicate the level of over-representation in the given cell, while signs "-" and "- -" indicate the level of under-representation in the given cell.

Table 2 Ethicality of the companies in the Hungarian economy

	Strongly export oriented	Struggling export oriented	Domestic market oriented	Big domestic monopolist	Non competitive
"eminent"		++		-	
"non-formalised"			+		
"stingy"	++			-	–
"satisficer"	--	-	-	++	
"underdog"		--		-	--

The relationship between the ethicality clusters and the strategic clusters of the companies suggest that the ethicality of companies is highly *context-dependent*. Those *companies* that are operating in well-developed Western economies display a significantly higher level of ethicality than *companies* (foreign or domestic) *operating* in the less-developed *Hungarian economy*. Also, *market-orientation* goes hand in hand with some level of the ethicality of the companies.

4.   PROSPECTS FOR THE FUTURE

According to socio-economics represented by *Amitai Etzioni* and his followers economic behaviour is basically determined by two major variables, namely *utility* and *morality*. (Etzioni, A. 1988) In a comparative perspective we can say that it is the *inherent morality* of the *actors* on the one hand and the *relative cost* of *ethical behaviour* on the other hand that really matter in economic life.

Ethical behaviour can be expected if the cost of the ethical behaviour is much lower than the cost of unethical behaviour in the same situation. If the relative cost of ethical behaviour is high, including opportunity costs and transaction costs, then unethical behaviour can be expected from individuals and companies.

Joining the *European Union* Central European countries will change the basic socio-economic context within which their economies function. In this *new context* the ethicality of companies and individuals can be considerably improved.

NOTES

1 This study was part of the "*Competitiveness of the Hungarian Economy*" research programme headed by *Attila Chikán* at the Department of Business Economics of the Budapest University of Economic Sciences in 1995-1997.
2 The research was financed by the *Austrian-Hungarian Action Found*. The empirical analysis and the first interpretation of the gathered data were done by *László Radácsi* at the Business Ethics Center of the Budapest University of Economic Sciences.
3 The cluster analyses were done by *Tibor Misovicz* and *László Radácsi* at the Department of Business Economics of the Budapest University of Economic Sciences.
4 The research was financed by the *Austrian-Hungarian Action Fund*. The empirical analysis and the first interpretation of the· gathered data were done by *László Radácsi* at the Business Ethics Center of the Budapest University of Economic Sciences.

REFERENCES

Angelusz, Róbert & Tardos, Róbert 1996: *The Social Reception of Market Economy in Hungary*. 1996. Budapest University of Economic Sciences, Department of Business Economics.
Angelusz, Róbert & Tardos, Róbert 1997-1998: Aspects of Transformation and Public Opinion" *Acta Oeconomica* Vol. 49. No. 1-2. pp. 207-229.
Epstein, Edwin M. 1987: "The Corporate Social Policy Process: Beyond Business Ethics, Corporate Social Responsibility, and Corporate Social Responsiveness" *California Management Review* 1987. No. 3.
Etzioni, Amitai 1988: *The Moral Dimension*. 1988. The Free Press.
Zsolnai, László 1997: *Ethics and Competitiveness of the Hungarian Economy*. 1997. Budapest University of Economic Sciences, Department of Business Economics.
Zsolnai, Laszlo 1998: "Business Ethics in Management Science" in Peter Koslowski (ed.): *Business Ethics in East Central Europe*. 1988. Springer Verlag. pp. 95-102.

Chapter 7

Economic Growth and Foreign Direct Investment: the Polish Case

Maria Romanowska
Warsaw School of Economics

Abstract:	In Poland the economy is still dominated by state-owned enterprises (SOEs) and government is still interfering with the economic processes; the access to many strategic industries is restricted by licences, duties, allowances and other barriers. However it does not discourage investors searching for highly attractive investment and ready to adapt their entry process to government's requirements and local competition. In 1997 Foreign Direct Investment (FDI) in Poland reached the level of 20 billion US dollars through purchasing of shares of privatised companies, establishing joint ventures, and recently more and more green field investments. Research and field studies confirm the strong positive impact of FDI on Polish companies and economy. FDI stimulates the transfer of capital and technology as well as foreign trade and contributes to GDP growth. At the microeconomic level FDI increases the competitiveness of Polish companies, a key factor for EU accession.

## 1.	INVESTMENT ATTRACTIVENESS OF POLAND

Some effects of globalisation of the world's economy led to the spreading of investments beyond the zone of the highly industrialised countries. Products now manufactured in the countries attracting investments have more and more often replaced the traditional exports. According to «World's Report on Investments» worked out by UNCTAD in 1996, direct investments abroad amounted to almost $350 billion, of which 40% was invested in developing countries. The countries of Asia, the Pacific, and Latin America have been very attractive developing markets for years. But after communism had collapsed some new markets appeared in Central and Eastern Europe (CEE).

Such a conclusion is proved by the still increasing level of investments in that region which amounted to almost $ 14 billion in 1996. The highest proportion of this sum was invested in Hungary, Poland, the Czech Republic, and Russia.

Two main factors, attractiveness and risk determine foreign companies' interest in investing abroad:
- attractiveness of a particular country characterised by present and anticipated market potential, labour cost and other cost factors, favourable tax regulations, protectionism of local markets, limited competition, export opportunities in neighbouring countries, low requirements of potential clients, and special incentives for foreign investors.
- risk connected with investing in a given country resulting from policy instability, different culture, high level of crime, lack of technical and capital infrastructure, and other unfavourable conditions.

Many studies define the level of investment risk as a potential degree of threat compared to actual economic results anticipated by the investor. The higher the risk, the lower the probability of achievement of intended effects. The investment attractiveness is defined as a complex of advantages and disadvantages of the investment place. If we define attractiveness and risk this way, we may recognise the market of high attractiveness and low risk to be the best one. Such a situation may occur in the case of natural monopoly or licensing of a profitable business.

A company that makes a decision to entering a foreign market will, first of all, look for very attractive markets offering a low investment risk. Then it will consider entering markets with an increased level of risk. We seem to deal with such a situation in the case of the former communist countries. Investors' attention is attracted to eastern markets when large demand and low trading costs are considered. However, in the very beginning at least, the high risk causes their entry into these markets to be cautious and on a small scale so as to enable them to pull out as quickly as possible if things go wrong. Investors from well-developed countries ready for investing in CEE countries monitor their international rankings of investment attractiveness and penetrate local markets searching for some extraordinary bargains at the same time. In the years 1991-1993, Poland was usually ranking in third position on these lists just after the Czech Republic and Hungary, but it always showed a tendency for improvement in its position. In some rankings, Poland took the lead among East European countries. Five post-communist countries were recognised as "rather free" in "The Report of Economic Freedom for 1998" published by the Heritage Foundation and The Wall Street Journal. Estonia was in 19th position, the Czech Republic in 20th position, Latvia in 63rd position, Hungary in 67th position, and Poland in 73rd position. The remaining countries were rated among the group being "rather controlled" and "fully controlled". Polish economy was officially classified in the first place among CEE countries at the EBOR conference held in London in April 1997.

It seems that the most representative are assessments of economic attractiveness based on the results of foreign investors acting in CEE. On the basis of their own experiences, foreign investors estimate the chances and threats connected with running a business in this part of the world and recognise that their opinions have a strong influence on other foreign investors' decisions. The views of large foreign investors have, for five years, been based on the data published by the Institute for Market Economy Research. The research into investment risk in Poland and other post-communist countries conducted by the Institute demonstrates that CEE has increased its attractiveness within the last few years. This is thanks to liberalisation and democratisation of economic, political, and social life, the modernisation of law regulations and the improvement of organising conditions, economic growth, the changes in consumers's habits, and the raising of qualifications in the labour force. Among the motives that encourage examined companies to invest in CEE countries, the following were the most often listed[1]:

- following a client which is active in these markets,
- searching for local domination of a market segment within a framework of global competition,
- searching for growing markets by companies operating in mature industries,
- looking for increased capacity of production,
- country-specific motives: duty levels, market protections, proximity of the investor's headquarters, local economic growth, similar culture.

In the light of presented research, Poland is constantly improving its competitive position in relation to the other countries of the region. It ranked number 4 for attractiveness in 1993 after the former GDR, Hungary and the Czech Republic and was given a satisfactory grade. The following criteria were taken into account while making the ranking: preconditions, available forms of organisation, accessibility of industrial sectors, taxes, duties, banking system, access to information, land property, privatisation process, and the "get out" clauses. Investment economic risk measured by the level of demand, the power of competition, the limited conditions of profitability and the high costs of production placed Poland on a level lower than middle risk i.e. fourth place in that period. Poland's situation changed in relation to the other countries in 1997. Nowadays, Poland comes in first as regards investment attractiveness and is ahead of the Czech Republic and Hungary. Poland however still has a higher risk index than those two countries, resulting from policy instability and lack of pace in reforming the economic structure (figure 1).

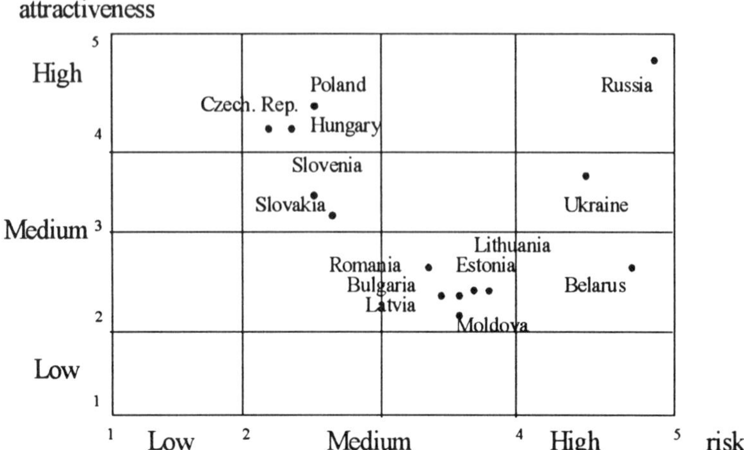

Figure 1. Investment Attractiveness of CEE Countries in 1997

Source: Z. Dworzecki. Map of investment risks... op. cit.

The most attractive countries on the map are Russia, Poland, the Czech Republic, Hungary and Ukraine. Russia, Ukraine and Belarus are the ones with the highest level of investment risk. Generally speaking, Poland is very highly evaluated in the rankings of investment attractiveness, but much lower in the rankings of investment risk. According to Deloitte & Touche, the highest threats to foreign investors in Poland are duty regulations, telecommunications, the banking system, local authorities, tax regulations, inflation, local currency, and the collection of debts. Investors also complain of policy instability, excessive claims of trade unions, and low work productivity. According to Polish Agency for Foreign Investment (PAIZ) in 1996, the low cost of the labour force, market size, fast economic growth, large work supply, and low cost of manufacturing are of the greatest importance for decision making concerning investment in Poland[2].

As we can see, despite many barriers in the form of business licensing and law volatility, Poland is a very attractive country for foreign investments. This is demonstrated by its good ranking position and proved by the increasing inflow of foreign capital.

2.   RANGE AND FORMS OF FOREIGN INVESTORS' PRESENCE IN POLAND

In 1998 Poland ranks first for FDI among CEE countries. The value of direct foreign investments in Poland amounted to over $ 20 billion at the end of 1997, of which $17 billion represented investments exceeding one million dollars. In order to complete the involvement of foreign capital in Poland we must add to the sum of direct investments, portfolio investments on the Warsaw Stock Exchange of $5 billion and the value of government bonds as well as treasury vouchers of $ 2,5 billion purchased by foreign investors. Altogether it is over $ 28 billion committed to Poland's economy within recent years. Dynamism of direct investments in Poland is presented in figure 2.

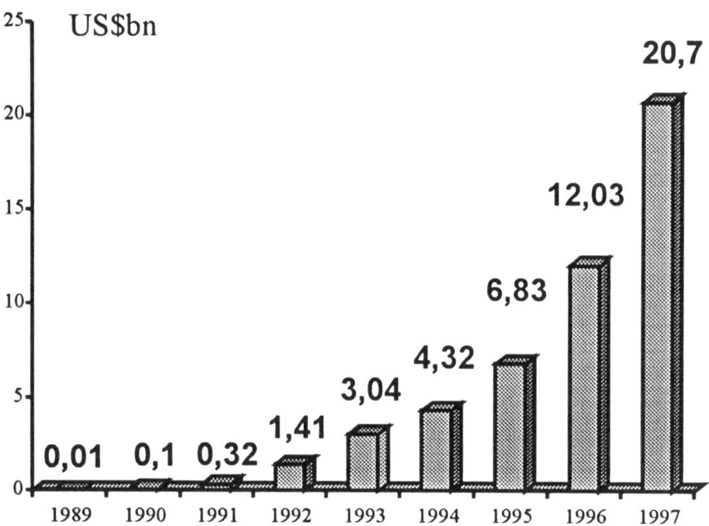

Figure 2. Dynamics of Foreign Direct Investments in 1989-1997

Source: Polish Agency for Foreign Investment (PAIZ)

A question comes to mind as to whether the level and dynamism of direct investments in Poland is satisfactory. As a matter of fact, Poland attracted the largest direct investment of this European region. It is higher than Russia's $9.3 billion, Hungary's $17 billion or the Czech Republic's $8.2 billion, however the other countries are ahead of Poland when the per capita index is considered. In 1997, $ 534 of direct investments could be attributed to each Polish person, $1666 per Hungarian, and $ 800 per Czech. Poland lowered its investment level risk later than Hungary and the Czech Republic and presently attracts more capital than those two countries.

Industries of electro-machinery, food, wood and paper, chemical materials, minerals, construction, as well as commerce and telecommunications have the largest share in direct investments. Such a specialisation of foreign investment points to foreign investors concentrating on high-technology industries which is a stimulus to favourable structural changes in Polish industry. Serious investment of capital into the old industries, which are connected with environmental pollution such as industries concerning cellulose, paper, chemicals, and food may, however, mean that the costs of these burdensome industries have been transferred to less developed countries.

As far as regional structure of direct investments is concerned the majority of joint ventures are found in the large cities. As regards the number of registered companies and the amount of investments, Warsaw comes first. Next come the regions of Poznan, Gdansk, Katowice, Szczecin, Wroclaw, Kraków, and Lódz. The map of the location of joint ventures correlates with the geographical map of investment risk.

Significant changes have occurred in the source of capital inflow within recent years. First of all, an increase is visible in the activity of investors from outside Europe, for example, American and Korean. However, international companies from Germany, Italy, France, Holland, and UK still enjoy a very strong position. Largest investments in Poland are those of Fiat and Daewoo in the car industry, EBRD and Polish-American Ent. Fund in finance and enterprise buy outs, PepsiCo, Coca-Cola in the beverages industry, IPC in the cellulose and wood industry, ING Group in banking, ABB in the machine industry, and Philip Morris in the tobacco industry. Over 70% of capital come from these seven countries and international corporations. Capital structure according to the country of origin is presented in figure 3.

Investors' decisions depend not only on the selection of a country but also on the choice of type, sector and scale of investment. A country's legal regulations also limit the investment potential. The problem is particularly important in Poland because the state's participation in the economy is too great. The state retains a right to control shares of foreign entities in so called "sensitive" sectors. The list of "sensitive" sectors for which special limits and requirements were determined covers:

– sectors inaccessible to foreign investors such as: lottery games and telecommunications. These sectors will, however, soon be opened for foreign investments, but on specific terms.
– sectors of limited access for foreign investors such as: banking, radio and television, fishery, telecommunications, sea and air transportation, insurance. Limitations concern the percentage share, capital or legal requirements.

accessible sectors but requiring a special permit such as: sea economy, commerce, culture, unlicensed defence industries, transportation, tourism, legal advice and others.

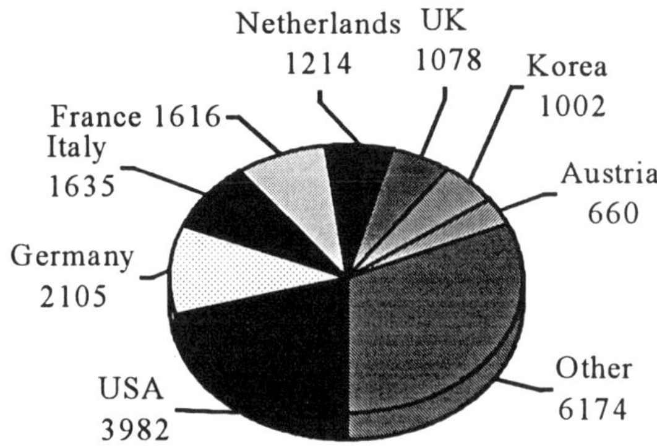

Figure 3. Foreign Investment by Country of Origin (US $ million)

Source: Polish Agency for Foreign Investment

Restrictions applying to some of the activity sectors make inflow of foreign capital difficult on the one hand, but on the other hand make these sectors very attractive for large investors who are capable of compliance with the requirements and restrictions. This is illustrated by foreign investors' strong emphasis on the banking sector and telecommunications. Foreign capital share in the "sensitive" sectors is insignificant so far, but we must expect liberalisation of government policy and the lifting of these restrictions. Since the middle of the 90's there has been is a tendency to treat foreign investments equally with national ones. It amounts to accepting the principle of equating the functioning conditions of companies and their subsidiaries, also under foreign control, or other forms of direct foreign investment, with the functioning conditions of their national equivalents. Although the principle of treating foreign investors equally with the national investors is expressed in Polish law, Poland also follows the requirements of international treaties, in particular the Uruguay Round of GATT.

The strongest legal restriction making the inflow of foreign capital to Poland difficult is a complex system of concessions imposed on trading. Polish basic law regulation on licensing is the Trade Bill from 1988. Basically, 11 licensed fields were listed in the bill, however it provided a chance of expanding that number by the Cabinet and the government made use of this opportunity. Presently, the list numbers 18 licensed fields.

However, a real field of licensing is much bigger than the bill provides, since the other bills i.e. The Radio and Television Bill, or Paid Highway Bill introduced quite different procedures of licensing which are not listed in the Trade Bill. Analyses of the range and principles of trade licensing in Poland lead to the conclusion that there is a tendency for expanding the fields of licensing which clash with the economic freedom and restrain the inflow of foreign capital into the most attractive sectors.

Licensing is usually applied to secured fields, which investors try to enter by purchasing a national company or establishing a private one. More possibilities of entering the Polish economy are dependent on the form of the partnership agreement. Regulations of Polish civil and commercial law define the legal basis of an alliance of non-share and non-capital forms. Various kinds of contracts and agreements on co-operation in the field of research, production or trade may be concluded in the forms of trade and civil contracts. Such contracts are not registered, so we neither know the real number of them nor the parties involved. We may also guess that Polish entrepreneurs, like their foreign colleagues, conclude «secret agreements» which are aimed at temporary cessation of competitive struggle in order to secure the sector profitability as well as their own incomes. Such informal, secret, and illegal agreements are only unearthed when they come up for trial and are publicised in the media. Price agreements are the ones that are commonly concluded between competitors in Poland.

License contracts have been very popular forms of alliances in Poland for years. Such contracts already concluded in the 70's gave Poland access to Western technology. However, for the sake of isolation of Poland from the world's markets they were not in the form of alliances. However, license contracts presently concluded with the companies from the same sector that may convert into direct competitors within the process of globalisation must be considered as competition threats. Franchising is a known, but not a common form of alliance agreement in Poland. It is, however a very favourable form of alliance for those Polish companies which neither have large capital resources nor are distinguished by product or trademark. Franchising lowers the costs of market entry since it gives a possibility of using a trademark, technology, know-how, and the advice of the franchiser. The most famous franchising agreements are chains of large foreign concerns such as Levi-Strauss and McDonalds. Polish entrepreneurs also apply franchising agreements. The Franchising Association is the institution that supports and propagates this form of development in Poland. A franchising agreement is usually concluded between a large and well-known company and a budding entrepreneur. Thus, it is more like a deliverer/ receiver co-operation than that of a competitor.

Capital alliances, when a company buys out a minority share of a competitive company are little known and probably underestimated in Poland.

Foreign companies prefer to purchase a controlling interest for a stake in a low priced Polish enterprise. Minority share purchases among national competitors are not common. This form of share purchase, is however, more often applied in relation to the buyers and deliverers in order to control their actions as well as to co-ordinate the chain of values.

International consortia set up to execute a joint and large venture such as the construction of a part of a highway or digital telecommunications are a new phenomenon. A good example is the Polish Digital Telephone System known as ERA that obtained a concession for constructing and operating one of two GSM networks. The consortium consists of Elektrim, the Polish capital group, DeTeMobil, and US West. In Poland, many foreign companies invest their capital not in their own subsidiaries, but in privatised Polish enterprises through the buy out of shares, or establishing joint ventures with Polish partners. Thus, they settle themselves on the Polish market at the lowest cost and are able to minimise the investment risk. Many positive examples may be noted when observing the alliances of Polish companies with their foreign partners, however there are many examples that such alliances threaten Polish products and may result in elimination of the Polish company from the market. The company that makes a decision on incorporation with a stronger and more experienced partner must take into account that apart from capital, know-how, and new product inflows some disadvantageous effects may follow such an alliance. These disadvantages may emerge as devious attempts at squeezing the Polish partner's goods out of the market, attempts at taking over the company or even declaring bankruptcy. Investments in commercial law companies are the most popular form of foreign investors' activity in Poland.

In 1996, 29,157 joint ventures were registered, including 429 companies, which invested more than $ 1 million. In 1997, over 30.000 such companies were operating on the Polish market. Approximately one third of joint ventures is represented by green field investments[3].

The largest part, over 61%, of the foreign capital has been invested into limited companies. Only 8.3% of business entities had an initial capital higher than PLN 1 million, but they represented almost 56% of all employees and 95.3% of foreign initial capital. The number of remaining forms of direct foreign investments is difficult to estimate.

The most attractive sectors are the pharmaceutical industry and the paint and lacquer industry.

The interest of foreign capital in the Polish pharmaceutical market was not high until 1997 but it is now assessed to be very attractive, large, dynamic, and with limited competition. the earlier problems were caused by privatisation restrictions, governmental regulations on medicine prices, and duty-free medicine imports. Nevertheless, the prospects of huge incomes attract the foreign investors' attention. Presently, foreign concerns act in

Poland in various forms: as franchisers, importers, clients, and shareholders of pharmaceutical companies. All the concerns in Poland distribute medicines manufactured abroad, however participation of Polish-foreign pharmaceutical alliances is growing. The most popular form of alliance is the commissioning of component production by the concerns as well as the granting of licences for medicine manufacturing. Polfarma – one of Poland's largest pharmaceutical companies with 65% market share works as a subcontractor for international companies. Herbapol plants, specialising in medicines and para-medicines of vegetable origin, deliver highly processed components to the West European countries that are then sold, after purifying, under the brand names of those countries. Most large Polish pharmaceutical companies manufacture medicines licensed by Western concerns and although licence conditions lower the profitability of Polish companies they enable them to maintain quality standards. The rise of interest in direct investments into the pharmaceutical industry came after the government had worked out a concept of privatisation of the sector. Recently, three large state-owned enterprises have been sold. Croatia-based Pliva purchased 60% of Polfa-Kraków shares, ICN bought 80% of Polfa-Rzeszów shares, Glaxo Welcome purchased Polfa-Poznan Company, and the next transactions have already been negotiated. The history of foreign investments into Polish industry shows that in the case of the regulated and risky sectors investors enter the market as franchisers, exporters, and allies and only later on opt for a buy out of national enterprises.

A good example of a sector in which government, to a small extent, regulates the market is the paint and lacquers market. This is the industry of a highly dynamic growth and Polish companies of the former Polifarm Group enjoy large shares in it. Not long ago, foreign companies acted as exporters only on the Polish market. The first large company purchased by a foreign company was Wroclaw-based Nobiles. In response to that Poland's two largest companies of Cieszyn-based Polifarb and Wroclaw-based Polifarb, which had a market share of 40%, merged. The fourth largest Polish company, Polifarb Debica, was partly purchased by Alcro Beckersfirma. Two smaller companies based in the cities of Pilawa and Kalisz were partly sold to other Western companies. The example of paints and lacquers shows how the first entry of a foreign company influences the situation within the sector and persuades other investors to take investment decisions. As in the car industry, Fiat's entry persuaded Daewoo to invest in a large Polish car factory, and General Motors to build a new factory in the town of Gliwice.

3. INFLUENCE OF FOREIGN DIRECT INVESTMENT ON POLISH ECONOMY

Research points to the favourable influence of foreign investments, not only on the enterprises that are involved, but also on the whole Polish economy. They provide the evidence that there is a strong relationship between foreign investments and Poland's economic development. Of all forms of foreign investments, direct ones contribute to restructuring and development of Polish economy to the largest extent. Influence of direct foreign investments is visible in three areas: macro-economic processes, privatisation, and the rising competitiveness of Polish companies.

3.1 Macro-economic Processes

Polish research shows that foreign capital was a main out-of-budget source of financing companies' development in the previous period. If substantial budget means are systematically squandered in ineffective restructuring processes of the large state-owned enterprises the investments by foreign companies may get into developmental channels that hold promise for future profits. Many sectors of the economy such as brewing or the motor industry were, to a large extent, restructured thanks to the financial means of foreign investors. These investments provide and support new fields of activity such as cordless telephones or highways. Macro-economic effects result from the positive influence of direct investment in companies acquiring new technologies and new production facilities as well as the extent to which they make use of them. But these effects also result from the dynamics of foreign trade and favourable influence on GDP formation[4].

3.1.1 Transfer of Resources and Technology.

In the years 1993-1995, global share of direct foreign investments in Polish GDP amounted to 3%, and share in global investments between 15% and 18%. It means that a considerable part of investment is achieved thanks to the inflow of the foreign capital. Joint ventures distinguished themselves by investment activity higher than average. Approximately 80% of joint ventures have invested in Poland while one third of them allocated the whole of the previous year profits to this end. The majority of joint ventures applied new technologies and equipment as well as modern methods of organisation and management. They enjoyed a higher than national average efficiency for the use of the labour force. Thus, a factor effect arises that increases the efficiency of investment outlay.[5] Linked to concentration of foreign investment in specific industries, the process led to modernisation of entire sectors such as furniture, juices, detergents, cars, and paper production. It was initially assumed that foreign investments would concentrate in the labour-intensive industries because of lower labour costs and in the industries that are detrimental to the environment because of fewer restrictive regulations. It turned out that a large and still rising part of investments was located within high-technology industries. Such an investment structure results in the fast substitution of the Polish economic structure for a more modern one. Joint ventures, using new equipment and technologies, are changing the economic structure in Poland. Research shows that the age of technologies and equipment in these companies does not exceed 5 years and over 60% of technologies and equipment being used is less than one year old. FDI is also conducive to quantitative and qualitative improvement of the human factor; research shows that direct foreign investments in Poland contributed to the creation of the new jobs and, on the way, to employment rationalisation as well as improvement of staff qualifications.

3.1.2   Acceleration of Foreign Trade.

Research shows that there is a positive and indirect link between the level of foreign investments and the volume of Polish exports. A rise of capital inflow by $ 1 million coincides with an average export raise by $ 2 million. This relationship results from the activity of joint ventures in exports. There is a tendency for exports from joint ventures to be twice as high as those of national companies although export sales remain low and do not exceed 20% of production. Only foreign companies take the first places in the 1997 ranking of largest exporters. They are Fiat Autopoland, Thomson Polcolor, International Paper Kwidzyn, Procter & Gamble and two tyre companies, Goodyear and Michelin. A Foreign Capital Bill is a factor that stimulates exports. This bill provides large tax relief for the companies that enjoy large export incomes. In spite of huge export dynamism in recent years Poland has had a negative balance of payments since 1992. The deficit exceeded US$ 15 billion in 1997 and Poland has had a negative trade balance with almost all the countries world wide. The reason is that, despite the increase in export dynamism, it has still been insufficient. On the one hand the overall structure and the disadvantageous prices charged for Polish products have prejudiced sales, and on the other hand, imports have been rising too fast. According to Polish economists, foreign companies acting in the Polish market are, to a large extent, responsible for the rise in imports. They contribute to it by importing consumer products as well as components and investment goods. Research of the Institute for Economic Situation and Foreign Commerce Prices shows that the imports of joint ventures grew faster than their exports and that 67% of the trade deficit was attributed to joint ventures. The example of Poland and other countries of the Visegrad Group show that a sudden rise in foreign trade deficit usually appears in the first years of increased inflow of direct foreign investments to developing countries. The increase in the competitive ability of companies and the higher dynamism of export should bear fruits only after some years of investment.

3.1.3   Foreign Direct Investment and National Income.

Econometric analysis of the influence of foreign investment on Poland's economic growth confirmed the existence of a positive correlation between the FDI and GDP growth.[6] One dollar of direct foreign investments in Poland is followed by a rise in GDP of $1.14, and growth of FDI of 10% is followed by a GDP rise of 0.31%. Research shows also the opposite relationship: GDP growth increases demand for foreign investments and contribute to raising its dynamism. 1% GDP growth is accompanied by average FDI growth of 4.9%. The last two years confirm that while Poland had high GDP growth it gathered a larger amount of foreign investment than it had anticipated.

3.2   Privatisation

FDI plays an important role in the process of the privatisation of economies of the former socialist countries. A well-prepared privatisation process is one of the main factors that raise a country's investment attractiveness. Also foreign investors' participation in such a process accelerates privatisation of economies having a modest national capital. The proportion between greenfield investments and the buyout of shares of state-owned companies may be a indicator of FDI role in the privatisation process of any given economy. According to the OECD, FDI share of already existing companies amounted to 67% in the Czech Republic, 63% in Russia, 60% in Hungary and only 37% in Poland. Poland in fact enjoys a relatively high share of greenfield investments. It may indicate that Poland provides better conditions for new direct investments than for buy-outs of already existing companies but this, as a consequence, slows down the process of privatisation which is not fast anyway.

Polish law enables two main startegies for privatisation of large state-owned companies (SOEs). The first one, called "capital privatisation", depends on converting SOEs into joint-stock companies owned by the Treasury Ministry (this stage is called "commercialisation") that are then partly or entirely sold to the investor. The second strategy, called "direct privatisation", is to "liquidate" a state-owned company that is then partly or entirely sold to the investor. Most privatisation transactions were carried out as "capital privatisation". Within the years 1990-1997 capital privatisation covered 228 enterprises including 48% of shares bought by foreign investors.

At the same time 80 enterprises were sold to the investors by direct privatisation. Burdensome and long-term privatisation procedures that discourage potential purchasers from investing are the main obstacles for broader participation of foreign investors in the Polish privatisation process. The time necessary to prepare a transaction for buying a company in a capital way usually lasts a year and sometimes even three years.

The same research was aimed at identifying the criteria that was important for Polish interests while making the selection of a foreign investor. It turned out that the criterion of the most favourable price was not decisive. The most decisive criterion was an investor's obligation to carry out further investment as well a conviction that the investor was also the best technical partner. The guarantees of continuity of employment came in third position and the last criterion concerned price and social conditions. Paying so much attention to the commitments connected with the further development of a privatised company points to the government's preference for privatisation advantages in the long term rather than current budget incomes. The greatest attention was paid to the investor's commitments to making technology available, maintenance of the present business profile, increasing initial capital, broadening the product range, taking decisions on modernisation and natural environment protection. . Foreign partners usually meet these commitments, which points to strategic and not spectacular treatment of direct investments in Poland and in this part of Europe. All Polish research confirms the opinion that the best way of privatisation is the "capital privatisation".

Additional effect of privatisation embracing foreign investors is the strengthening of market institutions such as the stock exchange as well as infrastructure development of market economy as a result of the creation of a demand for banking, insurance, consulting, and educational services by foreign investors.

3.3 Increasing the Level of Competitiveness of Polish Companies

Increasing the level of competitiveness of Polish companies and their products and, in fact, the whole Polish economy seems to be the most important, long-term, and irreversible effect of foreign investors' activity.

The research carried out within recent years shows that significant changes occur at all operational levels of joint ventures, i.e. economic, technological, production as well as employment policy.

Statistical research confirms a favourable influence of foreign investments on corporate competitiveness. Work efficiency measured by income per employee was 65% higher in joint ventures than the average for Polish companies. Performance in term of cost, return on stockholders' equity and asset management was also better. However, the net profit margin was lower but continuously increasing. Companies than have gone through the process of "capital privatisation" have better economic performance than all privatised companies.

Office of The Central Statistics carried out some comparative research in 1997 involving over two thousand companies. It used a method of testing the economic situation and produced a precise evaluation of the effectiveness of joint ventures.[7] This research showed that joint ventures were characterised by a higher degree of output capacity than the totality of the companies studied. They had better inventory management and better investment procedures; they maintained a higher level of employment than Polish companies. Research shows a convergence between effectiveness of Polish companies and joint ventures, which is undoubtedly an effect of benchmarking and raising the competitiveness of Polish companies.

Companies' representatives were asked about the barriers to their activity and their future forecasts. Poll research methods revealed characteristic differences of optimism level. Foreign companies complained more often than Polish ones about activity barriers, but they formulated more optimistic forecasts for production and employment as well as declaring a greater readiness to invest. Authors of the research point to a similarity of developmental goals formulating by both types of companies. Extensive development i.e. aspirations for increasing production, sales, exports, and for the introduction of new products came first. A desire for improvement in the efficiency of the production process i.e. reducing manning levels, reducing the use of materials and energy is hardly ever declared. Environmental protection is definitely a priority goal for all the companies. Research in 1995 involving 1750 joint ventures identified the following effects of foreign investments:[8]

- Educational Effect. This depends on improvement of employees' qualifications. Most of the managers claimed that there were qualification requirements to a much higher level including knowledge of a foreign language in the companies of foreign investors. Qualification growth results not only from the job requirement growth, but also from the importance that foreign investors attach to professional training and employee education. Higher work efficiency, the level of professional competence, and employee responsibilities are the outcome of improved investment in human resource management.

- Technological Effect Connected with the Introduction of New Technology. 85% of joint ventures' managers' claim that their companies' own equipment is comparable to that of foreign investors, which encourages staff to put technological improvements into practice. 37% of companies meet world standards as regards product quality, and 58% of them meet European standards, which is proved by the small number of claims and the growth in exports.

- Effect of Company's Organisation and Management Improvement. It was affirmed that joint ventures applied modern techniques of financial management more often than Polish companies. Cost control, financial planning, management accounting, and the efficiency of debt collection was improved. The studied companies show a high level of personnel management, an improvement in the clarity of the organisation, the motivational system, and better staff selection procedures were noted within all of them.

- Marketing Effect Connected With Companies' Market Reorientation. Joint ventures are fully versed in marketing activities. 32% of companies' workers are employed in sales and customer service departments and these companies spend nearly 6% of their budget on advertising and promotion. They participate in trade fairs and exhibitions. They develop detailed sales planning programmes and almost half of their goods are sold abroad.

Most of those scrutinised affirmed that the quality of customer service and market research as well as satisfaction of client needs had developed in their companies. The firms also broadened their trade contacts, increased competitiveness of their products, and improved the quality of the publicity and sales network. Researchers noticed that positive effects of foreign investments had appeared not only within joint ventures but also within the Polish companies, which follow the good examples of foreign ones and try to adopt higher standards of production and management. The imitation effect is particularly strong within competing companies as well as among the suppliers and clients of joint ventures. Results of presented research prove that the arrival of foreign investors is followed by a great improvement in all the elements of a company's management. It is a result not only of a capital transfer but also of partner's experience and ability. Moreover, these companies create good standards of management, which are quickly taken on board by domestic firms. One phenomenon is the return of management and engineering staff to Polish companies who had been «indoctrinated" in the management methods of a foreign company and now undertake an efficient rivalry.

The research into influence of foreign investment on the quality of national products, based on consumers' opinion, shows that the production of foreign companies in Poland squeezed out imports. The growth in the quality of national products is also enhanced by the imitation effect. In the consumers' opinion a significant part of the products being introduced by foreign companies in the Polish market results in a domestic equivalent appearing within three to six months. It follows that, in defiance of what economists say about the negative investment influence on imports, foreign investors reduce imports by making domestic products more attractive.

The influence of foreign investments on the quality of the work environment was studied as part of the same research. Like the managers, the employees of the companies studied appreciated the educational effect of foreign investors in particular as regards work efficiency. They also noticed the introduction of modern methods of work organisation connected with the precise description of workers' tasks, better use of work time, better equipment and workstation devices. 90% of those questioned noticed that their earnings had risen by nearly 70% in relation to the previous workplaces and almost half of them noticed an improvement in the welfare benefit. We commonly claim that workers' flexibility and their influence on a company's activity as well as the degree of their identification with the company rose significantly. The foreign investor's arrival also had a positive influence on the technical environment in the workplace: the range of automation and computerisation in production, the quality of equipment and devices, the quality of raw materials, standards of production and environmental care. Also Health and Safety at work was much better.

Statistical and inquiry research does not allow us to analyse the influence of foreign capital on a Polish company, sector, or economy. In order to understand the transformation process that a Polish company undergoes after being sold to a strategic investor, we must do very precise research using the case study method. Joanna Cygler did very interesting research into alliances of Polish companies with foreign investors. She investigated, among others, some examples of international alliances; Heineken with Zywiec-based Brewery Plant and Siemens with Telephone Devices Manufacturing Plant.[9]

The alliance between Heineken International Beheer B.V. and the well-known Polish brewery was converted into a minority equity alliance in 1994. This alliance had a very strong and favourable influence on the brewery's market position, strategic planning and on management itself. Large investments into production, distribution, and marketing were carried out as a result of recapitalisation. Marketing outlay in relation to 1 hectolitre of beer rose ten times. Beer production was doubled, the range of beer was broadened and diversified, thermo-sensitive labels were introduced, and pricing policy was changed by converting a cost formula into an elastic price formula which could be adjusted according to the actions of competitors, demand, and other market parameters. The distribution system was completely changed. A little-known model of a private distribution network based on distribution costs was introduced. Today, the distribution network of the Polish brewery is used for distributing Heineken beer in Poland. The system of promotion was also modernised and developed. In the face of Polish restrictions on alcohol advertising the promotional system was based on promoting the brewery trade name and not its products. Systems of sponsoring and merchandising as well as public relations were developed. Heineken's experience and its connections with marketing and advertising companies were of great assistance while working out a new marketing strategy for the Polish brewery. The foreign partner also participated in establishing the marketing budget.

The co-operation with the foreign partner caused significant changes in the system of Polish brewery management. Approximately 100 changes were made in the organisational structure within three years. Management was decentralised, many units were liquidated, and many were newly established. Reduction and rationalisation of employment and changes in labour time organisation accompanied these procedures. A new culture of organisation was created where brewery traditions and regional connections were united with the emphasis placed on modern management and innovations. We may notice outward symptoms of a new culture as well as changes in offices decor, and the employees' outfit. The resistance to culture changes suggested by the Dutch partner appeared at the least expected moment. The staff emphatically opposed the demand to remove dozens of cats from the plant. Thus, the cats, being the staff's favourites, are still running within factory boundaries. However, the staff was defeated by the partner's determination concerning many more important issues. Research into staff attitudes showed positive culture changes: changes and innovations susceptibility growth, independence growth, and more openness. Changes in management and strategy bore fruit in market share growth, the firm's image and product improvement, and a good reputation within business environments. Heineken's advantages are also obvious. Within a couple of years it took over a controlling interest in a modern company with an established market position.

Another example of co-operation between German Siemens and the Polish manufacturer of switchboards (ZWUT) also proves the importance of the restructuring power of a huge foreign partner for the Polish company. Siemens set up a joint venture with ZWUT in 1990. In 1993 it made use of a privatisation offer and purchased 80% of ZWUT's shares. The next step was liquidation of the joint venture. Effects of the investor's arrival in a large but outdated Polish factory bore fruit following a huge outlay for modernisation investments and putting Siemens' goods into production in Poland. The allies' co-operation concerned every department from the very beginning.

Siemens gave new technologies and modernised those already existing. It adjusted the logistics and delivery systems to the world standards. It had an influence on marketing policy and the customer service organisation. After the production of modern digital switchboards had been introduced the production of analogue ones ceased, some unprofitable plants were liquidated and the promotion and distribution systems were modernised. Changes in production and marketing were accompanied by changes in company management. A new system of personnel policy was worked out; specialists were trained in Germany and obligations to report in three languages as well as a requirement for a knowledge of German among all managers were introduced. After

Siemens had taken over ZWUT's controlling interest it carried out a total reorganisation of the Polish enterprise. A modern organisation and management system of the hitherto joint venture dominated the outdated ZWUT's structure. Within five years, manning levels were reduced by a factor of twelve and some young and educated employees were recruited. Siemens' success depended on entering the Polish telecommunications equipment sector with so little investment outlay in a short time. It also took advantage of simplified certification procedures for Siemens' products, its Polish partner's infrastructure, and tax holidays.

4. CONCLUSIONS

Research has demonstrated that FDI became one of the main factors of Polish economic success. High dynamism of production and national revenue, fall in inflation, and rise in the competitiveness of Polish products are to a large degree an effect of the investment of foreign capital as well as the introduction of higher management and employee skills.

Realisation of optimistic forecasts for Poland's economic development for the coming year will to a large degree depend on achievement of foreign investment growth. Economists estimate that the Polish economy is able to absorb an annual capital inflow in the order of $ 10 billion. None of the forecasts predict such an optimistic scenario, however it does not seem to be impossible in the light of data for the last two years. The newest forecasts for Poland's economic development are very auspicious. GDP growth up to 7% annually, fall of unemployment up to 6%, fall of imports dynamism, growth of exports dynamism, maintenance of a high, albeit, declining investment pace. Foreign investments would enable Poland to maintain high pace growth and would accelerate an economic integration with West European countries and other economically developed regions through raising the technological and marketing level of the domestic companies.

What are the prospects for the of maintenance of foreign capital inflow to Poland and which factors may prejudice this optimistic scenario? There are two possibilities: the first one is to put the most attractive sectors so far treated as «sensitive» up for sale. They are the oil industry, telecommunications, power, banking and the insurance sectors. The second possibility is to offer less restrictive preconditions for greenfield investments. As far as privatisation plans are concerned, such acceleration is feasible. The process of getting Poland's large state-owned companies ready for privatisation, but so far inaccessible to foreign investors, is coming to an end. These companies are Polish Telecommunication S.A, Pekao Bank S.A; a programme for oil and chemical industry transformation is being worked out;

and the power sector has already just been opened for foreign capital. An opportunity for purchasing shares of many attractive state-owned enterprises will appear within two years. On the other hand, the government offers better and better conditions for greenfield investments. Presently, there are 15 special economic zones in Poland, which offer tax exemptions and other special incentives for foreign investors. The most attractive is Gliwice Special Economic Zone where GM and Isuzu built their plants.

The Polish social climate is also favourable for foreign capital inflow. Research into a representative group of Poles, carried out over five years, shows that the number of avowed supporters of foreign capital inflow is stable around 40%. The numbers of people who voice an objection is also relatively stable and varies between 26% and 36%. The supporters are young, well educated people, inhabitants of big cities, who enjoy good living conditions.[10]   Research into management staff and employees of Polish companies showed that nearly 60% of them consider the presence of foreign investors to be good for the Polish economy and only 27% opposed this view.. The percentage of foreign capital supporters at 76% is definitely highest among the managing staff, which is proved by all the researches. The other employees are less enthusiastic about foreign investors since they are concerned about losing their jobs, welfare benefits, or just money.[11] These studies show that the opinions of workers being employed in a joint venture are very positive, so most of the fears seem to be practically unjustified. The social climate for foreign investments may be recognised as favourable and still improving.

Considering the prospects of FDI we cannot ignore the barriers, which still exist and discourage foreign investors. A considerable number of companies withdrawing from the Polish market trigger off some anxiety. Between 1995-1996, some 4,772 new joint ventures were set up while 3,893 companies withdrew. In the opinion of Commerce and Industry Chamber for Foreign Investors so many of these withdrawals result in these companies being treated less favourably than domestic companies. The foreign investors in most cases complain about:

- Lack of stable investment conditions caused by the many concession and permission procedures including difficulty with purchasing real estate.

- Unclear legal regulations – foreign investors' activities are regulated by as many as six Acts,

- Infrastructure underdevelopment, especially border checkpoints, customs administration, telecommunications, communications, banking, and real estate,

- Restriction imposed by tax, visas, and works regulations.

In the economists' opinion the withdrawal of smaller investors may be a result of some objective difficulties on the one hand, and cost underestimation on the other. The other reason may be competitive growth of Polish companies. These barriers are, however, gradually being eliminated and should not inhibit obvious opportunities for action within the Polish market i.e. high demand dynamism, large market, cheap labour force, proximity of eastern markets and the coming EU integration process. Poland's accession to OECD in November 1996 was preceded by number of liberalisations in the field of law and economy, which accelerated the progress of law and business activity standards to match world standards. This now gives a chance to maintain and even raise the inflow of foreign capital to Poland. In the face of slow reforms and policy instability in Russia, Ukraine, and Belarus, Poland's rising investment attractiveness provides an excellent opportunity to maintain or even increase the level of direct foreign investments.

REFERENCES

1 Z. Dworzecki. Map of investment risk in the Middle and East European countries. Studies of IBNGR» No. 5, 1998.
2 Foreign Investment in Poland; Private & Public Attitudes, Polish Agency for Foreign Investment, Warsaw 1996
3 Statistical evidence of Polish Agency for Foreign Investment
4 J. Misala. Macroeconomic effects of foreign capital involvement within the process of transformation of Polish economy. Foreign capital and privatisation process. Collective study edited by M. Jarosz. ISP PAN, Warsaw 1996.
5 ibidem
6 Analysis of foreign investments inflow on Polish economy. Polish Agency for Foreign Investment, 1996.
7 K. Marczewski. Foreign investors' activity within food processing industry in the light of economic situation researches. In: Foreign investments in Poland. IKICHZ, Warsaw, p.111.
8 Analysis ... op. cit., p.55
9 J. Cygler. Changes in Market Position, Strategy and Management System of Polish Enterprises as the Impact of Strategic Alliances with Foreign Partners. Warsaw School of Economics, 1998.
10 Pentor – Institute for Market and Opinions Research.
11 Foreign Investors ... op. cit., p. 260

Chapter 8

Transition and Democracy in Romania: the Pains of a Gradualist Restructuring

Sergio Alessandrini
University of Modena and University L. Bocconi, Milano

Abstract   Romania's democratic and economic transition has progressed more slowly than that of some of the other countries in the region. Differences in the initial conditions greatly affected the outcome. The National Salvation Front (NSF) governments, which succeeded after 1990, used to draw up economic macrostability programmes for one or at most two years. The transition strategy advocated slower, more cautious economic reforms and a social safety net, without ever defining the direction of development on a medium and long-term basis, which is necessary for the development of a sound and efficient private sector. The gradualist approach failed to produce the incentives since the institutional restructuring and the "depoliticisation" of the economy was inadequate, in particular in the industrial sector. Structural reforms were often delayed in comparison with the other CEE countries so the economic performance of Romania was poor and impoverishing. Political commitment to reforms has improved remarkably since the pro-market democratic coalition government came into office in December 1996. Monetary stabilisation brought inflation down and stabilised the foreign exchange. Privatisation and restructuring of major state-owned enterprises and the autonomous regions has been accelerated and the results are expected to improve efficiency and competitiveness and an enduring transition to a market-oriented economy. The application to European Union (EU) membership and the adoption of a "partnership for adhesion", with parameters and prospective timetable, will accelerate the adaptation of the right measures to support economic reforms and strengthen the democratic institutions in Romania. However, to do so successfully, the centre-right government needs to be sure it has broad based support to avoid popular backlash.

1.   THE ECONOMIC AND POLITICAL LEGACY

With an area of 237.500 square kilometres, and a population of 22.7 million, Romania is a medium-sized European country. Its population is predominantly of Romanian ethnic origin (89% with important minorities of Hungarian (8.9 %), Gypsy (1.6 %) and German (0.4 %), Ukrainian, Serb, Croat, Russian and Turkish origin. Minority populations are localised in Transylvania and the Banat, areas in the north and west which belonged to the Austro-Hungarian Empire until World War I. Ethnic Romanians comprised the overall majority in Transylvania, even before union with Romania, but ethnic Hungarians and Germans were the dominant urban population there until relatively recently, and still are the majority in a few districts. To complement this ethnic composition, the religion is almost entirely Roman Orthodox.

Besides being physically more removed from Western Europe, Romania is a complex mosaic of peoples and cultures which share certain traditions with the west. Nevertheless, the mixture of ethno-cultural groups seems to lead to inevitable conflict over basic principles for the management of their society and government. The historical memory of this country[1] shares many events in common with the Western European nations, as well as some authoritarian regimes. In the First World War Romania sided with the allies of the Entente and was occupied by Austro-Hungarian, Turkish and Bulgarian forces. Bukovina and Transylvania were claimed and annexed to Romania after the post-war settlement. As a result of a coup led by the General Antonescu and other pro-fascist elements, Romania entered the Second World War on the Nazi side in 1941. At the end of the war, in spite of the coup led by King Michael, which deposed the Antonescu dictatorship, Soviet occupation forces encouraged the appointment of a communist-led coalition government, while Bessarabia and part of Bukovina were annexed to the Soviet Union. During the sixties Romania maintained some distance from the Soviet Union in its external policy but internal policies become highly repressive and centralised under a personal and nepotistic dictatorship which lasted for more than two decades.

It was evident to many specialists that the Brasov riots of 1987 signalled that Romania was a country boiling under the surface and might erupt at any moment. In fact pressures for change mounted after Ceausescu launched a "sistematizare" (read de-villagisation) campaign in 1987. As a result, protests by ethnic Hungarians against Romanian rule escalated, with large demonstrations occurring in June 1988. Thousands of ethnic Hungarians also began fleeing the country, with hundreds reportedly shot while trying to cross the border into Yugoslavia. With the border situation clearly getting out of control, in mid-1989 Ceausescu decided to improve the defences along the Romanian-Hungarian border. When news of the construction leaked out, Romania was vilified in the West, embarrassing the Soviet policy beyond Eastern Europe, including Gorbachev's efforts to court Western Europe and to increase stability in Central Europe. Moreover, Ceausescu's call before the 14th RCP Congress in late November 1989 for Moscow to renounce the Molotov-Ribbentrop pact was an obvious call for the issue of sovereignty over Soviet Moldavia (former Romanian Bessarabia) to be raised again. Under international pressure Ceausescu eventually backed down from this plan, but one month later the regime ended with a coup d'état headed by a group of former communists, the National Salvation Front. In late afternoon of 22 December 1989 a new interim government was announced and the country entered into a difficult and volatile process of transition.

2.   THE POLITICAL DEVELOPMENTS

Ion Iliescu emerged as the leader of the National Salvation Front (NSF) and as the President of the interim government. He announced the establishment of a democratic multi-party system of government and the holding of new free elections. The electoral law was published on 14 March 1990 providing for the election of the National President and the Parliament, whose main task was to draw up the details of the new constitution. Shortly before the election, the NSF was openly criticised for the continued political and economic influence of members of the Ceausescu-era elite. Anti-communist and pro-democratic leaders had camped in Bucharest's University Square since April 1990 protesting about the dictatorial character of the Front until they were brutally dispersed by the miners who descended on Bucharest from the Jiu Valley in June 1990.

With this background of intimidation and open violence, presidential and parliamentary elections were held on May 20, 1990. Running against representatives of the pre-war National Peasants' Party and National Liberal Party, Iliescu won 85 % of the votes. The NSF, having captured two-thirds of the seats in Parliament, named a university professor, Petre Roman, as Prime Minister. His programme included cautious free market reforms such as the elimination of consumer subsidies, the liberalisation of prices and exchange rates and populist measures to restore living standards such as the reduction of the working week and the diversion of energy away from industry to households. Given the chaotic situation of the country, the Roman government was forced to negotiate and compromise the new laws directly with all groups interested to protect those affected, in particular the independent trade unions and with groups defending the rights for the minorities. He also put in place a tight monetary policy, but in the face of hostile demonstrations by coal miners, who returned to Bucharest to demand higher salaries and better living conditions, the government resigned in late September 1991. Theodor Stolojan, a technocrat, was appointed to head an interim government until new elections could be held after the approval of the new democratic constitution. In September 1992 national elections returned President Iliescu and his party by a clear majority and a new government led by an economist, Nicolae Vacaroiu, was formed in November 1992 with parliamentary support from three smaller parties, the nationalist PUNR and PRM parties, and the ex-communist PSM party. The NSF changed his name into the Party of Social Democracy of Romania (PDSR) in July 1993. The 1992 elections revealed a political cleavage between major urban centres and the countryside: rural voters, grateful for the restoration of most agricultural land to farmers but fearful of change, strongly favoured President Ion Iliescu and the NSF, while the urban electorate favoured the Democratic Convention (CDR) and quicker reform. The Vacaroiu government ruled until the three smaller parties abandoned the coalition in December 1995.

The 1996 elections revealed a major shift in the political orientation of the Romanian electorate. Opposition parties dominated the larger cities and made steep inroads into rural areas on the twin themes of the need to staunch corruption and to launch economic reform. Emil Constantinescu of the Democratic Convention electoral coalition defeated President Iliescu in the second round of voting by 6% and replaced him as Chief of State. The PDSR won the largest number of seats in parliament, but the constituent parties of the CDR joined the Democratic Party, the National Liberal Party, and the Hungarian Democratic Union of Romania (HDUR) to form a centrist coalition government holding 60% of the seats in parliament. Victor Ciorbea, a former labour lawyer and government prosecutor, was named Prime Minister. The new government outlined three top priorities, namely shock economic reform (including privatisation/liquidation of state enterprises and monetary and fiscal reform), decentralisation, and a campaign against corruption. After a reshuffle in December 1997, changing one third of the cabinet members and creating a new Ministry for Privatisation, Ciorbea resigned in March 1998 and was replaced by Radu Vasile, Secretary general of the influential National Peasants' Christian and Democratic Party (PNTCD) which facilitated return of the Democratic Party in the Government.

If one believes theories stating that democracy is only possible in a western-style country, it would seem difficult to automatically entitle Romania to the opportunity. The history of the country weighs heavily against the prospects of the reforms enacted in the Nineties. Romania was under communist rule for over forty years and the economic crisis had been growing steadily since 1982 when Ceausescu embarked upon a program designed to help Romania pay off nearly $10 billion in foreign debt. In doing so it engaged the country in a forced export drive and in a ruthless compression of vital imports, which starved the country of badly needed inputs, technology and even food. Ceausescu did achieve that goal in 1989, but only at an enormous cost in human suffering and deprivation. With investment slashed, Romania's technological infrastructure rapidly fell behind that of even its Balkan neighbours. The irrational plan to destroy eight thousand villages and move their residents into high-rise apartment complexes, as well as prestige projects with little economic return, absorbed a substantial proportion of the gross domestic product. In achieving these goals an enormous cost was plunged upon the population, making Romania one of the poorer countries in Central and Eastern Europe.

A largely obsolete industrial base and a pattern of output unsuited to the country's needs were additional burdens on the road of transition to the market economy. External shocks as well hit the country at a time of major political turmoil: the collapse of CMEA, the Gulf War and the disintegration of Yugoslavia. Both internal and external factors made even more difficult to implement changes and reforms.

The legacy of the communist regime and lack of experience of partial reforms, such as those undertaken in other Central European economies during the 1980s, left the country with a long and unstable path towards a market economy. All major parties espoused democracy and market reforms, but the three NSF Governments proposed slower, more cautious economic reforms and a social safety net, while the opposition Democratic Convention (CDR), which took the leadership in November 1996, favoured quick, sweeping reforms, immediate privatisation, and a reduction in the role of the ex-communist elite. The measures reflected a different attitude about the role of the market and its value as signal for the activities of the economic agents.[2] Having adopted a gradualist approach, over the past eight years, the transition to a market economy has been protracted and painful. Consequently, the economic restructuring has lagged behind most other countries in the region, with slowing GDP growth, ballooning budget deficits and inflation, a plunging exchange rate, and anaemic foreign investment.

3.   THE ECONOMIC PERFORMANCE AND THE STRUCTURAL CHANGES IN THE ECONOMY: THE THREE POLITICAL STAGES

In the context of the processes of economic and social reform, the Romanian economy passed through three distinct stages that overlap the political developments. Using economic and political data from widely available public sources, we can evaluate the performance and the sustainability of the Romanian transition to a market economy. We have seen that Romania started its transition from a difficult inherited position. The first stage ran from 1990 to 1993 and its main objective was the creation of a democratic state and an institutional framework for a market social economy, abandoning central planning and liberalising prices, trade and production. As a consequence the economic activity declined sharply during the period 1990-1992. The patterns of resource allocation matched neither real costs of production nor the preferences of consumers and the GDP declined 13 % in 1991, the worst decline reported by the transition economies. Inflation soared into triple figures and the currency devalued rapidly. In 1991 most prices were freed and small trading firms were privatised, while the former nomenclature appropriated larger firms. Collective farming remained almost untouched. The first measures of economic and social reform were concentrated almost exclusively on short-term objectives aimed at opening the domestic market for massive imports and ensuring productive output irrespective of the level of economic efficiency. The government's dedication to radical change was low for fear of social discontent. In fact the fall in GDP had been steeper than in other Central European countries, so that according to calculations based on PlanEcon estimates, the average consumption in 1993 was $1.412, down from $2.181 in 1989. The real national income per capita, had dropped by nearly 40 % in comparison with the maximum levels reached at the end of the 1980s. The same can be said of real wages, the fall in which closely followed the GDP drop. Therefore, several unpopular measures were postponed during the first three years and the final results were a worsening of the inherited structural macro-economic and sectional imbalances and the delay of the external financing from international institutions.

Starting in 1993, under pressure from international organisations, the government implemented a strict macroeconomic stabilisation, amplifying simultaneously the gradual processes of structural adjustment in order to give the national economy a competitive composition. This second stage was characterised by decisive actions in all fields of activity, using economic and financial key factors in order to halt economic decline, to release productive activity, and, in particular, to reduce the social costs of transition. Inflation rate was curbed to 62 % in 1994 and a GDP that fell 25 % in two years, 1991 and 1992, returned to grow in 1993 with a 1 % increase and a 4 % increase in 1994, slightly better than forecast, thanks to an extraordinary export performance. In this context, special importance had been devoted to assuring the functioning of the institutional system and to completing the legislative framework necessary to carry on market economy activities, permitting the principal producers to adopt suitable types of economic behaviour based on initiative and competition. Perceptible progress had been registered initially by the implementation of a programme of mass privatisation, development of managerial attitudes, the strengthening of the financial discipline of the autonomous regions, the regulation of bankruptcy procedures, and the promotion of competition within the Romanian economy.

Corrective actions, such as price liberalisation for most products, the elimination of certain subsidies for output and consumption, the introduction of new taxes and fiscal regulations, gradually influenced positively the behaviour of the economic entities, leading to a reduction of the inflationary expectations and to an increase of the perceived welfare. The economic recovery of the second stage had a negative effect upon the psychological attitude of a population so "naive" to the market mechanisms. Many Romanians, as indeed others across Central Europe, believed that the market economy would automatically and almost immediately bring affluence, improved living conditions and better qualities of all kinds of goods imported from the Western countries. The recovery of real incomes of the young and educated people, new entrepreneurs and the successful businessmen seemed to augur better days and they were trapped by private money-making schemes or pyramids promising huge dividends. At the beginning they returned highly spectacular payoffs to early investors but later they collapsed. The biggest fund in Romania was known as Caritas in the Transylvanian city of Cluj. Promising a 800 % profit within one hundred days, Caritas, run by a former accountant Ion Stoica, was a national celebrity from mid-1993 to early 1994, when the pyramid collapsed owing $1 billion to 3 million investors. In 1995 Stoica was convicted of misuse of funds and sentenced to six years imprisonment. His sentence was later reduced and he was released from custody. The Government accepted no "moral responsibility".

In spite of this incident, common to other CEE countries, the renewed stability was driven and sustained by the partial recovery of the external markets for the companies having comparative cost advantages and by the resumption of infrastructure investments. The business climate improved and the output of industry increased slightly. Economic recovery was much more accentuated by the good performance of the agriculture sector. In this respect, during 1995, several measures were implemented that permitted an upward evolution of the market demand for consumer goods and sustained the purchasing capacity of the internal market. The state has continued to be involved in agriculture by means of the specific mechanisms it used to assist small producers, namely: interest allowances and subsidies for production credits and investments, production allowances and compensations, fiscal advantages, guaranteed purchasing prices for agricultural products of national importance, and the provision of specialised technical assistance. The subsidies that were mainly oriented towards agricultural activities in 1995 represented 2.6 % of GDP or 7.5 % of the fiscal deficit [3]. In the framework of the process of transition during the 1994-1995 period, a renewed place was reserved for the privatisation of the commercial companies in the portfolio of the State Property Fund through the distribution of new vouchers instead of the direct negotiations with employees (management and employee buy-out: MEBO). Of course the easiest companies to privatise were those having few structural problems and therefore potentially profitable for investors. These were, respectively, those involved in agriculture, the food industry, textiles and clothing, wood processing, trade, tourism, transport, construction, and building materials. Consequently in the private sector, in addition to very small units created through individual initiative, some enterprises having a significant productive potential also began operations, a few of which were listed on the newly opened Bucharest Stock Exchange. However, the protracted privatisation of the large loss-making enterprises and the explicit support given by the banking sector, still under the control of the State, contributed to the deterioration of the fiscal deficit. The lack of financial discipline in the large SOEs contributed to the expansion of the money base and the acceleration of inflation. In the final analysis, the risks of the gradualist strategy materialised in December 1995, when, dissatisfied with the slow pace of reform, the IMF and World Bank halted their financial support.

Going beyond the immediate positive implications of the economic recovery of 1994, the results obtained in the last two years overshadowed the true picture of the socio-economic transformation and the risk factors that interfered with the evolutionary trend of the Romanian economy. That is, on the one hand, its high levels of subsidies to the autonomous regions and the extra-budgetary funds to agriculture, and on the other hand its high level of dependence upon exports of the energy-intensive branches of industry. In the context of accentuated international competition as a result of geo-political modifications and the stagnation of demand faced by the developed economies (in particular the European Union), the growth of output could not be based exclusively on external orders. Therefore when the export performance, based as it was to a large extent on unrestructured heavy industry highly dependent upon imports of energy and raw materials, fell behind the original expectations, the government decided to allocate the scarce foreign exchange to these priority sectors on the basis of a non-market "official" exchange rate. As a result, after a temporary recovery in 1994 and 1995, structural problems re-emerged as a serious obstacle to growth and the economic situation deteriorated in 1996. The 1996 budget deficit grew above 4% of GDP, exceeding initial estimates and reflecting election-year spending pressure. The excess demand for hard currencies led to the development of a parallel market and in November 1995 the significant deterioration of the current account deficit resulted in a sharp depreciation of the official exchange.

All this ended with the defeat of post-communist candidates in the presidential and parliamentary elections of late 1996. In the new political landscape the Christian-Democratic and liberal coalition launched the third stage of transition with a bold programme to address the problems that had caused previous programmes to fail. The Ciorbea government tackled the Romanian economic problems in two stages, with an emergency plan over 1996/97 to ensure social and political stability, followed by a radical structural reform programme over its remaining three and a half years aiming eventually at EU accession. The economic programme for 1997-98 supported by a new stand-by credit sought a decline in the external current account deficit to 4.5 % of GDP in 1997 from 6.6 % in 1996 and a sharp cut in the rate of inflation. Real GDP, however, was expected to decline by 1.5 % in 1997 in part due to a drop in output at a large number of SOEs as subsidies were withdrawn and input prices increased. To these ends the Ciorbea Government undertook a major fiscal adjustment, reducing the combined fiscal deficit and the quasi-fiscal subsidies provided by the National Bank of Romania from 8.3 % of GDP to 3.7 % in 1997. Fiscal measures did include increases in taxes on domestic crude oil and natural gas production and increases in excise and value-added tax rates. The programme was also supported by wage limits for loss-making state-owned commercial companies and the autonomous regions.

In the enterprise sector, the programme focussed on restructuring, involving liquidation or privatisation of many state-owned farms and industrial enterprises. Reform of the financial sector centred on strengthening the legal framework governing banks and other financial intermediaries and the privatisation of three banks in 1998. At this third stage, Romania has decided to break with the past hesitant and piecemeal approach to reform. In applying for membership, Romania accepted the objectives of the Treaty on European Union and the challenge now is to implement all measures set out in the White Paper, particularly the Single Market directives in the fields of taxation, public procurement, banking and intellectual property, or other important areas of the European Union's activity such as the environment, energy, agriculture, telecommunications, transport and social policy.

4.   DE-MONOPOLISATION AND THE PRIVATE SECTOR PERFORMANCE UNTIL 1996

Until 1996 the development of a private sector had been slow but noteworthy, accounting for 45% of GDP, well below the Czech or Hungarian levels in the same years. The expansion of private activities was the result of two phenomena: the creation of new enterprises and the transfer of property from the state sector. The 45 % figure covers up a wide variation by sector. For example, 80 % of agricultural land was transferred to private hands, although it was severely undercapitalised. That is important because agriculture accounts for 35 % of the workforce compared to 6.5% in the Czech Republic. Retail trade and consumer services were nearly 70 % and construction was 50 % privatised. Altogether about 500,000 private firms, about a third of which were small family-run enterprises, had been registered over the 1990-1996 period. Resource support for the SMEs from central and local government remained very modest. In this arena, a more active role had been played by semi-governmental and non-governmental foundations, entrepreneurs' associations, and chambers of commerce, with financial support from Western governments and international organisations (the European Union's PHARE Program, the World Bank, USAID, the Know How Fund, etc.). On the contrary the transfer of State enterprises offered for privatisation had been delayed and restricted by the poor performance of the companies and the poorly conceived methods of de-monopolisation [4]. This meant that the private sector accounted for only 15% of industrial production. One of the particularly serious consequences of the transition process has been the rise in unemployment, which has risen from 3 % (337.400 people) in 1991 to 10.9 percent (1.224.000) in 1994, of which the proportion of unemployed women in 1994 was 56.6 % and unemployed youth under 25 was 44 %. In terms of branch of activity, important reductions in employment were recorded in industry (especially in manufacturing), in transportation, and in construction. At the same time, an increase in the number of persons employed in agriculture and trade, as well as in financial and banking activities, was observed. The scarcity of jobs was a serious problem that distorted social balance. In Romania, unemployment tends to become chronic and is already a long-term phenomenon. It is unemployment caused by underproduction and economic decline, which is accompanied by emigration and the extension of the labour black market.

Romania ended 1996 with considerable structural problems. Inter-company arrears accounted for 16 % of GDP. The energy sector was propped up by hundreds of millions of dollars of indirect subsidies. Heavy industry was still largely in state hands and run with little concern for the balance sheet. Restructuring would require substantial labour shedding and capacity reductions. The agricultural sector had tremendous potential, but lacked the management, infrastructure, and capital necessary to produce and to market the products efficiently.

5. ECONOMIC POLICY REFORMS

Progress towards economic policy reforms is assessed from indicators drawn from the European Bank for Reconstruction and Development (EBRD) annual Transition Report[5], as well as other official sources. The indicators focus on critical economic aspects of liberalisation and institution building in the transition process, and are divided into "rounds", roughly corresponding to stages of development through which emerging economies pass.

The building of a new economic system involved two steps: increasing economic freedom and a comprehensive transformation of the economic institutions. The sequence and the speed of these steps are key issues in assessing the progress in different areas of reforms and their sustainability during the restructuring. For Romania the strategy over the period considered can be summarised as "a quick and widespread liberalisation and a slow institutional restructuring"; this means that liberalisation took place in a basically unchanged institutional structure, a source of errors and misallocation of resources, precluding the elimination of the massive shortages as well as the needed adjustment of the price structure to the market conditions. Besides, the gradualist approach advocated by the NSF benefited the "normal" politics conducted by political parties and the game of particular interests, but left an incomplete and inconsistent reform. The drawback of this strategy, with the high level of conflicts within the fragmented political system and the frequency of changes of government during 1991 and 1996 influenced negatively the expectations of the economic agents and therefore their willingness to engage in longer-term investments. Both stagnation of economic growth and increase of unemployment inspired the changes in the 1996 elections.

5.1 First Round Of Reforms

. liberalisation of prices

. external trade and currency arrangements
. privatisation of small-scale units

In many respects, these first rounds of reforms were designed to introduce a free market in as many sectors of the economy as possible. Since they required relatively little institution building, they have been the easiest. In fact, while in CEE the economic liberalisation by freeing up prices, eliminating subsidies, removing import restrictions and encouraging the establishment of private commercial ventures were generally adopted rapidly and quite thoroughly. The NSF governments which ruled Romania between December 1989 and November 1992 avoided serious economic reform, fearing "shock therapy" and its anticipated social costs. Confusion characterised 1990, with acute economic disorganisation, exacerbated by a breakdown of law and order and dramatic worker absenteeism. Half of the prices in the consumer good basket were liberalised by the Roman government in November 1990. The successive 1991 and 1992 liberalisation programmes were not fully implemented by the Stolojan government and they went off the rails. Indeed, the pattern of resource allocation matched neither the real costs of production nor the preferences of consumers, thus resulting in a temporary dislocation of production. Therefore, the down side of the price liberalisation was a sharp reduction of domestic consumer demand, which soon had a deadening effect on industrial and agricultural production. For Romania, the worst decline in GDP was in 1991, of 13 %.

These effects had a negative impact on retail consumer prices and quickly led the upsurge in unemployment. Although a reform agenda was developed and a large body of legislation enacted, little was done to actually implement reforms because of the fear of social unrest and social conflicts. Only the pressure of the International Monetary Fund and its imposed conditions for extending the structural adjustment loans convinced the Vacaroiu government, in 1993, to eliminate most of the consumer subsidies, while deciding to keep under direct control the prices of raw and basic materials, including all agricultural products, oil and energy products.

In the attempt to re-establish the correct signals to the producers and reduce the burden on the state budget, explicitly required by a new stabilisation programme, in early 1997 the Ciorbea government decided to complete price liberalisation by limiting the number of controlled prices to less than twenty items (essentially prices of public utilities and energy). For agricultural products the controls on prices were lifted following the decision to reorganise the state seed monopolies in March 1997.

The liberalisation of the foreign trade regime was completed by the end of 1992 leaving quantitative import restrictions only for a few products related to public health or security. The monopoly of foreign trade was abolished and enterprises were entitled to retain and trade in foreign currencies. However, a feature of Romania's trade policy has been the proliferation of discretionary and temporary reductions in tariff rates, in particular in the form of tariff quotas, which covered around half of Romania's imports. In 1996 additional trade restrictions (including export prohibitions and export quotas) were introduced in an attempt to curb a rising trade deficit.

The initial effect of economic liberalisation was an immediate escalation in retail prices, but also a rapid elimination of goods shortages that benefited the consumers after years of resignation and falling living standards. The primary objective, as advocated by transition economists, was to enable the emergence of effective price signals for the further development of a market economy. But in the case of Romania, the price liberalisation undoubtedly worked to the advantage of the monopolistic large-scale enterprises which continued to dominate the state sector, since the de-monopolisation was delayed in favour of the selective and piecemeal approach adopted by the NSF governments. They did so on a number of grounds: among others, the entrenched bureaucratic power potential of management in this residual core of the old system and the fear that domestic and foreign private buyers would "pick the eyes" out of the stock of state enterprises, leaving the state with only the poorest, least saleable performers, which would constitute a continuing heavy burden on the state budget.

This, too, was not unexpected. Problems with the monopoly position of some producers and buyers inherited from the previous system were acknowledged and, in other transition economies they were combated by a specific anti-monopoly legislation, which in Romania was enacted only in 1996 and therefore had only marginal effects. While conceding that privatisation was virtually impossible to complete in the short run, the government enacted orders and laws that changed the status and modus operandi of the state enterprises: above all, through Law No. 15/1990 they were immediately transformed into joint stock companies, with the state as the 100 % shareholder and with state-appointed supervisory boards of directors, until suitable divestiture provisions could be arranged. As a second step, a certain proportion of the shares would be sold and/or distributed to the Romanian citizens and other designated "financial intermediaries".

The scheme, together with the Law-Decree No. 54/1990 for "setting up small and medium-sized private firms", was clearly well tailored to address the major problems of the Romanian legacy, but it is worth illustrating the pitfalls awaiting serious programmes of economic reform. The ubiquitousness of state involvement in the economy during the previous regime has had qualitative, as well as quantitative dimensions; therefore one must consider its nature which leads to the "nomenklatura capitalism" or "spontaneous privatisation", where members of the former communist ruling elite take advantage of their old connections and new opportunities to gain control over state enterprises as their de facto personal property. This occurred on a massive scale in Romania in the first months after the 1990 elections, as managers and local officials colluded to gain control of the enterprise. Another problem inherited from the past, which illustrates the psychological legacy of the command system is the preference on the part of workers and former officials alike for worker ownership and worker self-management of the privatised enterprises. The ideological basis of this preference is clear since the beginning, as evidenced by Iliescu and Roman endorsement of this form of privatisation in their effort to retain a socialist element in the market reforms. The main drawback was a bias against long-term development and the likely isolation from domestic and international market forces.

5.2   Second Round of Reforms

- property restitution
- large-scale privatisation
- enterprise

The NSF governments had an essential role to play in modifying their own functions in the economy and in creating a more propitious framework for structural and systemic changes meant to encourage the progress of economic reform. But they failed. Despite attempts since 1989 to grant more freedom of initiative to lower management levels, decision-making power still remained largely with controlling ministries and their subordinated agencies. In addition, decentralisation without discipline and responsibilities continued to reproduce inefficiencies and losses.

The return of collectivised farmland to its cultivators was one of the first initiatives of the post-December 1989 revolution government, but it resulted in a short-term decrease in agricultural production. Some 4 million small parcels representing 80 % of the arable surface were returned to original owners or their heirs. Many of the recipients were elderly or city dwellers, and the slow progress of granting formal land titles was, in the succeeding years, an obstacle to leasing or selling land to active farmers.

For the industrial sector, having advocated moderation and gradualism, progress toward these reforms has been slower than that of the first round reforms; not surprisingly, because they require more preparation to build political consensus as well as to create the set of incentives needed to implement them. It may be that, according to the EBRD 1997 Transition Report, only the Czech Republic, Hungary and Estonia have progressed sufficiently in these regards (with an indicator of 4), since Romania scores only "2" for the large-scale privatisation, well below the threshold and "3" for small-scale privatisation. It was only with the programme launched at the end of 1993 that significant progress was achieved in accelerating the enterprise reform. But the momentum slowed down again in early 1996 in the face of mounting political resistance. So, at that time, the structure of the Romanian economy was still largely socialised and the privatisation programme continued to be plagued by political infighting, with only slight movement in the elimination of the former communists from positions of power. The preferences of the latter were clearly for retaining as much as possible of the old system, and substantial sections of the population were receptive to their socio-populist appeals. Thus, even though radical reform programmes were pushed through the legislature, in particular the law No. 15 of 8 August 1990, and suitably approved by the IMF and the EBRD, real progress towards the market and privatisation was not impressive. So, at the end, many large SOEs and state farms did not face any real risk of bankruptcy and they continued to obtain cheap credit easily from the state-owned commercial banks, which in turn refinanced them at the National Bank of Romania (NBR).

A number of legal and political obstacles undermined the integrity of the privatisation programme. The government owned virtually all industrial SOEs and controlled the state farms, which still accounted for about 10 percent of agricultural lands. While it is true that the development of a private sector had started to modify the structure of the economy, it was obvious that basic industries had seen little change, expectations being that they will remain under state control for the foreseeable future. Especially slow was the progress in enterprise restructuring and privatisation: at the end of 1996, the state sector accounted for 76 % of industrial production; only 1.100 of the 6.300 SOEs had been transferred to private owners and none of the large state-owned problem companies had seen any meaningful restructuring. In persisting with policies supporting SOEs and subsidies, Romania faced the risk of serious financial crisis. The old system had collapsed and the new, market-oriented replacements had hardly begun to be introduced. Much of what was achieved during 1990-96 in the transition to a market economy was due to private, small family-run enterprises operating very actively in the informal sector which accounts, according to Romania estimates, to around 20-30 percent of the official GDP. So the results achieved were relatively behind the progress in other CEE countries at the end of 1996: the private sector accounted for 52 % of GDP, 87 % of agricultural production, 78.5 % of domestic retail trade, 74.5 % of services, 47.7 % of imports, 50.7 % of exports, but only 24 % of industrial output. The chaotic and, in some cases, primitive state of the industrial and infrastructure networks in Romania offered few attractions for foreign investors, and the available pool of domestic savings, not to mention the structural and psychological preconditions for private investment, were still rudimentary.

The agriculture sector reflects most of these general problems, as well as a spectrum of special demographic and socio-economic problems unique to that sector. Former SOEs have inherited common problems from the command system, which seriously encumbered the attempt to create an efficient privately owned agriculture system. Given the decisive role of the state sector, this necessarily implied the privatisation of more or less intact state farms and producer co-operatives under the pressure of strong movements to legislate for the restitution of collectivised and nationalised land to their former peasant owners. In the meantime efforts were made to retain the most efficient large-scale farming enterprises and to give alternative parcels of land to private farmers. The resulting legislation implemented in 1991 (Land Law No. 18/1991) was one of the most radical land reforms in the region. More than four million new private farms were created, because the law favoured the division and the quick restitution of land. The new private farms were relatively small in size, even by the West European standards, and a limit of one hundred hectares had been established for private land holdings. Property rights were ill defined and the majority of farmers were assigned only temporary ownership titles. The resulting uncertainty about property rights meant that individuals were able neither to sell land nor use it as collateral for credit operations. Alternatively, encouragement was given to private farmers to farm or to join already existing co-operatives and maintain some form of large-scale joint farming enterprises on a share-holding basis. The scarcity of small implements and other farming inputs mentioned earlier was a good reason for adopting this strategy, at least as a temporary expedient until a fully fledged market in farm inputs and outputs was established.

The development of a private sector agriculture system was seriously hampered by the problems of inadequate and inefficient infrastructures, by insufficient mechanisation, and the lack of a fully functioning credit and banking system geared to meet the specific needs of small farmers. Also the presence of monopolistic input industries did not provide technology appropriate for the relatively small-scale private farmer. Exports had been directed to the Russian and other eastern markets to help pay for imports of needed fuels and raw materials, which were severely cut back by the collapse of Soviet trade in 1991. In short, the initial reliance on a totally free market in agriculture had effectively been abandoned, as the NSF governments came to grips with the realities of international agricultural trade. Prices were liberalised again in 1997, together with the reorganisation of State controlling enterprises for input and output. Whether this will inhibit the development of a rational agricultural development strategy in the context of a private farming system remains to be seen. Given their natural endowments and past trade patterns in Europe, there are reasons to believe that Romania will again become a major exporter of agricultural products, from horticultural to meat and dairy items and in some cases, food and feed grains as well. Given the likely persistence of import restrictions on their products by the EU, it is highly possible that they will appear as competitors of traditional exporters like Australia and New Zealand on the world market.

5.3   Third Round of Reforms

· banking reform and private non-bank financial institutions
· competition policy
· investment-related legal reforms.

These reforms are the most challenging, and progress is least evident in this domain. It may be that no CEE country has yet adequately restructured in this third round set of reforms. While the Czech Republic, Hungary and Poland have gone the farthest, Romania is far behind the leaders having failed to implement any form of radical reform. A two-tier banking system was introduced in December 1990: the National Bank of Romania assumed the traditional central banking functions, while its commercial operations were transferred to the newly created Romanian Commercial Bank. In addition, in April 1991, the general banking law No. 33/1991 provided for the transformation of the existing four banks into joint stock companies. A statute passed within the law No. 34/1991 granted significant autonomy within the regulatory framework defined by the National Bank of Romania for the bank's management to undertake lending and deposit-taking throughout the country. Consequently the banking sector consists of five state owned banks and a relative small number of private banks. The state-owned banks include the Commercial Bank, the Romanian Bank for Foreign Trade responsible for lending to the trade sector, the Romanian Development Bank (formerly the Investment Bank) responsible for long-term lending to the State Owned enterprises, the Banca Agricola (formerly the Agriculture and Food Industry Bank) responsible for lending to the agricultural sector and the Saving Bank mobilising the savings of the households. Romania adopted the universal banking system (banks that offer the entire range of banking services), granting equal treatment to foreign bank branches. The fairly high demand for capitalisation from the banks hindered the uncontrolled growth in their numbers - 41 banks were authorised to operate as at December 1997, one quarter being foreign banks - which in turn prevented numerous bankruptcies. A problem "inherited" from 1995 was the precarious situation of two private banks that found themselves in a de facto state of insolvency: Credit Bank and Dacia Felix Bank. Although the National Bank of Romania (BNR) declared them incapable of making any payments, operation regulations gave the banks the legal right to appeal BNR's decision, which they won thus provoking an ambiguous situation.

In addition to these specific features of 1996, some unresolved problems remained within the banking system which included delays in the system of payment and operation, loose application of the supervisory standards, reduction in attraction of resources and loans granted, and the seven-year absence of any banking privatisation. The need for modern clearing and payment procedures will reduce the delays in bank payments, which impose a kind of inflation-tax upon creditors. Perotti and Carare[6] conclude their investigation of the quality of credit allocation in Romanian banks by arguing that these banks have continued to play a passive role, funding large and unprofitable SOEs. Although there were some improvements in the allocation of credit among profitable SOEs, there was still a strong tendency for credit to be directed at larger firms and most recently to those with the most trade arrears. They found that for the worst performing SOEs, the evidence suggested that the quality of credit allocation was deteriorating. The evidence was not consistent with the hypothesis that as a result of a market oriented reform of the banking system, the allocation of bank credit would improve. There was still neither a real stock market nor a bond market. Their existence would increase eligible portfolio investment. Developing the capital market and increasing the number of actors which could mediate between foreign investors and the Romanian authorities on this market (like investment banks, etc) are two of the main issues which needed to be tackled in order to attract domestic and foreign investors.

In the seven years after the introduction of the banking legislation, important changes transformed the banking sector with the opening of new private banks and the diversification of its services. Despite plans to increase bank privatisation - three banks are planned to be privatised in 1998 in accordance with provisions of Law No. 83/1997 - the sector continues to present considerable segmentation and concentration. It remains dominated by state-owned banks, some of which have a high proportion of bad loans in their portfolio and are therefore exposed to difficulties in the course of the current restructuring process in the enterprise sector.

Overall, reforms in competition policy lag the most while investment-related legal reforms show the most progress. Foreign investors adopted a very cautious stance, reinforced by the defiance of some leading political forces to accept foreign investment. Only in 1994 did the flows of FDI picked up, but they have remained insufficient to make a strong impact on the economy. Foreign investors were authorised to own land and repatriate profits only as late as June 1997.

Until 1990, most real estate in Romania was owned by the state. Industrial and commercial property office and retail were state-owned. Agricultural land was either state-owned (or operated as state farms); nominally privately owned but under state control (co-operatives) or owned by individuals. The majority of the urban housing stock was state-owned, having been either nationalised or built after 1950. The new Romanian constitution, adopted in December 1991, guarantees the right to ownership of private property. However, mineral rights, air rights and similar attributes are excluded from private ownership. Commercial and industrial real estate has been assigned to various commercial companies into which state enterprises were organised under privatisation law 58/91. These commercial companies are now being privatised. As private owners take control of the companies, the land is moving to private control.

Most residential housing units built with state funds (generally after 1950) have been sold to their occupants. Prices and interest rates reflected the rent already paid and the condition of the units. The issue of how to privatise nationalised residential properties was resolved by the Romanian parliament only in June 1995. The new law on nationalised dwellings favoured tenants rather than former owners. In April 1997, law 35/1991 was modified to stipulate clearly that a Romanian legal entity with partial or total foreign capital could acquire ownership of land.

As far as the protection of property rights, Romania is a signatory to international conventions concerning intellectual property rights and has enacted legislation protecting patents, trademarks, and copyrights.

6.   EXTERNAL SUPPORT AND THE ROLE OF FDI

External support was clearly necessary and immediately after the revolution, humanitarian aid did flow into the country and some direct bilateral aid continued after the installation of the Roman government. However, some obstacles delayed the reintegration of Romania into the international community and the country was excluded from the numerous multilateral programmes of the EU and the G-24, because of the uncertainty of the direction of the NSF policy. The justifications were provided by the short-term orientation of the stabilisation programme, the populist measures for the consolidation of the electoral base of the NSF[7] and the violent events of 1990 and 1991, quite distant from the accepted Western standards of democratic politics. Discussion on resuming IMF credits did not begin until September 1990 and the first loans were not taken until April 1991. Bilateral relations with the Western European states resumed after the visit of President Mitterrand in April 1991, the first Western head of state visiting Bucharest since 1989, which made possible the attribution of special guest status to the Council of Europe. Other CEE countries received full membership early in 1990. Shortly thereafter in February 1991 the European Parliament ratified the commercial and co-operation agreement Romania had negotiated with the EU in 1990. As part of this package Romania gained access to PHARE and G-24 financial assistance.

This positive and open approach induced Romania to take the European experience as a model and adapt it to the specific conditions of the country. The Western orientation of Romania is also supported by the strong popular support for NATO membership, in excess of 80%, and both Iliescu and Constantinescu have made NATO membership the number one foreign policy goal of their administrations. In line with the stabilisation of their external relations, in September 1996, Hungary and Romania signed a historic treaty which sets the stage for deeper co-operation between the two countries, and which commits both to protection of ethnic minorities and to support for the entry of each other into NATO, EU, and other Western security and economic structures. The new Romanian government is also committed to completing a similar treaty with Ukraine. These moves marked a shift in the right direction after the signature of the European Agreement in 1995 and the application for membership to the EU. The Phare allocation for the period 1995-1997 has totalled $250 million. In the Opinion[8] submitted to the Council in July 1997, the Commission has recommended that negotiations for accession should be opened with Romania as soon as it has made sufficient progress in satisfying the three conditions for membership defined by the European Council in Copenhagen. These conditions include the political criteria (stable institutions, guarantees for the rule of law, human rights and the protection of minorities), the economic criteria (creation of a competitive market economy) and the ability to assume the obligations of membership particularly as regards the internal market.

A new foreign investment decree was announced in March 1990, but a law was not passed until 1991. The Law No. 35/1991, though granting wide privileges and tax holidays, stipulated that foreign investors could not own land or non-industrial property and could only repatriate a maximum of 15 % of earnings. Not surprisingly, while countries such as Hungary, Czech Republic and Poland surged ahead as sites for foreign investment, Romania lagged well behind. As a result, until 1993, given the great uncertainties about the political and economic course of the country, investors adopted a very cautious stance, reinforced by the defiance of some leading political forces to accept foreign investment. Most of the FDI occurred through foreign capital participation in joint ventures, of rather small size, with local partners, offsetting in this way the impediments of the land property. In a report prepared in 1994 by Management Counsellors International we find the causes of the problematic FDI environment in Romania. The "functionary bad attitude" seemed to be the main concern of the foreign investors. It consisted of non-co-operative behaviour and abuse of procedures on the part of some employees of the government institutions and agencies. There were cases where the civil servants had been found to be incorrect in putting the laws and rules into operation, generating frustration and irritation in the foreign investors' community. Projects were often blocked at the lower levels of officialdom in spite of promises coming from higher levels. There was also a lack of transparency and some confusion concerning procedures that must be followed as the privatisation of a former state enterprise when some foreign investor decides to invest. The information and the services provided to the foreign investors were dispersed among different institutions like the State Ownership Fund (SOF), the five Private Property Funds (POFs) and the Banks. Foreign investors planning to obtain some share of a Romanian company were confronted with conditions set by Ministers or their departments. Projects were approved under different conditions and suggested terms because each Ministry had its own rules. The SOF and the POFs, which have removed and taken for themselves the majority of the RDA's functions, are thus making the registration procedures more complicated.

There was also debate surrounding the ownership of industrial land. A constitutional provision prohibited land ownership for persons and notaries and courts - especially local ones - and also opposed land ownership for joint ventures, referring to the constitutional article and to Law no. 18/1991. These institutions were misinterpreting the law in assuming that foreign persons are those having total ownership of land instead of being partners in joint ventures. But the misinterpretation finally led to a selection of entrepreneurs (in favour of those with a preference for maximising profit in the short-term) and a restriction of total loan guarantees causing a reduction in capital stock. The tax system was also controversial because of its complexity. Different tax holidays were granted to different sectors that could be interpreted in different ways.

In the move to attract non-resident investors, supplementary incentives to large-scale industrial investment (over 50 million US $) were introduced by Law No. 71/1994 and the flows of FDI picked up. The investment stock almost doubled in the last two years owing to the conclusion of a number of investment agreements. However, they have remained insufficient to make a strong impact on the economy. In a clear change of policy, the Ciorbea government has been actively courting foreign investors, who are now authorised to own land. In addition, an emergency ordinance introduced in

December 1997 (Ordinance No. 92/1997) makes profit repatriation easier and clarifies the legal regime regarding guarantees and incentives granted to foreign investors. Cumulative Foreign Direct Investment (FDI) is low for a country of Romania's size: at the end of 1997, the cumulative stock of FDI amounted to about $2 billion, 40 % coming from the European Union.

7.   THE PRIVATISATION OF SOES IN ROMANIA

7.1   The Gradualist Approach

The route to privatisation was not easily discernible at the beginning of reform. The process started only in mid-1992, three years after the Revolution in 1989, when the essential elements of the legal framework for the privatisation of state-owned enterprises and private sector development had been put in place. The resulting approach is a mixture of political and pragmatic considerations that delayed structural reforms. Direct sale of public enterprises was immediately excluded by the NSF, because of the political orientation of the first government. The improvement living standards rather, was more politically rewarding than economic reform, the NSF also suffered from the inadequacy of means of evaluating assets and the lack of local financial savings relative to the likely value of the SOEs. The pragmatic approach was therefore to adopt a voucher system, similar to the Czech one, which would give the right to purchase enterprises without the expenditure of financial savings. The second strategic choice was to exclude the involvement of insiders (in particular the managers and the interested foreign investors) and the related risks of veto over the privatisation process, so the decision was compulsory for all SOEs and centralised into a Government agency. The legal framework is given by two laws referring to a process known as "conversion" of SOE and "mass privatisation programme".

The law n. 15 of 8 August 1990, known as the "STATE OWNED ENTERPRISE CONVERSION ACT", provided the transformation of SOEs into joint-stock companies and the operative distinction between two kinds of enterprises: the autonomous regions and the commercial companies. Some 900 autonomous companies were created by decision of Government or by decision of district or municipal authorities and they were organised within the economy's strategic branches - armament industry, power industry, mining and natural gas exploitation, mail system and railway transports. These corporations, whose social capital is entirely owned by the state, were, by law, entitled to budgetary subsidies to cover losses and they accounted for 47 % of the nominal value of industrial assets. The other State owned companies were organised as joint-stock or limited liability companies, whose equities were fully owned by the Romanian Treasury and which were jointly overseen by a Council of Administration, depending on the legal form of the company, and by a Council of State Representatives appointed by the founding ministry. With a view to preparing and organising the mass transfer of shares, the National Agency for Privatisation, being subordinated to the Government, was set up by the same law in order to conceive the law projects in the domain of privatisation. The privatisation programme and the principles of the process, as well as the employees' protective and preferential regimes, had to be presented and approved by Parliament.

All new commercial companies were ordered to submit to the Agency securities equivalent to 30% of the amount of the established nominal capital. On that basis, the National Agency for Privatisation issued nominal securities (vouchers) at 5.000 lei each that were allocated equally and free of charge to all Romanian citizens living in the country, who were over 18 years on or before December 31, 1990. With little understanding of the process governing the disposition of enterprises or the potential value of the property rights represented by the vouchers, many Romanians promptly traded them for a small amount of cash to speculators who accumulated them into large holdings.

The second legal instrument was Law No. 58 of 14 August 1991, which provided the legal framework for the transfer of ownership from the State to the private sector. It is interesting to note that the Government then in power, while considering that the citizens could be compensated in that way for the forty five years of communism, ensured that the majority interests in the newly created commercial companies remain in the public domain and, virtually excluding any interest from most foreign investors. In order to achieve this goal, this law sets forth the distribution of the shares of six thousand three hundred commercial companies and their partition between two kinds of financial institutions: the SOF and the five POFs. In particular, 70 % of commercial companies' shares were allocated to the State Ownership Fund (SOF) which is charged to divest itself of its holdings over several years by a variety of means depending on the size of enterprise. In order to administer the remaining 30% of the capital, five Private Ownership Funds (POFs) were established and named after the five great regions of the country: Banat-Crisana, Moldova, Transylvania, Muntenia, Dobrogea and Oltenia. At the end of 1996 the POFs were converted into private investment funds (PIF).

All companies were included in the portfolios of the five funds, according to the county they belonged to and their fields of activity. Each POF had in its portfolio 30% of the social capital of one thousand enterprises. By March 1993, certificates representing 30% of their shares (held on behalf of the population by five Private Ownership Funds) were distributed to seventeen million Romanian citizens and these titles were used for purchases of individual enterprises or in mutual funds to be formed by the Private Ownership Funds. To monitor this complex process, the Government created a Council for Economic Co-ordination, Strategy and Reform, an Agency for Privatisation, and an Agency for Industrial Restructuring.

When the privatisation started, there were about six thousand three hundred commercial companies organised according to Law No. 15/1990, with a majority of state-owned capital. In 1992 only two enterprises were privatised. Between 1993-1995, the most used privatisation method was MEBO, by which the stocks of the enterprises were bought by the employees of the respective companies, on instalments ranging over ten years. The interest rate charged was very low, in line with the intrinsic logic to subsidise the "private" stakeholders. That method was used for all small-sized companies, some of the middle-sized ones but very little for large enterprises. As an example of "nomenklatura capitalism", some managers established Employee Associations and purchased parts of the company share-stocks, benefiting from bank credit to pay the deposit to SOF. The instalments and bank interest could thus be paid from the profit of that company. Such a method proved very inefficient, as it could not guarantee the availability of the capital necessary for a company to make investments or modernise itself. On the other hand, MEBO did not allow all the citizens to participate in the privatisation as only those employed with a company in course of being privatised could have access to the necessary information. The OECD in its first assessment of the Romanian economy[9] pointed out the risks associated with delaying structural reforms without deep restructuring of the economy and imposing a stringent financial discipline upon the large SOEs. On the other side, the autonomous regions, representing around 20% of employment in the economy, had not even been included in the privatisation programme and remained largely unrestructured. Therefore, in 1994, that method was given up and a new set of measures, both institutional and procedural, was adopted to speed up the pace and quality of privatisation decisions. Substantial efforts were made to halve the number of autonomous corporations to less then five hundred, including those of local interest. Ultimately, the plan of the Vacaroiu Government was to control only forty-four public corporations of national importance.

Progress could be noticed in the programmes drafted by the State Ownership Fund (SOF) and endorsed by the Parliament for 1994: it was envisaged that two thousand three hundred and sixty commercial companies would be privatised. Nevertheless the programmes were too optimistic. The

SOF privatised six hundred and thirty five companies during 1994, which was 28 % of its programme. Of these, more than 80% were small-sized companies, employing an average of two hundred and eighty workers each. A number of twenty five million shares were sold to public and private investors with a total value of Lei 450 billion. The slowest pace was recorded in industry, where only 3% of the companies have been privatised so far. Since December 1993, when the process started, about one thousand small and medium sized companies employing four hundred and twenty thousand workers in the field of consumer goods, tourism, trade, light industry, food industry, and farm mechanisation were privatised and sold by the SOF, which is 13.3% of the total companies in its administration. However, their number rose to over eight thousand as a result of the division of some autonomous administrations into several commercial companies.

7.2   The Fears Of The First Privatisation Programme

Progress in the privatisation programme has been far from easy and the most serious problem was the fear of mass unemployment and the associated reduction of consumer demand with its negative influence on production. These fears undermined the integrity of the government programmes and Prime Minister Vacaroiu was forced to scale back the scheduled privatisation of more than five thousand state enterprises, which had been intended to be handed over to private investors. The government policy demonstrated the Romanian authorities' reluctance to relinquish control of the country's large firms. Reform at enterprise level was progressing slowly and had been generally limited to cost reduction through downsizing. Furthermore, having avoided imposing any discipline on the managers, the government continued to subsidise loss-making industries. Moreover, the lack of authority encouraged fraudulent activities from small groups with the necessary capital to invest. The evidence of the results justifies the criticism of the behaviour of the NSF governments during this phase which gained the confidence of those dependent upon the state by reconciling de-facto divergent policies, such as the privatisation of large-scale industries and the avoidance of lay-offs of workers. The chaotic, and in some cases primitive, state of the industrial and infrastructure organisation in this country offered only few attractions for foreign investors, and the available pool of domestic savings, not to mention the structural and psychological preconditions for private investment, were still rudimentary. Although their intention of speeding up the process of privatisation was quite clear, so far the country's three NSF governments failed to move any further than a moderately successful management buyout scheme. This first attempt at privatisation is generally considered to have been a failure because few SOEs were sold, thanks to the unattractiveness of the terms imposed by the 1991 law.

The relaxed pace of privatisation, as well as the absence of a genuine privatisation programme, accounts for the fact that the share of the capital transferred from the state into private property represented in 1995 only 6.7% of the nominal capital of the six thousand three hundred companies to be privatised.

According to the critics[10], the main reasons for the slow pace of the first privatisation were:

(1) the inadequate use of ownership vouchers in the privatisation process;

(2) the absence of a unitary procedure through which the ownership coupons might have fulfilled their role. As a result part of the population disposed of the certificates for a very small amount.

(3) assessment of the ownership certificates was difficult as different values had been ascribed to each Private Ownership Fund (POF).

7.3   The Acceleration Of The Second Privatisation Programme And The New Financial Institutions

Under pressure from the international institutions, the Vacaroiu Government announced an acceleration of the privatisation process with the intention of building a western-style market economy. The second round began with the adoption of the new privatisation law No. 55 passed on 21 March 1995, but it led to the same criticisms of complexity and inflexibility[11]. In addition, a fractious parliament held up legislation that would provide a legal order to secure the rights of citizens. For speeding up the mass privatisation about three thousand state companies, nearly one half held jointly by SOF and POF's, were included in the programme. The public offer differed from the first mass privatisation programme. The companies had to be valued in order to establish their selling price, an issue prospectus was to be drawn up, endorsed by the National Commission for Securities (NCS), which offered the citizens detailed data on the financial state of the company identifying debts, stocks, work in progress and prospective contracts. In March 1995, the five POFs launched a public offer of about 10% of their shares in one hundred state companies. POFs shares could be swapped for ownership vouchers, revalued at 25.000 lei, which 17 million Romanians got in 1992, but since some of the citizens had already sold their certificates, the members of the Government decided to issue new titles, named "nominal privatisation coupons", distributed in August 1995 at a price of Lei 875,000 (US$ 467), which was approximately four times the average Romanian's monthly wage. To avoid further speculation, the new coupons were non-transferable. Neither local nor foreign investment funds would be able to buy them. All five funds (POFs) offered more than four million shares each - or some 10% of their stake, while the remaining 20% of the POFs stake would go into the private sector through management and employee buyouts. At the time, the opposition parties claimed that the measure had a domestic political character and was aimed at winning the elections in the following November. On the basis of that law, a list of three thousand eight hundred enterprises was made up, to which the holders of certificates and nominal privatisation coupons could subscribe until March 1996. Likewise, they could subscribe to one of the five POFs, which had developed during the four years of government thanks to the dividends obtained from the companies in their portfolios.

Learning from experience, the strategic choice this time was not to adopt a specific set of principles governing the disposition of ownership rights. Here are the main characteristics defining the second mass privatisation programme: (1) the size of the action: three thousand eight hundred commercial companies to be privatised in 1995, i.e. some 50% of the total companies to undergo privatisation; (2) wider flexibility: 60% ceiling of the registered capital of the companies and sales of shares by auction on a cash basis of the remaining 40% of the registered capital; (3) re-establishing equal access to all eligible Romanian citizens; (4) stepping up and concluding privatisation in 1995; (5) the possibility of jointly using new and already operational privatisation methods (MEBO, "case-by- case" negotiation, etc.); (6) virtual conditions, appeared as an outcome of the programme, favouring, for the second privatisation stage (i.e. 1995), distribution shares, against liquidities and increasing foreign capital inflows; and, (7) partial capitalisation of commercial companies by auction stake of shares with a view to improving their economic situation and overcoming the economic-financial deadlock.

The methodology and the implementation of the second mass privatisation have been considered fairly positive by the international institutions[12]. As mentioned before, the privatisation methods used by SOF have been diversified by the 1994 and 1995 Laws. Gradually, the MEBO method has been replaced by auctions and negotiations. This privatisation approach will help to create "public" companies whose shares can be traded on the new Bucharest Stock Exchange opened in June 1995. Regulations established by Romania's new National Securities Commission would guarantee the transparency of the operations, requiring the disclosure of information and the enforcement of appropriate corporate governance for the privatised companies. SOF started selling share-stocks on the stock market only in September 1995, when 40% of Bucharest "Electroaparataj" company stock was sold. The entire stock was sold in only three hours. Moreover, other companies were preparing to do the same, since through the process of mass privatisation potentially about 17 million Romanians could became shareholders. In order that they might be able to trade in their shares, Romania inaugurated a system of electronic OTC market transactions, RASDAQ, patterned in part after the UN NASDAQ. The OTC market became operational in November 1996.

In the context of implementation, not all of the three thousand eight hundred companies could be traded and only 13% percent of the large companies could be transferred to private investors. Initially about eight hundred medium-sized companies were quoted, at present there are two thousand, compared with only fifty-two on the Bucharest Stock Exchange. Most times, the sellers were share-certificate holders and the buyers were those interested in obtaining the majority of the share-stock from the SOF. Whenever SOF announced that 51% of a company's stock was to be sold, the interest towards that company rose. The second Mass Privatisation Programme contributed positively to larger shareholder participation in the economy, and thereby jump-started the fledgling Bucharest Stock Exchange that began trading on June 1995.

The relaunching of the privatisation programme for 1997 was included in the so-called "Contract for the First Two Hundred Days" of the incoming new centrist government. The programme endorsed the main provision of the agreements signed with IMF and the World Bank. As a result, one thousand three hundred and four companies were privatised in 1997 by public bid, direct negotiations and auction on RASDAQ OTC market. Another two thousand are expected in 1998. The programme also brought some measure of corporate responsibility to privatised companies, transferring the responsibility for failing companies out of the hands of the government thereby allowing them to restructure themselves or to be liquidated and their assets sold. This provided some encouragement to foreign investors through the increased availability of the most ordinary exit strategy - selling stock to the public. The other important move was the privatisation of the capital of some autonomous regions, reducing in this way their number and their monopolistic position on strategic sectors such as telecommunication, energy and transport.

7.4   The Timid Support of Foreign Investors

Since the fall of the Ceausescu regime in 1989, the Vacaroiu government has sought to build a Western-style market economy. The pace of restructuring has been slow, but by 1994 the legal basis for a market economy was largely in place. Parliament enacted laws permitting foreign entities incorporated in Romania to purchase land and it identified a large number of government enterprises for rapid privatisation or restructuring. Foreign investment is subject to routine and non-discriminatory screening by the Romanian Development Agency, which checks on the compliance of company incorporation documents with Romanian laws and keeps a record of all companies with foreign participation established in Romania. In accordance with European legislation, foreign investment must comply with environmental protection regulations and must not negatively affect Romania's national security, defence interests, public order, or public health. Foreign capital started to flow into Romania, although less than in some other Central European countries, since the State Ownership Fund, which currently holds 70% of the shares of the state-owned enterprises to be part of the Mass Privatisation Programme, was authorised to sell to foreign investors controlling interests in attractive commercial companies. Should a foreign investor be interested in buying the stock of a company in the portfolio of SOF, he may forward a Letter of Intent to SOF. This organisation is obliged, within five days from the receipt of the potential investor's letter of intent, to advertise the company with a view to privatising it. The list of the companies likely to be privatised is published in the Official Register Part IV and in the mass media. One Letter of Intent is enough to start such a process, which should result in the continued availability of controlling interests in significant investment opportunities for foreign investors.

7.5   The Results So Far

By end of 1997 SOF had privatised three thousand eight hundred and sixty two enterprises out of a total number of eight thousand six hundred and seventy one and the private sector accounts for about 55% of GDP, up from 35 % in 1994. Employment originating in the private sector rose sharply from 23 % in 1995 to 47% in 1997[13]. Out of two thousand seven hundred and ten companies included in the programme of SOF offerings, one thousand and sixty five have been sold, of which eight hundred and ninety three were sold by direct negotiation and one hundred and seventy two by auction. Ordinance No.15, recently approved by the Government, stipulates that the activity of SOF must be completed by 31 December 1998 although, with the approval of Government, its term may be extended once - but only for six months. This means that by July 1999 the privatisation process in Romania should come to an end.

8.   THE ECONOMIC AND FINANCIAL RESTRUCTURING OF INDUSTRY

While the restructuring of state-owned enterprises was acknowledged as an essential complement to privatisation, the process began with slow and unclear liquidation procedures; there was no bankruptcy law until 1995 and progress was hampered by the rudimentary financial sector. A law was passed in 1995 to establish the Bucharest Stock Exchange and the institution became operational in August 1995. As in other Central European countries, foreign investment could not become a realistic alternative means of privatisation and private sector growth because, among other reasons, the implementation of the privatisation process had been so slow. Infrastructure and land ownership issues were also important barriers, not only for foreign investment but also for private-sector development generally.

A radical change came in the third phase of the transition process when Emil Constantinescu of the Democratic Convention electoral coalition campaigned on the twin themes of the need to staunch corruption and to launch more radical economic reforms. The appointed Prime Minister Victor Ciorbea immediately discovered that the financial situation of the Romanian state-owned enterprises was much worse than anticipated. Faced with a larger-than-expected accumulation of inter-enterprise arrears, mostly at the expense of the national electric, gas, and railways monopolies, which were forced to deliver services to insolvent state factories, the government turned its immediate attention to administering a policy of strict fiscal restraint and to speeding up industrial restructuring and privatisation. A comprehensive shock-reform package was drawn up. Its objectives were to eliminate price controls, to free the exchange rate, to eliminate subsidies, to establish a more efficient banking system, to allow bank privatisation, to introduce a modern tax system, to establish clear and efficient privatisation and restructuring procedures, and, most importantly, to encourage foreign investment. This new programme was intended to enable Romania to make a rapid transition to a market economy. The restructuring of key industries has been initiated by identifying large inefficient state-owned enterprises, which had created severe problems in the past because of their huge debts, idle capacities and under-employed work force. The Council for Economic Strategy and Reform was given the monumental task of drawing up plans for the restructuring of about two hundred of these firms which accounted for at least 75% of all losses. In addition, in June 1997, all "régies autonomes" were established as joint-stock companies.

Restructuring was partly associated with the privatisation efforts, since the funds gained by the sale of the state-owned assets would be re-channelled into revamping and modernising strategic firms. The Council would prioritise activities and plans on an individual enterprise basis. The first thirty problem enterprises, operating in such energy-intensive sectors as the chemical, petrochemical, machine building and metalworking industries, were put under economic and financial surveillance. If incapable of recovery, they would either be shut down or split and privatised by the selling of shares. Liquidation of eight companies began in February 1997.

Romanian national assets in industry are, in many sectors, antiquated and both energy intensive and inefficient. Likewise, much of the nation's infrastructure shows signs of prolonged neglect. Because of this situation, the success of industrial restructuring will depend, to a large extent, on the availability of investment funds. Despite the fact that private sector activities in trade, construction self-sufficient agriculture and service industry have grown rapidly, private investment capital has remained insufficient to support the process. Therefore the state remains the predominant owner of productive resources and provides nearly a quarter of national investment. State-owned commercial enterprises provide another 48% from their own sources. Of considerable importance, in this context, would be the response of foreign capital, which currently is still growing at modest levels.

Of course, investment funds needed for industrial restructuring vary from sector to sector. An estimate of allocations for the next three years prepared by the Ministry of Industries shows that about 70% of available funds will go to energy and energy-related sectors (mining, oil, gas, chemical/petrochemical), which will be developed to facilitate recovery and enhancement of the other sectors. Restructuring of industry will rely in many cases on the ability of companies to generate the needed financial support, since budgetary allocations will be restricted to very few basic industrial projects in energy, mining and geology, and environment protection.

9.   AGRICULTURE

Agriculture reflects most of these general problems. Given the decisive role of the state in this sector, this would necessarily involve not only the creation of new private farms, but also the privatisation of more or less intact state farms and producer co-operatives. In Romania, after the coup, immediately emerged a strong movement to legislate for the restitution of collectivised and nationalised land to their former peasant owners, but efforts were made to retain the most efficient large-scale farming enterprises and to give alternative parcels of land to private farmers. One of the most radical pieces of land reform legislation was enacted in 1991, according to which 4.9 million Romanians were entitled to reclaim plots of up to one hundred hectares of arable land from State holdings. More than 90% of the new landowners received "temporary property certificates". There, encouragement was being given to private farmers to form or to join existing co-operatives and maintain some form of large-scale joint farming enterprises on a share-holding basis.

The mechanism of land privatisation did not contribute to the creation of a transparent and supportive market. Approximately 55% of the arable land are farmed by producer associations, which leased the land from absentee landowners and pensioners resident in towns. These arrangements are informal; often the compensation was in kind according to the value of a particular crop, and the lack of an effective land market allowed for a wide disparity in the type of land lease agreements. A further distortion was concerned with the SOEs, which were allowed to continue operating on the basis of soft budget constraints, as their losses were subsidised by soft loans or cancelled. The total agricultural support both directly from the government and indirectly in subsidised prices rose significantly from 2% to 4% of GDP over the period 1993 to 1996 and most of this support was directed to the SOEs, despite the fact that the private sector provided the majority of food output.

Producers were also asked to contract their production to economic agents recognised by the state i.e. State "integrators" or intermediaries. For example, still in 1995, the proportion of the total harvest, which had to be contracted, depended on the product grown and was 40% for bread quality wheat, 40% for seed wheat and 90% for seed maize. The scarcity of small implements and other farming inputs mentioned earlier was a good reason for adopting this strategy, at least as a temporary expedient until a fully fledged market in farm inputs and outputs could be established. This mechanism was modified in 1996.

With such mechanism a reliable market for producers would hardly emerge. Throughout the region, with the introduction of relatively uncontrolled prices for farm products, private farmers have experienced serious problems in making ends meet. The decline in real wages had created shrinkage in demand for food products. This, combined with a flood of subsidised imports from the EU, had reduced farm incomes and increased discontent in the farming sector, sometimes expressed for example, in Romania, in a refusal by the farmers to bring their produce to market. Production helped to balance supply with declining domestic demand, but in the meantime exports had been directed to the Russian and other eastern markets to help pay for imports of essential fuels and raw materials, which were severely cut back by the collapse of Soviet trade in 1991. The role of government in this sector, through its intervention agencies, remain higher than in most other CEE transition economies and its results were perceived being particularly risky as changes in tariffs, quotas, price controls and restrictions on internal trade affected output and profitability.

Another problem for the small farmers, who account for 30% of the Romanian workforce, was the severe shortage of working capital, machinery and equipment and the increase of prices of fuel, fertilisers and pesticides as well as the transport costs which were not matched by the retail prices. In addition, as pointed out by many economists[14] the slower progress in reforming property rights and establishing land titles impeded the creation of an effective rural land market. In the current climate of rising unemployment and the closure of large-scale enterprises, private farming undoubtedly represents an attractive alternative to many Romanians for starting a private activity and earning an extra-income which remains largely unknown (un-taxed) as long as it is not recorded in official fiscal statistics. However, the absence of traditional peasant expertise and application to this type of employment after decades of socialist indoctrination suggests that the number of people willing and able to make a success of private farming will not be large, and that a major shakeout of the farming sector will have to occur before it can become a viable contributor to the domestic and foreign trade of the respective economies. Therefore the sector is expected to undergo a much-needed comprehensive reorganisation as a result of the changed government policy. The agricultural policy was implemented in 1997 with a liberalisation of prices of all agricultural products, a review of import taxes and the improvement in credit policies.

10.   FOREIGN EXCHANGE CONTROLS AFFECTING TRADING

In concert with the policies of gradualism, the NSF governments opted for a policy of gradual liberalisation of the exchange regime, which was intended to lead to eventual convertibility. In the process, the lei has undergone a substantial devaluation. By the end of 1993, the lei was trading at 1,276 to the dollar from rate of 20 to the dollar in October 1990. After the stabilisation efforts during the first part of 1994, the lei settled at about 1,650 to the dollar, a rate which remained in a narrow trading range for several months. The devaluation continued and by the end of 1997 the exchange rate was 8.500 to the dollar. Historically, the course of exchange policies has been dictated by a wish to avoid a vicious spiral of inflation-depreciation which it was feared would occur if the rate were freed in the absence of supporting macro-economic policies. But, in reality, the NSF governments used the exchange rate policy to secure access for imports of energy and raw materials. Nevertheless, these policies failed as government intervention was not adequate to stem continuing depreciation. Large fiscal deficits occurred, highly negative interest rates created unreal pricing through most of the period, and episodical price liberalisation contributed to continued pressures on the exchange rate.

Moreover, parallel markets flourished at premiums often much above the official rates. At the end of 1993, it was estimated that only about 15% of exchange transactions were passing through the auction in the official banking system. About two-thirds of the flow of foreign exchange was passing through an unofficial "grey" market, consisting largely of enterprise transactions, at a premium generally between 25-35 % of the official auction rate. The wide disparity between the official and parallel rates created, in effect, subsidies to those importers who were able to get foreign exchange at the auction. In addition, pricing of energy and agricultural products used the official rate as the benchmark for domestic price setting, giving considerable cost advantages to energy users. Meanwhile, the many changes in the foreign exchange regime undercut Romania's drive for sustained export growth and reduced confidence in the lei. Recognition that these policies were harming Romania's prospects for sustained income growth became more apparent in late 1993.

As of February 1994, NBR started to implement a programme for the gradual liberalisation of the national currency's exchange rate and the transition to an interbank currency market. By the end of July 1994 the interbank currency market would fully replace the currency auctions organised by the NBR. The interbank currency market would integrate all authorised intermediaries, both banks and exchange offices, which would be able to sell and buy currency without any limitations at freely negotiable rates.   The currency market would be in agreement with international standards, being decentralised and continuous.

11.   CONCLUSION

Over the past year, Romania has made progress in privatising the economy and establishing the legal framework for a market economy. Parliament approved the most relevant legislation affecting the transparency of the market, including copyright and anti-trust legislation, and partially completed work on the bank privatisation law. The NSF governments sponsored two Mass Privatisation Programmes and transferred partial equity in three thousand nine hundred state-owned enterprises to Romanian citizens, but it still owns the large loss-making commercial companies and about nine hundred "régies autonomes".   In October 1996, Romania inaugurated an OTC stock market (RASDAQ) which operates in the Bucharest Stock Exchange.

The private sector is composed of small and medium sized entrepreneurs, primarily in agriculture and services, a co-operative sector and, which is what concerns us, a number of large privately owned enterprises concerned mainly with import-export activities followed by manufacturing and service businesses. This has accumulated large amounts of capital because of market distortions, their privileged connections and because of the lack of economic transparency. The greatest distortions of all which generated the large 1990-1992 incomes, were caused by the managed exchange rate regime in the currency market and by the managed distribution of raw materials, export and import goods.

There were frequent changes in legislation, and sometimes the laws were issued in unpredictable and uncorrelated ways. Known laws were modified by amendments and ordinances which contradicted others already issued. There were in addition frequent changes in some governmental institutional structures: for example, although the RDA was organised in 1992 under a modern structure, the Government Decision n. 216/1995 put it into an old-fashioned ministerial formula, transforming it from an active modern institution into a passive and bureaucratic one.

The political factors were important for Romania, as they influenced the expectations of the economic agents and therefore their willingness to engage in longer-term investments. In a political context Hungary can be singled out as the country with the most stable political system so far, followed perhaps by the Czech Republic. Romania has displayed much more political instability. The negative results of the Romanian economic programme have been the consequence of this instability and also because most of the changes were not introduced during the first four years when there was continuity in the economic leadership.

The new centrist government faces the challenge of reforming an economy, which is still dominated by state-owned enterprises and public utility networks. The principal focus will be on restructuring the inefficient energy and agricultural sectors, freeing up the foreign exchange market, and accelerating privatisation. The new government also realises that Romania lags far behind its principal Central European neighbours in attracting foreign investment. By promising to accelerate economic reform, to restructure and privatise, to introduce fiscal and monetary austerity, and to reduce the state's role in the economy, it will create a country open and attractive to foreign investment. The government is tackling its formidable economic problems in two stages: an emergency plan over the winter of 1996/97 to ensure social and political stability, followed by a radical structural reform programme over its remaining three-and-one-half years, aimed eventually at EU accession. The results are essential to improve the economic efficiency as a pre-condition for lasting stability and sustained growth. Furthermore the government should be prepared to face external, structural and political constraints and avoid the temptation to resume populist measures to accommodate the adjustment costs of the liquidation of some large loss-making companies. A reversal of the economic hardship of the shock therapy will rest largely on the rapid and successful restructuring of the economy under hard-budget conditions. Its negative development risks pushing Romania into an undesirable fourth phase, dominated again by a gradualist and piecemeal approach intended to minimise the social costs, with a further delay in reforms. But this time, failure will foster the legitimate aspiration towards more freedom and democracy and diminish the hope of European reunification.

NOTES

1 For a comprehensive history of Romania see R.W. Seton Watson, History of the Romanians, Cambridge University Press, Cambridge UK, 1934; Andrei Otetea, A Concise history of Romania, London, R. Hale, 1985; Kurt W. Treptow (editor), A history of Romania, Iasi , The Romanian Cultural Foundation, The Center for Romanian Studies, 1995; Martin Rady, Romania in Turmoil, London, IB Tauris & Co Ltd, 1992 2 Mary Ellen Fisher, an American political scientist, see the NSF period characterised by overlapping structures of two authoritarian regimes. The transition moved toward a "liberalised authoritarianism" during which a growing private sphere of industrial and group rights emerged into the political arena. See M.E. Fisher, "The New Leaders and the Opposition", in D. N. Nelson (editor), Romania after Tyranny, Builder, Westview Press, 1992.

2 Mary Ellen Fisher, an American political scientist, see the NSF period characterised by overlapping structures of two authoritarian regimes. The transition moved toward a "liberalised authoritarianism" during which a growing private sphere of industrial and group rights emerged into the political arena. See M. E. Fisher, "The New Leaders and the Opposition", in D. N. Nelson (editor), Romania after Tyranny, Builder, Westview Press, 1992.

3 See Junior R. Davis, Paul G. Hare, "Reforming the System of Rural Finance Provision in Romania: Some Options for Privatisation and Change", CERT Discussion Paper No. 97/13, May 1997, table 2.

4 A study from Per Ronnas commented this poor performance as "a failure to carry out an adequate institutional restructuring and "depoliticise" the economy which kept Romania to a pre-industrialised stage of development. See. Per Ronnas, "Romania: Transition to Underdevelopment", in Ian Jeffries (ed), Problems of Economic and Political Transformation in the Balkans, Pinter, 1996 5 Sufficient progress must entail an adequate threshold of reform as well as a favourable trend over time; that is, no significant policy backsliding. Nine indicators are taken directly from EBRD's Transition Report 1996 (November 1996) and compared with comparable indicators from EBRD's previous two annual reports, measured on a one-to-five scale. A "five" represents standards and performance norms typical of advanced industrial economies. Depending on the particular indicator, a "3" or a "4" may very well be the threshold that we seek.

5 Sufficient progress must entail an adequate threshold of reform as well as a favourable trend over time; that is, no significant policy backsliding. Nine indicators are taken directly from EBRD's Transition Report 1996 (November 1996) and compared with comparable indicators from EBRD's previous two annual reports, measured on a one-to-five scale. A "five" represents standards and performance norms typical of advanced industrial economies. Depending on the particular indicator, a "3" or a "4" may very well be the threshold that we seek.

6 See Enrico C. Perotti and Octavian Carare, The Evolution Of Bank Credit Quality In Transition. Theory And Evidence From Romania, CERT discussion paper no. 97/02, CERT.

7 See Ronald H. Linden, "After the Revolution: a Foreign Policy of Bounded Change", in D. N. Nelson (editor), Romania after Tyranny, Builder, Westview Press, 1992.

8 See European Commission, Economic Reform Monitor. Romania, Brussels, September 1997; European Commission, Romania. Accession Partnership, Brussels, September 1997; European Commission, Agenda 2000 - Commission Opinion on Romania's Application for Membership of the European Union, DOC/97/18, Brussels, 15 July 1997.

9 See OECD, Romania, An Economic Assessment, Paris, 1993, chapter 3.

10 Among others see OECD (1993) and OECD (1998).

11 See, for example, "Romania: A Wasted Chance", The Economist, June 1995, p. 69.

12 See the World Bank country report, Summary of private and financial sector development, p 2.

13 Data derived from several private sources and from the World Bank country profile

14 See for example Junior R. Davis and Paul G. Hare, Reforming the systems of Rural Finance Provision in Romania: Some options for Privatisation and Change, CERT Discussion paper no. 97/13, CERT.

REFERENCES

Davis, J. R., Hare, P. G . (1997), "Reforming the System of Rural Finance Provision in Romania: Some Options for Privatisation and Change", CERT Discussion Paper No. 97/13, May 1997.

EBRD (1996), Transition Report 1996, London.

European Commission (1997a), Agenda 2000 - Commission Opinion on Romania's Application for Membership of the European Union, DOC/97/18, Brussels, 15 July 1997.

European Commission (1997b), Economic Reform Monitor. Romania, Brussels, September 1997.

European Commission (1997c), Romania. Accession Partnership, Brussels, September 1997.

Fisher, M. E . (1992), "The New Leaders and the Opposition", in D. N. Nelson (editor), Romania after Tyranny, Builder, Westview Press.

Linden, R. H . (1992), "After the Revolution: A Foreign Policy of Bounded Change", in D. N. Nelson (editor), Romania after Tyranny, Builder, Westview Press.

OECD (1993), Romania, An Economic Assessment, Paris, 1993.

OECD (1998), OECD Economic Surveys: Romania, Paris, February 1998.

Otetea, A. (1985), A Concise History of Romania, London, R. Hale.

Perotti, E.C., Carare O. (1997), The Evolution Of Bank Credit Quality In Transition. Theory And Evidence From Romania, CERT discussion paper no. 97/02, CERT.

Rady, M. (1992), Romania in Turmoil, London, IB Tauris & Co Ltd.

Ronnas, P. (1996), "Romania: Transition to Underdevelopment", in Ian Jeffries (ed), Problems of Economic and Political Transformation in the Balkans, Pinter.

Seton Watson, R.W. (1934), History of the Romanians, Cambridge University Press, Cambridge UK.

The Economist (1995), "Romania: A Wasted Chance", June 1995.

Treptow, UK. W (editor) (1995), A History of Romania, Iasi , The Romanian Cultural Foundation, The Center for Romanian Studies.

World Bank (1998), Romania, Country profiles, Washington.

Chapter 9

Company Co-operations between Eastern and Western Europe

A Key Role in the Development of Eastern Europe

Martin Zagler and Christian Ragacs
Vienna University of Economics and Business Administration

Abstract:　In this paper the effects of co-operations of small and medium-sized firms between the economies in transformation and the developed regions in Europe will be examined. A discussion in the framework of the new theory of economic growth offers a relevant starting point for analysing macroeconomic effects. In this course, economic development essentially stems from process innovations. Starting from a description of the model, expected effects of co-operations between SME in transforming and developed region are first analysed and then accompanying measures are proposed. In the analytical setting used, the opening of the economy and especially SME co-operations of Eastern and Western European companies within identical market segments clearly lead to positive growth effects.

1.　REASONS FOR A MACROECONOMIC ANALYSIS

This chapter examines the economic effects of co-operations among small- and medium-sized firms. While the small- and medium-sized enterprises (SME) are usually analysed on a business or microeconomic level, the economic importance of SME as a group justifies a macroeconomic analysis. The fact that SME have a significant macroeconomic importance can be seen in the following illustration.

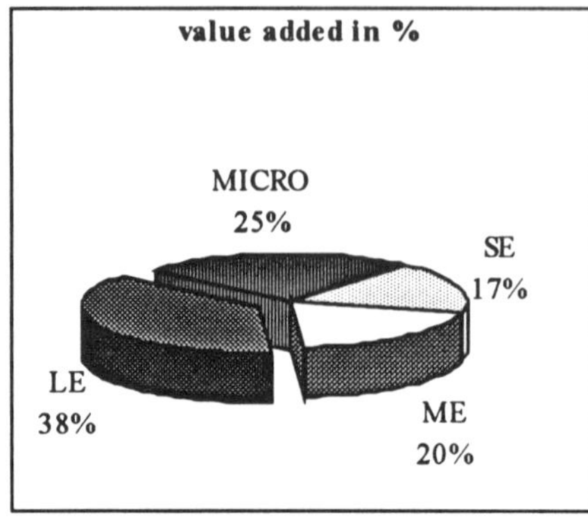

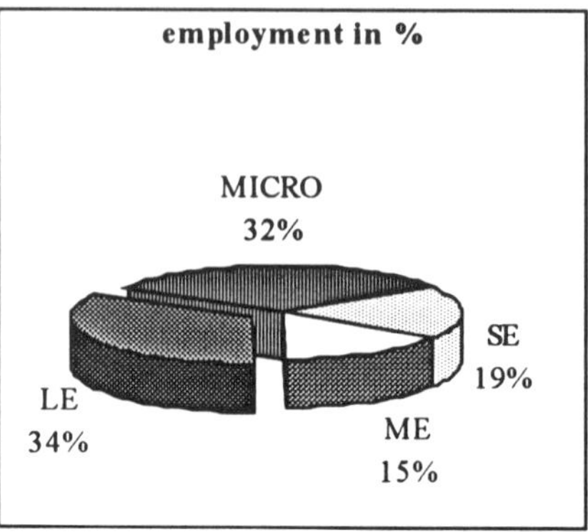

MICRO (micro enterprises: 0 - 9 employees, SE (small enterprises): 10 - 49 employees, ME (medium-sized enterprises): 50 - 249 employees, LE (large enterprises): 250 employees and up. *Source:* Pichler et al, 1996, p. 15

figure 1 added value and employment by firm in EU and EFTA

We find that 62,46 % of value added and 66,51 % of employment can be attributed to SME. The situation is similar in Central and Eastern Europe (CEE), as the following figures indicate. As data are not comparable across CEE, we have used Hungarian data to provide an example.

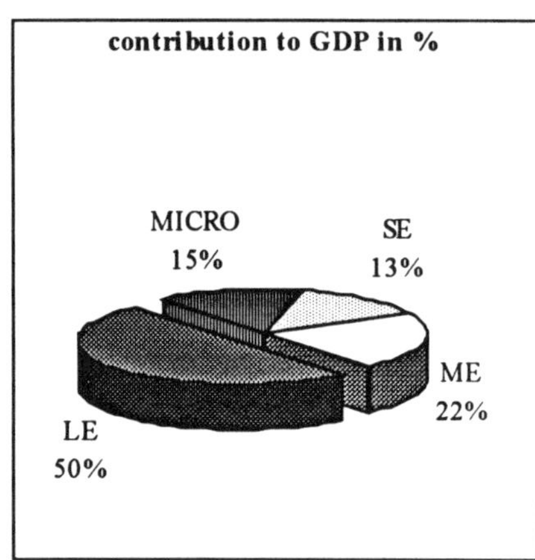

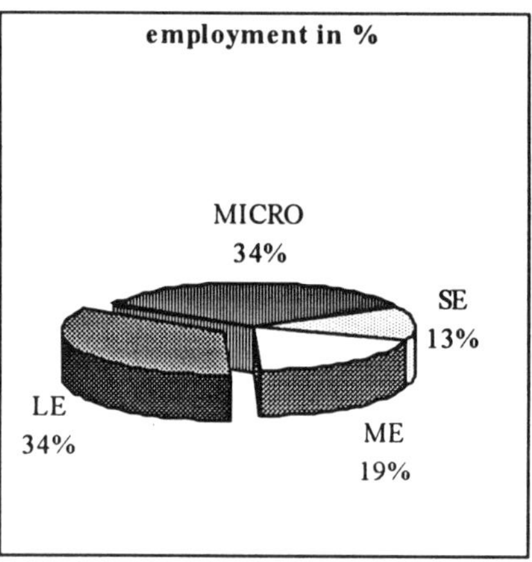

MICRO (micro enterprises: 0 - 9 employees, SE (small enterprises): 10 - 49 employees, ME (medium-sized enterprises): 50 - 249 employees, LE (large enterprises): 250 employees and up. *Source:* Kallay, 1998

figure 2. added value and employment by firm size in Hungary

In terms of employment, the Hungarian data match nicely with other CEE countries and developed economies in Europe. In terms of value added, however, SME in CEE lack far behind, contributing only half of GDP.

Indeed, much of the analysis that will follow tries to explain how this gap can be closed.

Macroeconomic effects arise on several levels. In particular, one should mention the manifold effects on the supply side of the economy, which stand in the centre of the following examination[1]. Because of their economic heterogeneity, co-operations of SME between the economies in transformation and the developed regions in Europe are especially interesting. Economically relevant aspects of co-operations are the enlarged goods markets, the access to new technologies and management structures, and the potential for small- and medium-sized firms to operate at significantly lower costs. As there are advantages for both enterprises in Eastern and Western Europe, there is the possibility that both sides may benefit.

Because of the small short-term macroeconomic capacity to control SME (for instance by fiscally motivated subsidies), the effect of SME on the state of the economy will only have a small importance. However, SME co-operations constitute a structural, hence long run, change for the affected economies. Insofar, a discussion within the framework of the theory of economic growth offers a relevant starting point to analyse the relevant economic effects. Thus the central question for this investigation is, what contributions can, respectively could, SME and in particular co-operations between SME make for the long-run economic development in Europe. We are particularly interested in the present and potential growth process in Europe as well as in differences of the growth process between developed EU countries and the emerging economies in Central and Eastern Europe (CEE) and in possibilities that both regions achieve beneficiary effects, however, to a different extent.

2. ANALYTICAL FRAMEWORK

The following analysis is methodologically oriented on the modern macroeconomic theory of growth, the workhorse of modern development economics, which is based on a general micro-based equilibrium model, taking into consideration market power (price setting) and external effects. Following orthodox economics, the result of this class of models is a so-called dynamic steady state, a condition under which all markets are cleared and relevant variables follow equilibrium growth paths. Exogenous interferences in this system (e.g. by economic policy or by opening an economy) influence these growth paths.

To explain the growth dynamics, this class of models is oriented on the following approaches. First, according to Joseph Schumpeter's concept of the

"Schumpeterian Entrepreneur" (Schumpeter 1912), the right to profit is based on the creative ability of innovation, imitation and invention. Second, Robert Solow (1956) stressed the significance of technical progress as the main source of economic development. Third, Paul Romer (1986) presented for the first time an approach in which technical progress is endogenised by introducing human capital, thus explaining growth within the model. Fourth, besides the empirically disputed human capital approach, the research and development approach by Paul Romer (1990), Gene Grossman and Elhanan Helpman (1990) became decisive for the discussion. This concept is based on the idea that research and development themselves are subject to the economic urge to obtain surplus. Therefore, a constant size of the research sector generates permanent innovation and thus long-run growth.

Consequently, there should be an empirical relation between research- and development spending and economic development. It can be noticed however, that there is at least no direct relation between R&D expenditure and economic development, as to be seen in table one.

We observe relatively small shares of R & D in Central and Eastern Europe in comparison to the European Union, whilst CEE countries exhibit faster rates of growth. Moreover, the share of public R % D is larger, and should follow less economic reasoning. A similar picture would also arise amongst developed economies, so that we cannot accept the causal relation indicated by theory.

The theory of economic growth is not a theory on the advances towards potential output, but on the evolution of potential output itself. The engines of economic growth can therefore only be found on the supply side of the economy. There is no doubt, however, that a variety of transmission mechanisms[2] may open demand side channels for economic growth.

For these reasons the methodical necessity arises to adapt the models with respect to the explanation of the economic development itself. It should still incorporate all channels of growth, both the aggregate channels, via physical and human capital or public infrastructure, as well as the desegregate channels via research and development. Particularly the inclusion of small and medium sized firms turn out to be promising. Hence we describe a model-theoretic framework, based on the formal model of Zagler and Ragacs (1998).

The model comprises three sectors of production. A retail sector, in which final (consumption) goods are furnished, a small and medium enterprise (SME) manufacturing sector, in which intermediate goods[3], which are inputs for production of final goods, are produced and a sector for innovation, where the blueprints for intermediate goods are produced[4].

Table 1: Research- and development spending and growth in the European
Union and selected Central and Eastern Economies

	1991	1992	1993	1994	1995
Hungary					
Private R & D in % of total	60,00	58,40	59,50	46,60	52,10
Public R & D in % of total	40,00	41,60	40,50	53,40	47,90
R & D in % of GDP	1,07	1,05	0,98	0,89	0,75
GDP Growth Rate in %	..	-3,10	-0,60	2,90	1,50
Poland					
Private R & D in % of total	..	..	..	36,00	35,30
Public R & D in % of total	..	..	..	64,00	64,70
R & D in % of GDP	..	..	..	0,82	0,75
GDP Growth Rate in %	..	-7,00	2,60	3,80	5,20
Czech Republic					
Private R & D in % of total	..	..	..	..	67,70
Public R & D in % of total	..	..	..	..	32,30
R & D in % of GDP	2,12	1,83	1,35	1,25	1,15
GDP Growth Rate in %	..	-6,40	-0,90	2,60	6,40
European Union					
Private R & D in % of total	58,80	60,00	59,80	60,70	60,90
Public R & D in % of total	41,20	40,00	40,20	39,30	39,10
R & D in % of GDP	1,95	1,93	1,92	1,87	1,85
GDP Growth Rate in %	2,46	0,58	0,78	3,75	2,61

Source: OECD Main Science and Technology Indicators, 1997

Because of high transaction costs, it is assumed that small and medium
sized firms do not have access to both the domestic and the new final-
product markets in Central and Eastern Europe, and therefore operate as
industrial suppliers. The access to the final product markets is provided by
either retailers or large companies. As mentioned earlier, R & D is not by
itself a sufficient explanation for economic growth. Process innovations,
which are not captured in the traditional R & D indicators, are at least as
important as product innovations. An important share of process innovations
occurs in firms with low capital labour ratio, in particular SME. Therefore
the separation between SME and the innovative sector is merely an
analytical device to ease the exposition. For simplicity reasons innovative
firms discover new, innovative processes, which they sell to SME by
collecting the economic surplus. The price for new innovations can therefore
be interpreted as expenditure for process innovations within the SME.

Agents in this model are, on the one hand, households, with labour supplied in the retail and in the innovative sector and with goods demand in the retail sector. On the other hand agents are firms in the final goods sector (retail trade), in manufacturing (SME) and in the innovative sector. Additionally, the public sector has a range of revenue- and expenditure-side possibilities in its economic policy, in particular taxes on consumption and all forms of income as well as expenditures for public consumption, education and infrastructure. In this context, we always assume a balanced budget to take into account the current narrow fiscal margin throughout Europe.

3.   INNOVATION AND STRATEGIC CHOICES FOR SME AND OTHER ECONOMIC AGENTS

Through their urge for profit, SME costly acquire special abilities in a specific market for innovations in order to operate in a new market segment with higher profit expectations[5]. New specialisation will be demanded as long as the costs of the innovation do not exceed the expected returns. The supply in this market is provided by research institutions under standard market conditions.

The different intermediaries of SME will be demanded by large enterprises or retail chains in intermediate-good markets[6]. Because of the assumption of monopolistic competition, SME achieve economic surpluses in these markets.

We are assuming a fully conventional downward sloping demand function of retailers and large enterprises for intermediate-goods. In a specific intermediate-product market, the function shifts outwards with aggregate demand, falls with its own price and rises with the average prices of the competition. Because of the segmentation of the intermediate-good markets, every SME determines the quantity of supply in their own market segment corresponding to the rules of monopolistic competition, as the following illustration shows.

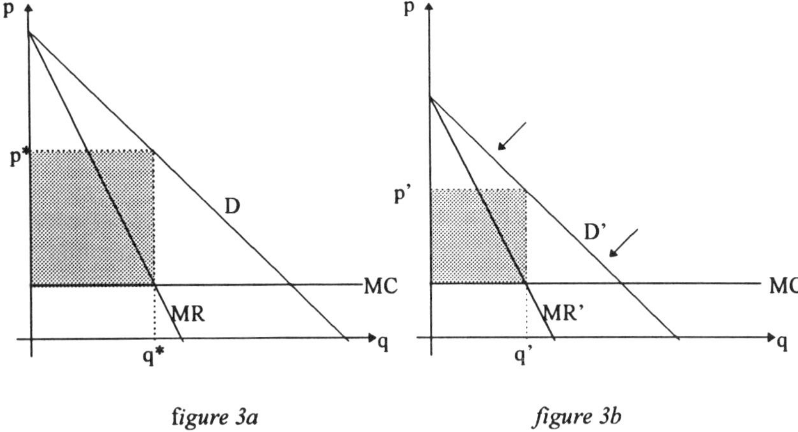

Figure 1. innovation and strategic choices for SME

Figure 3a displays one of many existing intermediate-good markets, with the price of the good (p) and the quantity (q) as the axis labels. The demand for goods follows the above-mentioned traditional course. Through a variation of the quantity supplied, the SME strategic option is to choose a particular point on the demand function. The price rises through a reduction of the quantity, which may result in a change of revenue. The marginal revenue (MR), is defined as the additional revenue from a rising quantity of supply. The marginal revenue function follows the well-known Amoroso-Robinson rule. Profit maximisation requires that the quantity supplied is increased until the additional revenue does not exceed the marginal costs (MC), or at the point MR = MC.

The emergence of new innovations has consequences on the existing markets for intermediate products as displayed in figure 3b. New SME partially displace existing ones, which results in a shift of the demand function for goods to the left for an existing SME to D' as well as the respective marginal revenue function to MR'. Price and quantity in the new equilibrium are lower. As a result, with increasing innovations the economic surpluses (grey areas in fig. 3) of every single SME decline.

4. SME AND DEVELOPMENT

In order to dynamically extend the model, the creation of new (process-) innovations (through applied research) must be discussed. Let us assume that an innovative firm strives for new specialisation because it can sell them to SME to levy all of the above-defined economic surpluses. In the market for innovations, a conventionally falling demand curve (due to falling surpluses) meets a supply function that is determined by the marginal costs of the innovative firms for a specific innovation.

The marginal costs of innovative firms depend negatively upon productivity in the innovation sector, because higher productivity causes lower costs in the provision and hence lower prices. Further it can be assumed that the marginal costs and hence the price for new innovations decrease with an increasing amount of technological knowledge, measured by the number of existing innovations. Economic growth can be stimulated by either an increase in demand for innovations or by decline in marginal costs of innovations.

In this approach, in addition to traditional explanations like human capital or research- and technology, economic growth is seen as a result of SME diversification (given that all SME produce either in different market segments or with different technologies). In addition economic growth stems from profit expectations of the innovative firms in case of a newly developed invention.

Although the supply of labour is limited, qualitative growth takes place in this model. This is because an existing potential of workers in the innovative sector permanently creates new specialisation. Because of that, SME are constantly engaging in new fields of activity, creating jobs (job creation) by attracting labour either from existing firms (job destruction) or from an unbalanced labour market, whereby the total factor productivity increases and hence steady-state growth is generated.

5.   DEVELOPMENT AND SME CO-OPERATIONS WITH EASTERN EUROPE

So far the model has been discussed without national boarders. In the following we want to discuss the possibilities and perspectives of integration. For the sake of simplicity, we analyse the integration between EU-15, as the more mature or developed region, and Central and Eastern Europe as an emerging region. This separation is for theoretical convenience, as Slovenia or the Czech Republic exhibit a similar level of GDP per capita as some EU-15 nations, e.g. Greece or Portugal. However for the regions in total, the difference in income remains substantial. Note that the analysis could also be applied for two specific countries. Even if CEE economies have achieved a certain degree of integration with the EU, we assume for simplicity that before the integration, the growth processes of both regions occur independently but by the same economic principles as mentioned above. Even under some degree of integration, the following results hold qualitatively. In the language of our model, this can be expressed simply through different levels of the corresponding variables that are aggregate demand for goods, level of innovation, productivity and therefore wage and price levels.

Three central issues of the opening are decisive for the growth process with or without co-operation.

Individual firms see generally an enlargement of the goods market potential. The existence of surpluses shows that both regions are located beneath their potential output. Hence an increase in demand leads to improved sales conditions for the consumer goods industry, which leads to an increased demand for intermediate products, which shifts the demand function for the intermediate goods outwards (D in fig. 3). This increases the incentive for further innovations and exhibits a positive effect on growth.

Through outsourcing, the production costs of the innovative firms in the developed region decrease, which brings about further impulses for innovations, leading to a decline in marginal costs of innovative firms, hence to an increase in supply of innovations, inducing growth.

Furthermore, a broad market opens up for small- and medium-sized suppliers in both regions, which intensifies the diversification of production and management technologies in both regions. Of course the integration of two regions does not lead to a linear increase of knowledge about production and management, since it has already been partly applied in both parts. It is evident that a stronger increase in know-how will occur in Eastern Europe. This leads to higher productivity in R & D, which leads to an increase in the supply of innovations too, followed by relatively higher rates of growth in Eastern Europe.

One has to decide whether SME of different regions operate in differentiated or identical markets. In the prior, the model reduces to the one country model introduced earlier. Due to the three points mentioned above, both regions would exhibit higher growth rates. Only in the latter SME of different regions have principally two alternatives. There is either the option of competition, or that of co-operation. In the first case, competition as defined by Bertrand or Cournot will take place that would destroy or at least substantially weaken the economic surpluses following standard economic theory. Therefore competition will stop or at least slow down the growth effect in these market segments in both regions. While firms from economies in transformation have lower costs (MC in fig. 3), the old market economies possess competitive advantages from their higher productivity, which will determine the division of the common market accordingly. Alternatively, in the case of co-operation, the economic surpluses continue, so that company co-operation plays a key role in the development of Eastern Europe, as growth effects must still occur.

Size and nature of the growth effects for the case of SME co-operations can be described by an increase of the demand for innovations and a decrease in the costs of new innovations. The demand for innovations increases in comparison to the case of autarky by an increase in aggregate demand for goods and by a deeper differentiation of the innovations. That is because an increase in the number of varieties, due to the integration, results in lower marginal costs in innovation, which as mentioned above, leads to a higher growth rate. The costs decrease comparably due to the higher number of existing innovations. Additionally, they decrease because of lower aggregate factor prices.

Finally, we like to draw the attention to three special issues. First, as mentioned above, human capital accumulation reduces costs of innovation and hence fosters economic growth. In principle, the acquisition of human capital is a long-term process. Particularly, the creation of human capital in the field of business specific and market specific qualifications requires an extensive effort even when the existing basic training is of high quality. Co-operations speed up and facilitate this process mainly in economies in transformation, so that firms in Eastern and Central European countries receive the necessary human capital, which leads in turn to relatively higher growth rates, in which the western co-operation partners can participate.

Second, despite high rates of economic growth, CEE economies still suffer from inefficient allocation and diffusion of innovations, as the relevant market mechanisms have not developed under the command economy, and the emergence of "innovation markets" requires a considerable initiation period. It is quite likely, that co-operations between SME in CEE and EU will improve the process of diffusion of innovation, and thus reduce time and cost for the acquisition of innovations, corresponding to a decline in marginal costs of innovation, as described earlier.

Third, another important aspect in the transformation process is the diffusion of investment capital. Traditionally, the financial sector is organised through markets (the Anglo-Saxon system) or through banks, in particular, the continental European system of "Hausbanken". The financial sector in CEE is borrowing characteristics from both the Anglo-Saxon systems, with the emergence of dynamic stock markets throughout the region, and the continental system, with close ties between the banking sector and industry. It is not decided yet which elements will dominate the future financial market in CEE.

In any case, (international) financial markets should exhibit the function of transferring funds to the best host. Yet there is little evidence why financial intermediators make decisions efficiently under high risk, which innovation evidently is. Moreover, as there is an intrinsic lack of innovation in the economy, allocation by the financial sector would lead to a systematic rate of under-innovation in both regions. The advantages of co-operations of SME are such that affluent firms in the developed region can, combined with a considerably better possibility to assess risks due to their own knowledge of the industry and the experiences of the co-operation partners in the economies in transformation, coupled with a standing interest in profits, at least reduce the below optimal under-investment and under-innovation.

Summing up the results obtained,

- opening the regions in differentiated market segments leads to relatively higher rates of growth, even if co-operation does not take place,
- opening the regions in identical market segments, co-operations between SME of Eastern and Western Europe are a necessary precondition for continued growth in these segments in both regions,
- additionally co-operations in identical market segments yield higher growth as compared to autarky,
- and finally co-operations are a central ingredient in the development of Eastern Europe, compared to the situation of autarky, because growth rates in Eastern Europe will be relatively higher than in Western Europe.

Co-operations are formed for economic interests. Because of the importance for economic development the question arises to what extent should there be public interference (which may be executed by the respective local governments or by supranational bodies or agencies such as the EU and EBRD) in the structure of incentives for macroeconomic interests. They seem meaningful, when the positive dynamic effects outweigh the short-run costs. In this sense, policy variables for macroeconomic measures can set in at the productivity in the innovation sector, at infrastructure and at the institutional framework.

An obvious economic policy is to increase productivity, or directly the success probability of innovation. In spite of different possible policy strategies, the underlying basic idea of all these attempts is "picking the winners" in industrial policy. However, there is no reason to assume, that public institutions know which projects yield the largest revenue expectations. Hence there is a big possibility for policies that support firms with old and unproductive technologies, which is in complete contrast to the basic idea. Thus, direct subsidies for research projects seem to be much more effective, since they increase the incentive for new innovations by increased profit expectations. In the language of our model this is equivalent to a promotion of not-yet-established SME versus established SME.

In our model an indirect channel to increase economic growth due to an increase of productivity is, according to Barro (1990), to improve the production conditions of the firms via infrastructure investment. Improved infrastructure conditions clearly reduce the costs of co-operation between firms. This argument may be interpreted for actual policy decisions. Hence, increasing trans-european networks by the EU for instance would accelerate economic growth.

Finally, growth-specific options arise through the reduction of the institutional framework, which prevents fast conversion of new technologies. This would allow new SME to obtain economic rents more easily and faster. As a consequence, a higher discounted yield increases the incentive for innovations. Examples would be a faster approval of concessions within the craft legislation and the unconditional admission of any new company establishment by domestic and foreign companies. Of course this category also includes the dismantling of tariff- and non-tariff barriers.

CONCLUSION

In this paper the effects of co-operations of small- and medium-sized firms between the economies in transformation and the developed regions in Europe have been examined. A discussion in the framework of the new theory of economic growth offers a relevant starting point for analysing macroeconomic effects. In this course, economic development essentially stems from process innovations. Starting from a description of the model, expected effects of co-operations between SME in transforming and developed region are first analysed and then accompanying measures are proposed. In the analytical setting used, the opening of the economy and especially SME co-operations of Eastern and Western European companies within identical market segments clearly lead to positive growth effects.

NOTES

1 Of course there are also demand-side effects, especially via distorted prices. These are discussed in Ragacs and Zagler, 1997. See Zagler (1998) for a more profound discussion.

2 These may be interpreted as "useful capital goods to produce final goods", Sala-i-Martin (1990), 36.

3 This model builds upon the work by Romer (1990), Grossman/Helpman (1991).

4 As defined by Grossman and Helpman (1990), instead of new market segments one can also implement new procedures within an existing segment.

5Tangible assets or other factors of production are not used in this model for reasons of simplicity. However, their implementation would not change the conclusions from this model.

REFERENCES

Grossman, G. M. and Helpman, E., 1990, *Innovation and Growth in the Global Economy*, The MIT Press, Boston

Barro, R. J., 1990, 'Government Spending in a Simple Model of Endogenous Growth', *Journal of Political Economy*, Vol. 98, S103-S125.

Kalay, L., 1998, The State of SMES IN Hungary as the Tax Returns and a Representative Business Survey Shows: Implications for a SME Policy, Paper presented at the SME Forum and Conference, Budapest

OECD, 1998, WWW-Database „Basic Science and Technology Statistics", http://www.wifo.ac.at/cgi-bin/wzrp/wzrphome.cgi, from March 11

OECD, 1998, WWW- Database „National Accounts", http://www.wifo.ac.at/cgi-bin/wzrp/wzrphome.cgi, from March 11

OECD, 1998, WWW- Database „Science and Technology", based on STI Database and Industrial Outlook, http://www.oecd.org/publications/observer /figures/st_a.pdf, from Feb. 9

OECD, 1997, Main Science and Technology Indocators, Vol. 2, Paris

Pichler, J. H., Pleitner, H. J., and Schmidt, K.-H., 1996, *Management in KMU*, Verlag Paul Haupt, Bern

Ragacs, Ch. and Zagler, M., 1997, Economic Policy in a Model of Endogenous Growth, *Vienna University of Economics & Business Administration*, Department of Economics, Working Paper No. 37, Vienna

Ragacs, Ch. and Zagler, M., 1998, Wachstumsstrategien für Österreich in einem veränderten Mitteleuropa, In: Tagungsband der WU Jahrestagung, *Service-Fachverlag*, Wien, (forthcoming)

Romer, P. M., 1986, Increasing Returns and Long-Run Growth, *Journal of Political Economy*, Vol. 94, 1002-37

Romer, P. M., 1990, Endogenous Technological Change, *Journal of Political Economy*, Vol. 98, 71-102

Sala-i-Martin, X., 1990, 'Lecture Notes on Economic Growth (II): Five Prototype Models of Endogenous Growth', *National Bureau of Economic Research, Cambridge, Working Paper* No. 3564

Schumpeter, J. A., 1912, *Theorie der wirtschaftlichen Entwicklung*, Duncker & Humblot, Leipzig

Solow, R. M., 1956, A Contribution to the Theory of Economic Growth, *The Quarterly Journal of Economics*, Vol. 70, 65-94

Zagler, M. and Ragacs, Ch., 1998, Endogenous Growth, Division of Labour, and Fiscal Policy, in: Zagler, M., *Endogenous Growth, Market Failures, and Economic Policy*, Macmillan, Basingstoke, (forthcoming)

Zagler, M.,1998, *Endogenous Growth, Market Failures, and Economic Policy*, Macmillan, Basingstoke, (forthcoming)

Chapter 10

Swedish Multinationals in Central and Eastern Europe - entry and subsequent development

Jan-Erik Vahlne, Kjell A. Nordström and Styrbjörn Torbacke
Stockholm School of Economics

Abstract: This paper reports on the findings from the first phase of a larger longitudinal project that focuses on the establishment process of Swedish multinational corporations in Eastern Europe. The first step of identifying and explaining the establishment mode, type of activities intensity and type of control applied in local operations of five of the firms is reported and commented here. The tentative key conclusions at that stage indicate that (1) entry into the region has been sequential and gradual, (2) old relationships are extremely important, (3) early entries are looked as « learning devices » in several case firms, (4) the attitude to risk varies in size and ownership, (5) there is a difference in how risk is perceived between local managers and the head office, (6) the head office generally closely monitors the operations, and (7) several case firms see the potential for using Eastern and Central Europe as a production base. [This paper was first published in *Journal of East-West Business* (International Business Press, an imprint of The Haworth Press, Inc) Vol.1, n°4, 1996, pp 1-16.][1]

1.   THE PROJECT

The research presented in this paper is conducted within the framework of a larger project, called "Evolution of International Business Institutions - Models of Involvement in Central and Eastern Europe by Corporations of Advanced Industrial Countries". The project is based on the belief that Central and Eastern Europe provide an environment of great potential but also of large uncertainty and risk. These characteristics vary from country to country within the region. In that sense, it provides a testing ground for new

---

[1] Copyright 1996 by The Haworth Press, Inc.

ways of doing business, adjusted to the characteristics of the environment. Differences between national markets provide a quasi-experimental situation, and comparisons between countries and companies will hopefully make for interesting conclusions. The research is performed by teams from Japan, the United States and Sweden. Access to multinational corporations in the respective three teams' home nations will allow for some comparisons between multinationals of different origin. The objectives of the project are firstly to study how modes, activities, and monitoring and control of these activities evolve over time as a consequence of the characteristics of the environment. Secondly, we will study how these variables are changed over time through learning from past experiences and adjustments to changes in the environment.

2.   OBJECTIVES OF THIS PAPER

The focus of this paper is, consequently, to identify and explain the mode, type of activities, intensity, and type of control applied in the local operations of some Swedish multinationals in Central and Eastern Europe.

At this stage, we have paid a first visit to the Central and East European operations of half a dozen Swedish multinationals, and material on these operations have been collected. We report on the frame of reference used for this data collection, provide highlights from the cases, and offer some general conclusions which should be regarded as very tentative.

3.   FRAME OF REFERENCE

3.1   MODES OF INVOLVEMENT

Over time, companies have developed new modes of doing business in foreign markets. Most of these, however, are variations on a few themes. Figure 1 summarizes the main categories we need to pay attention to.

The source for this figure is the latest standard book on modes, but it suffers from an export orientation which belongs to the past. So, for example, category #1 is named "Export Entry Modes", and there is no category labeled "Import Entry Modes". It is true that most companies started their internationalization from the "export" side of their business, but some companies also started from the "import" side (cf. Swedish IKEA), and this is believed to become more common. Consequently, we need to add the Import Entry Modes to the other categories in the figure.

<table>
<tr><td>1.</td><td>Export Entry Modes
(a) indirect
(b) direct agent/distributor
(c) direct branch subsidiary</td></tr>
<tr><td>2.</td><td>Contractual Entry Modes
(a) licensing
(b) franchising
(c) management contracts
(d) turnkey contracts
(e) contract manufacturing/international sub-contracting
(f) collaboration agreements</td></tr>
<tr><td>3.</td><td>Investment Entry Modes
(a) wholly -owned /majority-owned: new establishment
(b) wholly-owned /majority-owned: acquisition
(c) joint venture: new establishment acquisition</td></tr>
<tr><td>4.</td><td>Corporate Coalitions and Strategic Alliances</td></tr>
</table>

Figure 1. Foreign Market Entry Modes

Source: Young, S. & al., 1989, *International Market Entry and Development: Strategies and Management*, Hemel Hempstead: Harvester Wheatsheaf.

It is well known from the literature (cf. Young et al., 1989) that these modes have different characteristics in some important dimensions, such as risk (size of investment), potential for learning, and controllability, including control of proprietary knowledge. There is a trade-off, given the context, between these characteristics: The more the company invests, given the context, the higher is the risk, but the better it actually controls the operations. Because of this, companies seem to prefer a gradual internationalization process starting with less risky, but also potentially less rewarding modes. As experience is accumulated and relationships become established, firms move towards the use of riskier modes (Johanson and Vahlne, 1977, 1990). No doubt, performance of the riskier modes is generally superior from the companies' point of view so that riskier modes are usually preferred when the market potential is high.

According to Wolniak (1991), exporting is the dominating way of exploiting the East European markets. Since foreign participation was allowed, the number of joint ventures has increased. Licenses, which were quite common up to the mid-1980s, have lost much of their popularity once joint ventures were allowed. Further to note is that, once the rules were relaxed to allow majority ownership by foreigners, this became the dominating mode, judging from a small sample (Nigh et al., 1990). The same source states that companies with previous experience from trade and licensing relationships used this as a base on which equity joint ventures were built. Another observation is that U.S. venture partners tend to limit their exposure by keeping capital investment low. Most inward investments are so far made through acquisitions (Wolniak, 1991; Hood and Young, 1991).

3.2   ACTIVITIES

The basic typology of activities applied by us is based on Porter's (1985, ch. 2) value chain. At the highest level of description, the typology is: support activities, in and outbound logistics, operations, marketing and sales, and service. Where relevant, we have used a more detailed classification.

The general expectation we started with was that entry is connected with the performance of only a few activities. Gradually, more activities will be added. The motivation for this expectation is the same as the one provided in the section on the choice of mode.

3.3   MONITORING AND CONTROL

Any organization is concerned with how to focus resources towards attainment of organizational objectives. It is through the set of instruments and processes that usually is referred to as the control system, that goal congruence and goal achievement is assured (Leksell, 1981). A prerequisite for exerting any form of effective control is an efficient monitoring function. The monitoring function - through its focus on measuring performance in various aspects - provide the necessary data for exerting control.

Following Leksell (1981), we can distinguish between three key systems subject to monitoring and control: organizational, administrative, and social systems. Organizational aspects include aspects such as allocation of responsibilities, organizational specialization, vertical and horizontal differentiation and formalization. The administrative system includes budget, planning and goal-reaching procedures, as well as the corresponding reporting and evaluation systems. Within the frame of the social system, we find selection and recruitment procedures, executive relations and development procedures as well as incentive systems.

Most empirical research indicates that effective organizations facing environmental uncertainty created by heterogenous and unstable environments, adopt more flexible and adaptive organizations (see Leksell, 1981). It could be expected that operations in Central & Eastern Europe and the former U.S.S.R. are regarded as "more risky" than similar operations performed elsewhere, due to a very high environmental uncertainty. In effect it could be expected that operations in this area have the following characteristics:

a)Performance requirements will be higher than in comparable operations in more stable environments.

b) decision-making on operations will be highly decentralized (Thompson, 1967) and subject mainly to social monitoring and control.

c)Any decision-making in matters considered to be of strategic importance (e.g., the national market is important in the global competitive game, local manufacturing for the global system, etc.) will be centralized and involve top management. It will in these cases be difficult to differentiate between monitoring and control, on the one hand, and the various systems of monitoring and control on the other. This is due to the active participation of top management in the decision-making process.

3.4   METHODOLOGY

Having the possibility to follow the objects of study over a three-year period, will allow us to observe the development of the operations in Central and Eastern Europe and the way they are controlled. In one extreme case, we will follow the development closely by being present fairly often at critical meetings. In others, we will confine ourselves to return 3-4 times to the same managers to enquire about the development since last time. Our approach will be processual (see Pettigrew, 1985).

Our sample is two-dimensional: countries and companies. We wanted to vary perceived uncertainty and risk by including operations in Hungary, Poland, the Czech Republic, Russia and Ukraine. The companies are all well known Swedish multinationals, albeit of somewhat varying size and experience from international business.

4.   FIVE CASES ON EUROPEAN MULTINATIONALS' ENTRY INTO EASTERN EUROPE

4.1   THE ENGINEERING GROUP Ltd.

The Engineering Group Ltd.[2] is a highly internationalized US$ 43 billion company. Since its formation, the Group has expanded from its European base to become one of the world's leading producers of engineering products and systems within its area of competence.

From its substantial manufacturing base within EC and EFTA countries, the Group has during the last two to three years positioned itself as one of the largest investors in Eastern Europe and the former U.S.S.R. Although the group, through a large number of acquisitions and joint ventures, employ between 27,000 - 30,000 people in this region, Eastern Europe and the former U.S.S.R. account for only 1.5 - 3.0 percent of the sales.

It is the outspoken ambition of the management to further increase its commitment to this region for two reasons. Eastern Europe and the former U.S.S.R. is, on the one hand, considered to be an excellent low cost/high quality manufacturing base for a company in this industry. It is, on the other hand, a huge potential market per se, in need of enormous investments. Significant local presence is considered a necessity in order to be able to exploit any major share of this potential. Judgements of potential as well as of risk vary to a large extent with, for example, geographical location or, as one manager in the Engineering Group's Russian operation puts it: "We see it from the local market's perspective and market the possibilities internally, why should they bother about starting business in Russia when they are located in a business area in Houston?"

According to the present plans, the turnover of the Group's total operations in this area should represent no less than 6.0 - 7.5 percent of the turnover by 1995.

The Engineering Group's expansion into the former COMECON area was initiated by top management immediately after the 1989 liberation wave. Poland and Hungary - both countries that had been significant export and licensing markets during the communist era - became the initial target markets. Apart from relatively stable political conditions, historical ties in the form of exports or licensing arrangements to these markets enabled the

---

[2] We have promised confidentiality until the companies have agreed to publication. As time has not allowed us to ask for permission to publish, some company names are not disclosed in this version.

Group to quickly identify the most interesting acquisition candidates. Frequently, it was former licensees that actually were acquired.

Complete takeovers, i.e., a 100-percent ownership, was in general preferred by the Group, but even minority positions could be accepted, as long as the Engineering Group had the management responsibility and an option to increase their share in the future. By 1993, the Engineering Group has about 13,500 employees in Poland in twelve different operations and about 10,500 employees in Hungary in eight different operations.

The Czech republic and Romania - considered to be more difficult and unstable markets - were entered at a later stage and on a smaller scale, following roughly the same principle as in Poland and Hungary. By 1993, the Group has about 1,000 employees in eight operations in the Czech Republic, and about 2,600 employees in two operations in Romania.

The market considered to be one of the most unstable in the region - Russia - was entered on a larger scale in 1991. Russia, or rather the former U.S.S.R., had like the other countries in the region historically bought certain equipment from the Group. In spite of the uncertainty, top management considered this market to be of strategic interest to the Group and local presence a necessity. So far, a set of smaller acquisitions of 48-49 percent stakes in firms focussing on engineering, service and local marketing support have been made in the region. The ten Russian operations with 1,000 employees in fifteen different operations are considered to be a training ground. Further knowledge and acquaintance with Russian market conditions is considered to be needed before any investments of a larger scale are conducted.

The investments in Eastern Europe and the former U.S.S.R. have been closely monitored by top management and its controllers, both in strategic and financial terms, ever since the first acquisitions. The Central & East European operations report directly to the highest corporate level. The person responsible for the area spends a lot of time travelling around to more closely follow the operations. Profit requirements have - with the exception of Russia - been lower than Group average during the first years. The particularly unstable conditions in Russia have implied that a higher ROI than Group average is required. However, it is the ambition of top management that the various operations in the former COMECON area, as an effect of significant technical as well as administrative support, by 1995 should be well-integrated units of the Engineering Group without any need for special treatment.

The newly acquired firms have, in spite of some problems, particularly in Russia, performed surprisingly well. Polish and Hungarian turbine components are, for instance, now sold by the Engineering Group on the world market. It is the firm belief of Group management that the investments in this region are well-motivated in a long-term perspective. A number of further acquisitions and joint ventures are presently being investigated and negotiated. The Russian operation is, for example, expected to go from eight operating companies and 800 employees to fifteen operating companies and between 2,000 and 4,000 employees before the end of 1993.

Distinctive features

• The Engineering Group Ltd. has enjoyed long-term relations with companies and government bodies in Central & Eastern Europe for the past fifty years.
   • Initially, the group saw the potential for the area to become a Taiwan of Europe, with low-cost and high-quality production. However, with time the group has come to appreciate the market potential in the area as such.
   • The Engineering Group Ltd. is currently enjoying acceptable profit margins in the area, thus proving that they are not there to distribute aid but doing business.
   • Monitoring and control of the operations in Central & Eastern Europe are handled by the highest corporate level.

4.2   ELECTROLUX

Electrolux is one of the world's largest manufacturers of household appliances. After an aggressive acquisition program - particularly in the 1980s when more than 200 acquisitions were completed - Electrolux is today a global company with more than 600 subsidiaries in 40 countries, 150,000 employees worldwide, and foreign sales representing about 85 percent of total sales.

In spite of being highly internationalized, the East European markets and the former U.S.S.R. did not even account for 0.1 percent of the firm's turnover by the end of the 1980s. The non-convertibility of the currencies had effectively hindered any expansion.

The company had, by 1989, discussed for years various ways of circumventing the currency problem. Early penetration was believed to provide an important psychological basis - a sort of training ground - for further expansion in a region which was considered to be of future interest. Hungary was preferred as a first step because it was believed to be the most well-functioning among the East European countries.

The major political changes in Eastern Europe initiated Electrolux' acquisition of its former supplier of refrigerators for decades - The Lehel Group of Hungary. Initiatives to begin discussions between the firms came from both parties. Electrolux saw a potential acquisition candidate, and

Lehel was interested in finding a financial partner. After two years of negotiations, the acquisition was finalized in 1991. At the time, it was the single largest investment ever made by a foreign firm in Hungary. Lehel had about 5,000 employees and it was considered to be one of the best functioning firms in Hungary.

For Electrolux, the acquisition of Lehel of Hungary not only meant that a former competitor and capable supplier was added to the corporate portfolio. By acquiring this company, Electrolux had gained access to the strongest indigenous local brand name in Hungary, and taken its first major step towards entering the new markets in Eastern Europe. Further acquisitions in the non-covered area of Eastern Europe and the former U.S.S.R. could be expected, due to competitive reasons and anti-trust problems within the EC/EFTA region.

The acquired firm was in a first phase swiftly integrated into Electrolux global structure and norms. An immediate major re-organization in line with Electrolux global standards, significant educational efforts, the appointment of foreign "shadow" managers that could assist local management in certain key positions, and a swift introduction of the Group's standardized reporting system, here enabled Electrolux to maximize the use of local management. In the new organization, only two marketing managers and one product manager are foreign.

The time required before Lehel of Hungary could function as an independent unit within Electrolux without any particular need for support, is still too early to tell. However, Lehel is expected to perform in line with Group standards by the end of 1993.

Distinctive features

• The relationship between Electrolux and Lehel was a supplier-producer one, which turned into acquisition discussions which resulted in Electrolux buying Lehel.

• Electrolux wanted to build a low-cost, high-quality production base in Hungary.

• Hungary was seen as a good training ground for a continued launch into the area. Electrolux saw Hungary as the least risky country where to start.

• By acquiring Lehel, Electrolux bought the brand name Lehel, which totally dominates the Hungarian market, thereby assuring sales of a healthy magnitude.

• Electrolux, as rapidly as possible, included Lehel in its worldwide computerized reporting system to better be able to monitor and control the operations in Hungary.

4.3   THE OCPOC GROUP

The Ocpoc Group - a highly internationalized US$ 2 billion company primarily active in the areas of heavy engineering goods - has historically had very little interest in Central and Eastern Europe. Ocpoc's contacts have been limited to occasional exports from Sweden.

Ocpoc's history in Hungary goes back to 1964 when the first order from Hungary was received. Three years later, an agency agreement was signed with a state-owned import organization, and by 1981 the cooperation had been extended to encompass also a local service organization and a consignment stock. Due to the lack of hard currency, Ocpoc's market was severely limited. Local manufacturing could to a certain extent solve this problem, and in 1984 a license agreement for small-scale equipment was concluded with a Hungarian partner. However, Ocpoc was not satisfied with neither the agent nor the licensee by the end of the 1980s. The locally made equipment price as well as quality was not competitive when import restrictions gradually were lifted. Furthermore, Ocpoc was convinced that the agent - due among other reasons to an inefficient administration - did not capture the whole potential market. In 1989, Ocpoc - after some negotiations - had terminated its previous relations, hired the key personnel of the former agent, and established a wholly-owned sales subsidiary.

Although Russia has been, and still is, the single largest mining country in the world, the amount of imported goods has been limited to less than US$ 100 millions a year. Ocpoc's arch-rival has, for historical reasons, completely dominated the market.

In spite of the fact that there are about 1,300 mines in Russia, Opcop has basically only had one customer in the region during the last twenty years - the Northern No.7 Mine. This mine had, due to its size and exports (about 40 percent of the former U.S.S.R's total exports), been granted the right to select its own suppliers.

The management of the Ocpoc Group stands firmly behind entering East European countries as well as Russia and other C.I.S. countries. In early 1993, the group established its first sales subsidiary in Russia. However, local manufacturing seems for the moment to be of less interest. It is the establishment of further sales subsidiaries in countries like Romania, The Czech Republic, Poland, Bulgaria and C.I.S. countries other than Russia that is the top priority. The latter group of countries are presently planned to be served from the Russian operation. However, apart from significant geographical distances to customers in certain of these countries, like for example Kazachstan, the political distance is gradually becoming wider.

The risks are considered to be moderate, even in the case of Russia. Most of the buyers are exporting organizations with a significant cash flow in hard currency. Furthermore, the mines are of extreme importance - particularly to Russian exports - and badly in need of modern equipment. Even in the case of significant turmoil it is expected that the mining sector will be protected. Furthermore, in the case of Russia, Ocpoc foresees that its arch-rival will lose market share, the more decentralized the buying process becomes. In spite of this, the operations are still being meticulously monitored from central headquarters.

Distinctive features

• The interest shown in the region by Ocpoc, has been preceded by some twenty years of doing business in Hungary and with the U.S.S.R.

• There is money to be made in the area; the group is not present for the goodwill nor to support the new nation states.

• All operations report directly to a member of the executive committee.

4.4   SCHNURR Ltd.

Schnurr Ltd., with a turnover of US$ 4.5 billion, is one of the world's most internationalized firms, with subsidiaries in more than 130 countries. The core business, a component for the engineering industries, account for more than 75 percent of total turnover. Schnurr is the market leader in all of the industrialized countries except Japan, and it has a worldwide market share of approximately 20 percent.

The relations between Schnurr and the former U.S.S.R. goes back to the turn of the century. The local manufacturing operation of Schnurr was nationalized right after the Bolshevik revolution and renamed Engineering Factory No.2. This factory was later "cloned", and by 1993 there were about 33 such "clones" in operation all over the former U.S.S.R., together making the C.I.S. group of countries, in terms of volume, the by far largest producer in the world in this industry.

The Group has wholly-owned, well-established sales subsidiaries in Hungary and the former Czechoslovakia. In the case of Hungary, the subsidiary was established as early as 1928. For a few days, the operation was nationalized at the beginning of the 1950s. However, after some political and commercial negotiations, it was re-established as Schnurr property and has remained - although with severe restrictions until 1988 - a part of the Group ever since. More recently, wholly-owned sales operations have been established in Bulgaria, Croatia, Poland, Albania, Romania and Russia.

Schnurr responded to the political and economic transition of the former COMECON countries by, on the one hand, implementing a comprehensive process of change towards Group standards in the established subsidiaries in Hungary and the former Czechoslovakia; on the other hand, it established wholly-owned subsidiaries in those countries where Schnurr had no representation of its own. For example, in the case of Russia (where Schnurr actually had a subsidiary which was nationalized), this implied that the national head of the foreign ball bearings procurement organization, in 1986 was invited to become a Schnurr employee and to build up the local sales organization. A gentleman who by that time had been working in this industry since 1974 buying from Schnurr. He was very well-known to Schnurr, and Schnurr was very well-known to him, when he was recruited in 1974.

Schnurr is committed to the region and further investments are planned. Presently, a handful of the above mentioned "clones" are considered to be interesting acquisition candidates, and they are being closely monitored by the Russian operation. Schnurr believes that they, as well as their competitors, are well aware of which of the "clones" are the most interesting and well-run ones.

Distinctive features

• Schnurr recruited the former state official in charge of purchasing equipment of the type that Schnurr sells, thus getting not only him, but also his knowledge of the market and his network of contacts.

• Their former presence has merely been extended into a more determined launch of their products on the market.

• All monitoring and control of the operations are carried out at the highest corporate level.

## 4.5	IKEA

IKEA of Sweden, is one of the world's largest furniture retail operations in the world, with a turnover of close to US$ 4 billion in 1992. IKEAS's straightforward business idea, is to provide high-quality furniture and accessories at such a low price, that the average person can afford them. The core competence of IKEA is a sophisticated design, logistics and distribution concept.

IKEAS's relation to Eastern Europe and the former U.S.S.R., has a somewhat peculiar history. The immediate success of IKEA during the 1960s in Sweden as well as abroad, led to a boycott by major suppliers in Western Europe. IKEA was considered to be a threat to the whole industry as its prices were considered to be too low. The company was at that time more or less saved by Polish suppliers. Ever since, the founder and sole owner - Mr Ingvar Kamprad - has had a special relationship with Eastern Europe in particular, but also the former U.S.S.R. IKEA has over time established procurement operations in Hungary, Poland, The Czech Republic, Slovakia, Romania, Yugoslavia and Russia.

By 1988 - after several attempts in Czechoslovakia as well as Hungary - the first IKEA outlet was established in this region. A joint venture was set up with Hungary's largest furniture retailer, which three years later became a wholly-owned operation. The Hungarian outlet was considered to be a pilot case and a way of testing the IKEA concept in the Eastern European context, without taking too much risk. Hungary was considered to be the most advanced market in the former COMECON area.

As of 1993, one more outlet has been established in Poland, and land acquired in several big cities in the region to ensure future expansion possibilities. Apart from further investments in outlets, IKEA plans to acquire fifteen manufacturing operations in the region within the near future. It is argued that IKEA's manufacturing capacity in the region has to be protected from competitors and further rationalized.

Distinctive features

• IKEA entered the area some 25 - 30 years ago, although not voluntarily. They have with time come to know the area and understand the people.

• The old supplier network has simply been broadened in scope, to now embrace a distribution organization as well. It is, however, built on the old relations established through decades of cooperation.

5.   TENTATIVE CONCLUSIONS

The points given below are observations we have made as direct and indirect outcomes of interviews made in the nine companies visited so far. Their status is that of propositions made very early in the research process. It should be born in mind that our sample consists of large, experienced multinationals.

1. Old relationships are extremely important. Licensors and licensees from the time of the command economy <u>both</u> often have found reasons to deepen relationships which, on the limit, led to an acquisition, as in all the five cases presented. (Because of this, we should add to our sample some companies not having a history in Central and Eastern Europe.)

2. Entry into the region has been sequential, starting from the Western side and gradually moving eastward (as in the cases of the Engineering

Group Ltd. and IKEA, and as is the intention of the Electrolux Group.) It so happens that geographical and psychic distance as well as degree of risk and uncertainty are correlated: the further to the northwest, the smaller the psychic distance and the lower the risk and uncertainty. In some cases, the former contact point, Vienna, has been used as a bridgehead for establishing business ventures in the Central European national markets.

3.Some of the early entries, particularly those in Hungary and Poland, have been looked upon by the investors as experiments and learning devices (this goes for the Engineering Group Ltd. and Electrolux, among others.)

4.In each national market, there is a strong tendency for the individual investor to start out with less committing modes (e.g., a sales subsidiary) and later on to invest in more committing modes (manufacturing subsidiary). This is entirely consistent with general models of internationalization (see Johanson & Vahlne, 1990).

5.Western multinationals have different attitudes to risk-taking. Clearly size and ownership matter, whereby large size and private ownership allow for higher degrees of risk taking (as is the case of the Engineering Group).

6.Interviews with representatives of the MNCs in the local markets have given us the impression that there is a difference between the perceptions of two categories of management: the "field personnel" see the potential as larger than do HQ-representatives, while the latter perceive risks as higher than the former. Obviously, geographic as well as hierarchical distance to a particular market seems to affect how risk and potential are perceived. Again, this is consistent with our expectations.

7.The higher risks as perceived by HQ in some cases seem to motivate a demand for higher returns or alternatively a demand for a shorter pay-back period. In some cases this was not so as when the huge potential seemed to motivate a classification of the investments as "strategic", allowing for patience concerning the return.

8.On top of standardized reporting back to HQ, controllers and the responsible individual in group management spend considerable time learning about the companies' operations and about the local environments. Although formal decision-making concerning the operations is decentralized, this opens up avenues for HQ to affect the decisions (as has been explicitly stated by most of the corporations in the study).

9.Most of the industries of which our sample companies are members, can be regarded as global or at least regional oligopolies. Hence, watching, matching, and preempting competitors' moves should be important. No doubt, competitors' activities are generally monitored. To our surprise, preemptive moves seemed important in smaller markets only. For large markets, statements such as "There is room for everyone" were common.

10. Many of the companies see the potential of exploiting the Central and East European environment for group purposes, e.g., export of certain products to West European markets (the Engineering Group is already doing this). Again, these conclusions are highly tentative. We will now try to include HQ views and the experiences of smaller companies. Later on, we will return to the companies from which the above reported material was collected, to catch their learning and adjustment processes.

REFERENCES

Hood, N. & Young, S., 1991, "The Internationalization of Business and the Challenge of East-European Development". Paper presented at the Annual meeting of the European International Business Association (EIBA), Copenhagen, 13-15 December.

Johanson, J. & Vahlne, J-E., 1977, "The Internationalization Process of the Firm - A Model of Knowledge Development and Increasing Market Commitments", Journal of International Business Studies, spring/summer, pp. 23-32.

Johanson, J. & Vahlne, J-E., 1990, "The Mechanism of Internationalization", International Marketing Review, Vol. 7, No. 4, pp. 11-23.

Leksell, L., 1981, Headquarter-Subsidiary Relationships in Multinational Corporations. Stockholm: Institute of International Business and the Economic Research Institute, Stockholm School of Economics. (Doctoral dissertation)

Nigh, D., Walters, P. & Kuhlman, J., 1990, "US-USSR Joint Ventures: An Examination of the Early Entrants", The Columbia Journal of World Business, winter, Vol. 25, No. 4.

Pettigrew, A.M., 1985, "Contextualist Research: A Natural Way to link Theory and Practice". In Lawler, E.E. III, ed., Doing Research That Is Useful in Theory and Practice. San Francisco, CA: Jossey-Bass, pp. 222-274.

Porter, M.E., 1985, Competitive Advantage. New York, NY: The Free Press.

Thompson, J.D., 1967, Organizations in Action. New York, NY: McGraw Hill Book Company.

Wolniak, R., 1991, "Foreign Investment in Eastern Europe: Emerging Trends and Policy Prescriptions". Paper presented at the Annual meeting of the European International Business Association (EIBA), Copenhagen, 13-15 December.

Young, S., Hamill, J., Wheeler, C., & Davies, J.R., 1989, International Market Entry and Development. Hemel Hempstead: Harvester Wheatsheaf.

Chapter 11

The Enlargement Challenge

Franck Debié
HEC School of Management, Paris and Ecole Normale Supérieure

Abstract: The present enlargement of the European Union to Eastern Europe is a new step in a lasting historical process. The gap existing between Western Europe and Eastern European applicants is wider than the gap existing between the original member states and Mediterranean countries integrated in the late eighties. The lack of public support for integration (even in some of the applicant countries), the lack of political consensus on the method, the scarcity of resources likely to be allocated to the process have created a difficult challenge for European governance. The answer has been a cheap assistance scheme (most of the funds for transition will be available after accession) and a bureaucratic approach to the enlargement in which the Commission will play a decisive role. The enlargement is conditional - conditions are clearly stated in accession partnerships - but no clear deadlines have been set up in the medium term and the consequences of delays and lack of co-operation have not been made very clear. This unpredictable conditionality creates in turn challenges for corporate governance: dramatic changes are going to be introduced by the enlargement process but the agenda remains unclear and strategies have to be adapted to uncertainty and risks difficult to measure.

INTRODUCTION

The enlargement of the European Union was at the beginning a constitutive objective of the European Community's founding fathers. A solemn commitment was taken by the first six member states under article O of the Treaty of Rome that they should discuss any application for accession made by a European state: "Every European State may ask to become a member of the Union". According to that first definition, the first test for enlargement was a political, cultural and historical one. The applicant country had to demonstrate a "European identity" if geography was not clear enough. The case was discussed for Malta and Cyprus, which were finally found to be "European countries". Turkey is likely to be considered as having already met that first test of European identity, as the Ankara Agreement between Turkey and the EU clearly stated that Turkey could have access to the Union "one day". Moldavia, Belarus, Ukraine and Russia may be eligible on the basis of those first criteria of European identity. The question would be more difficult to debate for Armenia or Georgia.

The objective of Union's enlargement to Eastern Europe was defined as a revolutionary challenge in 1989, at a historical summit commemorating the bi-centenary of the French Revolution. Criteria for enlargement were defined very broadly in Copenhagen in 1993 and a pre-accession strategy established at the Essen Summit together with a specific budget and a first list of candidates. Candidates' profiles were investigated by the Commission in 1997 and a final list for the first phase of enlargement agreed upon at the Luxembourg Summit. Actual negotiations for accession started in spring 1998 and the Commission at the end of 1998 will submit a review of achievements.

The benefits from the enlargement to Eastern Europe were described as early as the Paris Summit of 1989: enlargement is a unique chance to reunify Europe, to ensure lasting peace and stability, to develop the world's largest consumer market, to provide a framework for Western assistance to Eastern Europe, a method and an inspiration for economic transition there.

In fact, the transition to market economy started independently from the European integration process and market liberalisation started much earlier than the accession process itself by courtesy of "association agreements" with the Union and bilateral agreements between Eastern European countries. Impressive results were achieved before the start of the Essen pre-accession strategy. As negotiations for accession are now underway, accession is no longer a debate in the Union and a prospect for Eastern Europe but a challenge for European governance as well as for European companies.

1.   EUROPEAN GOVERNANCE AND THE ENLARGEMENT CHALLENGE

Since the last enlargement encompassing the three remaining strong market economies of the continent (except Switzerland and Norway), enlargement has become a delicate political issue within the Union, as any further step would now dramatically change the economic and social characteristics of the Union.

Table 1. Successive enlargement impact

(Source: Eurostat, 1997)

Based on 1995 figures	Increase in size	Increase in population	Global increase in GDP	Change in GDP per capita	GDP per capita compared to first 6 members
1973 : 9 members/ 6 founding members	31%	32%	29%	- 3%	97
1992 : 12 members/ former 9 members	48%	22%	15%	- 6%	91
1996 : 15 members (including former GDR) /former 12 members	43%	11%	8%	-3%	89
2005 (?) 26 members/ 15 former members	34%	29%	9%	- 16%	75

1.1   The East-West gap challenge

1.1.1   East-West Gap and European security agenda

The enlargement to Easter Europe is likely to be the greatest challenge for the Union since the integration of the three Mediterranean countries in the 1980s and 1990s. The gap existing between Western members and Eastern European applicants creates political challenges difficult to deal with. It has created a potential for illegal worker migrations (from Eastern Europe), social dumping in Eastern Europe and criminal activities in Western Europe by Eastern "Mafia's": drug smuggling, prostitution and car robbery. The Threat to European security is clearly perceived by the European themselves, and 78% are in favour of increased assistance to Eastern Europe to fight against violence, terrorism and drug smuggling. This appears to be the first priority before assistance to declining regions (71% in favour), education and training systems (70%), small or medium size companies (58%). There has been a strong pressure from Germany and other European partners on Poland to re-organise border management with Belarus, Ukraine and the Baltic states. This objective is stated as a priority condition for Poland's accession.

One of the purposes of the enlargement and the structured political dialogue is to design common strategies to fight against those developments. But for some politicians, exclusion and barriers may be advocated as an alternative to the deal "enlargement against stability". A large part of the Balkan region has already been excluded from the enlargement process: for example, the new Yugoslavia was excluded in the two first waves of accession. The same thing is true for the peripheries of Russia: Moldavia, Ukraine, Belarus are clearly excluded.

1.1.2   East-West socio-economic gap and budgetary implications

Eastern Europe is likely to attract a large portion of European financial resources if enlargement is to be carried out seriously. The present poorest member states, such as Greece or Portugal, are not ready to accept that sort of huge reallocation of resources. At the Luxembourg summit, the poorest members have extorted the promise that they will continue to receive substantial amounts of structural funds for regional development, even after the accession of the new poorer Eastern European member states. However, wealthier member states are not ready to accept an increase in European fiscal pressure. As soon as financial commitments are involved, the support for a quick and extensive enlargement tends to weaken. The short comings in East-Germany, where huge budgetary transfer took place, is a further argument for those who want to limit the resources devoted to enlargement: time and a free market economy, they advocate, will do better than subsidies.

Eastern Europe was cut off from the rest of Europe for forty years. It is poorer and has not developed the same social values and mores. It is not considered by western Europeans as much European as are Sweden or Austria. Western Europeans do not necessarily feel any strong attachment for Eastern Europe despite increased tourism and exchanges. In this context, those who advocate solidarity, financial support and quick political integration are likely to lack strong political support.

Western European collective governance is strongly challenged by the issue of enlargement: on one hand, there is a historical chance to reunify the continent, provide lasting stability and create prosperity; on the other hand, public support and resources appear limited and member states divided. Finally, every decision about enlargement has a significant impact upon the already hottest and less consensual debates within the Union, such as common budgetary policy, common Agricultural Policy, Structural Funds, and institutional questions. The process of Amsterdam left many questions unresolved on those issues and created the need for a new inter-governmental conference around 2001-2002.

1.2 Building public support and political consensus

1.2.1 Lack of public support

The lack of support expressed by European public opinion for the enlargement is quite as clear, among the main member states of the Union as among the most advanced candidate countries.

Enlargement is not considered a priority for the Union by around 60% of its citizens. In Germany, despite obvious economic interests, the enlargement is not considered a priority by more than 70% of the population, in France by more than 75%. More European citizens would like the Union to remain as it is (16%) than to enlarge it (13%), but a vast majority (55%) would favour more integration within the present border of the Union instead of enlargement. Integration and solidarity within the existing Union benefit from much more support than any enlargement scheme. This vision is shared by the newly integrated member states such as Austria or Finland. Further enlargement is not a priority for 67% of Finnish citizens and not a priority for 57% of Austrian citizens, although those two countries may benefit from the economic consequences of the enlargement in Central Europe and the Baltic region. The only European countries where enlargement appears to be largely popular are Greece (47% in favour) and Denmark (61% in favour).

As far as the applicant countries are concerned there is clear support, even if not massive, only in four countries: Hungary, Poland, the Czech Republic and Cyprus. In the core countries of the Union, Germany and France, there is even a majority against the integration of Poland, Czech Republic and Cyprus. The decision to integrate Estonia and Slovenia in the first wave of accession has no popular legitimacy, such a decision being opposed by a majority of Europeans.

In the applicant countries, public support for accession is not extremely strong and even appears to be declining over time. In the Baltic states, only one third of the population would be ready to vote for accession to the European Union in case of a referendum. Only 29% of Estonians — a country selected to be in the first wave of accession — would vote for European Union membership. In Hungary, the Czech Republic and Slovenia, a huge majority in favour of European integration at the end of the cold war, and still strong in 1995, has decreased to a less impressive majority of around 45% of citizens who would still vote in favour of the integration in European Union at a referendum. Public support for European integration has remained huge only in two countries: Poland and Romania, a country excluded from the first wave of accession and for which there is limited public support within the Union.

Lack of public support for the enlargement puts the issue on a second priority agenda. Within the Union, monetary union, common action against unemployment, institutional reforms, regional development, new agricultural and environmental policies and common foreign policy are strong priorities over enlargement. As Euro-scepticism is widely spread across the Union, there is a strong incentive for Euro-optimists to show to their firm belief that the Union matters in every day life and that European people may directly benefit from its action. In the applicant states, European integration is also a second priority agenda. Security and stability are the top priorities for most governments. Membership of NATO, American support and military build up are key priorities for most of them. Economic transition is the other priority.

In applicant states, there starts to be a clear potential for Euro-scepticism. Civil servants feel threatened by European integration. Pensioners, employees of state owned companies, farmers and small independent companies may be disappointed with the coming reforms of social welfare, privatisation, market liberalisation and regulation, and may hold Europe responsible for those changes. As in Western Europe, the European integration process may be an easy scapegoat. Euro-scepticism may also result from a lack of vision, a lack of resources and the bureaucratic style of the accession partnerships.

1.2.2   Lack of political consensus

Enlargement of the European Union and the strategy to integrate Eastern European Countries into the network of European institutions has been a subject of debate and dispute much more than an element of political consensus between the major European players. Three main positions may be described as follows:

For UK and Denmark, the enlargement of the Union is an historical opportunity to re-establish liberal democracy, free trade and a more flexible approach of the Union. The Union should insist on the development of the rule of law, parliamentary democracy, personal and economic freedom. NATO should be extended to ensure the security of the new democracies. The establishment of a new free market (for goods, services and investment) deregulation and privatisation should happen as quickly as possible. Eastern

European countries should then be allowed to "opt out" as Britain and Denmark did, on issues like monetary Union, Schengen security package or the European social chapter, and yet still qualify for full membership. Criteria for accession should be kept quite general and admission policy pragmatic and flexible. This approach was taken at the Copenhagen summit when criteria for enlargement were defined for the first time in 1993, they were:
- Existence of democratic practices and rule of law,
- Transition to a market economy,
- The respect of human and minority rights
- Substantial internal reform of the Union itself

In the process of enlargement, emphasis should be put on subsidiarity: assistance should be reduced and candidate states should decide the path and the pace to reform by themselves. Finally enlargement to new members shall not prevent further trade liberalisation with other European and non-European partners, especially the US and Russia, nor with local forms of integration as in the Visegrad Pact or the Baltic Forum. This ad hoc and liberal approach to enlargement is popular in Eastern European countries and especially the Baltic states.

For a reunified Germany, the enlargement of the Union to Eastern European countries has to follow the same path as the former German Ostpolitik: enlargement has to be selective, conditional and cost-effective.

Negotiations have to be bilateral. Liberalisation of the entry into the European single market for Eastern European products, European assistance and finally accession to the Union have to be based on regular and scheduled progress by Eastern European countries. Straightforward objectives and explicit economic criteria have to be set up. One has to be serious about those criteria even if the respect of criteria may create some delays for accession and multiple waves of entry. The Essen summit of December 1994 strongly reflects this German approach to enlargement:

Ten official applicants for accession are named, including 8 that had not formally applied. Turkey is excluded from the first wave, as well as any country from the Community of Independent States.

Pre-accession strategy is thus defined and the candidates for membership have to:
- participate in structured political dialogue
- follow European Commission White Paper on how to prepare for integration into the European Single Market (May 1995)
- finalise an association agreement
- be seen to benefit from PHARE programme

Germany would favour a "slow, narrow and deep" enlargement, ideally to Hungary first, then the Czech Republic and finally Poland. As the end result for enlargement is to be increased security, prosperity and stability around Germany, the Germans support the parallel integration of their neighbour countries into NATO and other Western institutions as the OECD or the IMF.

This pragmatic German approach to enlargement with a strong emphasis on economic convergence and criteria based selection, matches quite well the bureaucratic style of the European Commission which has found economic assistance to Eastern Europe and the monitoring of accession partnerships new fields of activity and new grounds for legitimacy.

For France, the enlargement of the Union to Eastern Europe has to be a political process that will give the Union more strength on the world scene. This is the reason why the political construction of the Union should be carried out before (or at least together with) the enlargement process. France is not ready to accept an enlargement that would lead back the European idea to a free market and lead to vague political accord. This is the reason why France has been rather cautious about enlargement and has always stressed its political dimension.

In the early 1990s, President Mitterand for a while pushed the idea of a European Confederation, clearly distinct from the Union. France then pressed for the establishment as a structured and regular political dialogue with future candidates as a first step towards integration. France also launched the idea of a stability Pact between Eastern European neighbours as pre-condition for accession. Considering that the enlargement is a political challenge, France has been more reluctant than its partners to distinguish between candidates on the basis of economic criteria. For that reason the accession partnership will be applied equally to countries that are not qualified to be in the first wave of enlargement. For the same reason, French President Jacques Chirac did not hesitate to promise Poland an early accession by 2000, a deadline impossible to meet on the basis of economic criteria. But on the other hand, France does not want the enlargement to be "à la carte" and insists that there should be no exceptions for the new member states and that they should fully assimilate - after a possibly long transition period - the European acquis, including security arrangements, social chapter and monetary union. France does not want the enlargement process to dilute, "Germanise", or "Americanise" the European construction. France has strongly pushed for the integration of the last Mediterranean country, Cyprus at the Madrid summit.

European Union Member States in 1998

States in accession partnerships,
short-listed in Luxembourg Summit (1997), negotiating full membership since april 1998,
likely to integrate the Union soon after 2000

Other applicant states in accession partnerships with the European Union

Special cases :
* Malta, applicant state short-listed at Essen and Madrid Summits whose application has been suspended
* Turkey, applicant state not short-listed that shall benefit from full custom union with the Union soon after 2000

Figure 1. The enlargement process

1.3   **Western European Response to the Enlargement challenge**

The lack of political consensus over enlargement, together with weak public support, has produced:

- A minimal consensus on "cheap" enlargement: the resources devoted to Eastern European countries will be limited, the fiscal pressure on European citizens or further transfers from national budgets to the European budget will not take place. Growth in the Union is necessary to meet the financial requirements of enlargement.

- A methodological consensus on bureaucratisation: enlargement has been transformed into a complex bureaucratic process of assistance, training, investment and assessment. This process was launched at the Essen Summit (December 1994). At that summit, a list of ten likely applicants for accession was established and a pre-accession strategy defined.

- A paradox that may called "unpredictable conditionality": as member states are in fact divided about purposes, delays and criteria for enlargement, what would happen if one country failed finally to meet the required criteria was not clear: would assistance be reduced or suspended, would accession partnerships be revised or extended? "Unpredictable conditionality" is well demonstrated by the fact that:

a) accession partnerships bear no deadlines for "medium term" measures

b) enlargement negotiations and the assessment of accession partnerships will be kept separate and will be carried out by different teams

c) there is no sanction mechanism in case of clear violation of self-accepted European regulations by applicant states.

Table 2. Lack of resources for enlargement

Activity	Budget	Population (millions)	Budget per capita
1995-1999 European assistance to Union's less developed regions	ECU 150bl	60 m	ECU 500 per year
1991-97 German budgetary transfers to former GDR	ECU 450bl	16m	ECU 4000 per year
1995-1999 Pre-accession & accession partnership	ECU 7bl	110m	ECU 13 per year
2000 – 2006 Accession Partnership	ECU 21bn	110m	ECU 27 per year
2000-2006 EU budget allocated to new member states	ECU 53,5bn	65 m	ECU 117 per year

2. UNCERTAIN ENLARGEMENT AND CHALLENGES FOR CORPORATE GOVERNANCE

2.1 A Country-Risk Approach

Even in the most advanced Eastern European countries, local sources for investments remain limited and expensive. Self-financing is a common rule for a large number of local companies.

For foreign companies, operations, acquisitions or joint ventures in those future member states, financing relies on resources from their home market or, for the bigger groups, from the international markets. The availability and the cost of this type of financing depend on country risk assessment. Country-risk is integrated as a premium to pay on interest rates, insurance premiums or opportunity cost of provisions. The enlargement affects this evaluation of country-risk.

2.1.1 Political Risk

Political risk is supposed to be reduced by the enlargement process as enlargement is to be associated with democratisation, rule of law and transparent and fair business practices. The issues usually related to political risk such as confiscation of assets, contract frustration or discrimination against foreign companies should disappear. Yet some political risk is associated with the new phase of the enlargement. With accession partnerships the time has come for applicant countries to start the implementation of European regulations and pre-conditions (the so-called adoption of the European "acquis"). This process may be unpopular. Delays in implementation may occur that would create a risk for foreign investors, the rules applicable remaining unclear for a period of time. Worse, the process of implementing the European "acquis" may be stopped by newly elected governments, this could raise Euro-scepticism, anti-capitalistic attitudes and nationalism. This risk appears rather limited for the moment as the main political forces, including former communist parties or new nationalistic right parties still officially favour European integration of most of the applicant states. Yet, such a reversal of European commitment has already taken place in Malta. Euro-scepticism is almost an official point of view in nationalistic Slovakia and has gained strong support in Turkey, Croatia, Bosnia, and Albania.

Should such a reversal occur at a later phase of the European integration process, the unpredictable conditionality that results from the lack of political consensus in the Union, makes the "exit scenario" rather unclear. Free access to the European single market may be postponed or denied, European financial assistance reduced, sanctions taken. A more pragmatic "suspension" process may also be started in which some advantages such as market access would be withhold, some assistance would continue, some opportunity to join the process of integration later would be kept open and opt out clauses could finally be negotiated.

The risks of delayed implementation seem to exist for every country. The risk of reversal of the integration process is high in those countries where the popular support for integration is weak and deteriorating as in the Baltic states, or in those countries in which the road to travel is very long, such as Bulgaria and Romania.

2.1.2   Financial Risk

Financial risk is even higher than political risk for foreign investments and local companies. As the enlargement decided upon is a cheap one there is no direct macro-economic help from the European Union to ensure the stability of the currencies likely to join the monetary union one day. There is no monetary stabilisation package.

Unpredictable conditionality is quite evident in the monetary field: although applicant countries are not expected to opt out as far as monetary union is concerned, explicit monetary or macro-economic criteria (comparable to those of the EMU) are not defined nor any delays set up. Will the Eastern European countries join the old European Monetary System, still working for Greece, as the first step to monetary Union, will a fluctuation margin between their currencies and the EURO be defined at a precise moment: the questions have not yet been answered. For the time being, monetary solidarity has not been organised by accession partnerships. The European Union members certainly expect Eastern European currencies to value and gain stability through self-discipline of the applicant states, economic reforms (especially in the financial sector), increased exportations and foreign investments.

Budgetary discipline is quite difficult to realise in the context of enlargement: commitments taken by applicant states under the accession partnership agreements -as reform of social systems, administration, environment policy- will certainly, in a first phase, increase public spending. The principle of co-financing -i.e. a project is eligible for European financial assistance only if the local state makes a prior financial commitment on the same project- is also likely to increase the incentive for more public investments in the short term. The reform of local taxation is not going to be ready to provide additional resources immediately and European assistance is likely to be in-sufficient to bridge the gap. The solution will certainly be to increase the public debt.

The need for public debt as well as anti-inflation policies will certainly keep interest rate at high level, making the best Eastern European debt market quite attractive for investors. With the rather high interest rates and rather high exchange rates, decided by central banks to prepare for monetary union, difficult budgetary exercises, and uncertain financial reform especially in the banking sector, the best Eastern European financial markets may offer strong potential to attract of short term capital, speculation and devaluation, in a European context elsewhere stabilised by EURO.

As conditionality is unpredictable and no disciplinary or solidarity mechanism has been set up between applicant countries, it may be tempting for European (second) best economies to use competitive devaluation once the European single market open to their products. This policy may increase tensions between Eastern European applicants, strengthen speculation, and reduce the already weak support in the core member states, at that time under EURO, they will certainly consider those old European practices as being unfair to them.

As political risk is reduced but not suppressed and financial risk remains at a high level, the risk premium costs for operations in Eastern European countries has remained relatively high in recent years. Financing for international investors in the "emerging countries" of Eastern Europe is expected to remain expensive. Local companies will still operate with local interest's rates at a high level and may find it difficult to borrow on foreign markets at a much cheaper price (as they will be subject to country-risk premium by the foreign banks). For the same reason, the development of Eastern European private options markets as a source of direct short term debt for local companies may remain limited.

Lastly, it is not clear what influence a crisis in Russia would have on Eastern Europe economies. Such a crisis is likely in the coming years with the drop of petrol prices, the huge Russian debt, the poor fiscal system and the bad state of the banking system. Should a deep financial and confidence crisis occur in Russia, one is not sure that, despite reduced trade with Russia and CIS countries, the Eastern European economies may not be assimilated with Russia, as bearing some of the same type of macro-economic risks. Should an Asian style crisis occur in Russia and Eastern Europe, the Union is unlikely to be very helpful, because of limited resources that would be stretched out to face several crises at the same time and maintain the enlargement process on track. In case of a financial crisis in Russia and Eastern Europe, the key player would rather be the IMF, under strong US influence, which might impose "tougher conditionality" and agendas not necessarily compatible with the European enlargement calendar.

2.2 Corporate Strategies in Uncertain Time and Uncertain Space.

Resulting from the lack of consensus on the pace of integration, the medium-term agenda of accession partnerships has been changed into a very long and detailed checklist of objectives to be fulfilled but without any specific deadlines. This situation negatively affects two strategic aspects: the valuable chain of corporations operating in Eastern European applicant countries and the barriers those companies may face in the future.

2.2.1 Uncertain strategic agendas

The valuable chain of corporations, whether local companies or foreign affiliates, operating in Eastern Europe is likely to be quite dramatically changed by the enlargement process.

The privatisation of energy, telecommunications, suppliers of raw material such as coal, iron, and agricultural products will affect production. The competition likely to be introduced during the accession process is supposed to reduce some of those costs. As more Western companies will be able to supply the local markets with duty free industrial equipment, computers, and high technology inputs, production costs are likely to decline if financing for investments remains accessible and relatively inexpensive. In such a favourable context, some Eastern European countries may experiment with a Mexican type of development: decrease input costs, increase industrial outputs, take advantage of economies of scale (with the bigger European market), higher added value as local industry turns to more elaborate products and patterns of production. The problem for that nice scenario is that Eastern European countries are far from being Mexican under-regulated "maquiladoras". Production costs may indeed rise if Europe imposes its safety and quality norms, environment regulations and social chapter criteria as pre-conditions for full accession and free access to the European market. If the time lag is too short between market deregulation (imposed and accelerated by the European integration process) and comprehensive market "re-regulation" (as condition for accession, economic subsidies and full opening of Western European markets), the benefits that are likely to be drawn from the initial restructuring, social gap and market extension (with the progressive unilateral opening of Western European market to Eastern industrial products) may be reduced. The process of integration, instead of accelerating the emergence of new entrepreneurs may lead to sharp selection and rapid concentration, as only a few new Eastern European entrepreneurs will be able to apply on successfully to introduce the European regulations and remain competitive. This danger is well understood by the Commission that has put a strong emphasis helping small or medium size companies adjust to the European market conditions.

Subcontracting has a strong potential in Eastern Europe, where wages are lower and workforce training quite advanced and available. The unilateral opening of Western European markets to Eastern European manufactured products has already accelerated the move. Subcontracting will develop further as other segments of Western European markets open, for example the agriculture industry. Processing trade will also develop when Western products will be able to enter Eastern European countries free of any duty, be processed there and re-exported or sold locally. At the same time pressure on sub-contractors for quality, and European standards, just in time productivity and low costs will be increased. Instead of having several sub-contractors in each of the countries where new plants have been established, a Western company may well choose to mutualise the sourcing of its plants with one or two Eastern European subcontractors, as tariff and barriers disappear between the different Eastern European countries as a result of the European enlargement process. Western suppliers may come in Eastern European markets together with the Western companies already familiar with them and buy local companies in the same industry. The move has started but will be accelerated when regulations for foreign investments, property rights and export of dividends are clarified, as is required in the accession conditions. Increased competition between subcontractors, increased perspectives for processing trade, arrival of more Western subcontractors, increased demand for acquisitions may reshape a large part of the subcontracting industry.

Distribution will be changed as enlargement makes further progress. Western European distributors may try to enter Eastern European markets and reshape distribution channels and networks as soon as Eastern European markets are fully open to Western competitors. Their key advantages would be easy and cheap access to Western European products for which the local demand is high. They may supply Eastern European markets with those products at cheaper prices than local wholesale distributors and retailers buying directly in Western Europe. Those Western European distributors may also put some strong pressure on the local producers, as they would distribute their products in the rest of Europe. For markets where cost effectiveness is the key to success, the potential development for European big distribution channels appears quite high as soon as Eastern European markets cut off tariffs and deregulate market access. The newly established "import companies" that flourish presently and that use exclusive distribution agreements with Western producers will certainly suffer from that evolution as well as from the introduction of the European anti-trust regulations.

A large part of the competitive field as well as key elements in the value chain of many companies and industry are likely to be affected, hopefully positively, by the enlargement process. Some key elements need to be carefully watched such as:

- When will the full opening of European Union market take place, for energy, agro-industry, and services? What will be the regulations applicable to the incoming products (those of today, those of that day, specific ones?)? What kind of help and information will be provided by the European Union so that small or medium size companies may be able to adjust?

- When will the opening and full deregulation of Eastern European markets take place? Will there be specific niches that will remain for a while protected from Western competitors?

- When will the investment codes, property rights, fiscal regulations for foreigner be defined and stabilised?

- When will the "re -regulation" of Eastern European markets on the basis of existing European regulations take place?

For the time being, resulting from the "unpredictable conditionality" of accession partnerships, those key elements for any strategic agenda are still far from being clear and the steps to be taken are far from being explicitly defined. Will there be a standardised method for accession or will each country be allowed to follow its own specific path? Even that question is not clearly resolved. There is a striking difference with the Acte Unique, the Maastricht Treaty and the EMU processes in which conditions, steps and deadlines were much more explicit.

2.2.2   Barriers in enlarging Europe.

The enlargement process is designed to reduce existing barriers between Western and Eastern Europe. Yet the impact of enlargement on existing barriers should be discussed.

Western European barriers will not disappear. Tariff barriers will disappear unilaterally for industrial products in a short period of time. Tariff products for the agriculture industry will be reduced but will also remain in place for a while, maybe even after full accession to the Union of important agricultural countries like Poland or Hungary. But Western barriers to Eastern products are not tariffs but safety and product regulations. Those regulations, rapidly changing over time for certain products, are the true barriers for entry to the European market. There are the ones on which industrial lobbies and companies try to bear some influence to keep their positions on the core European market. Those regulatory barriers are not likely to be abolished in the near future. The enlargement process rather moves eastward those regulatory barriers, introducing the need for Eastern European countries and companies to lobby in Brussels as their Western partners do.

Internal barriers will be created in Eastern European economies. The accession partnerships are likely to introduce those regulations within the Eastern European countries themselves, creating a de facto barrier between those that will be able to adapt to the complex European regulations (and will hopefully get some assistance to meet the challenge) and will be able to supply the European market with European standard products and will fully benefit from its opening. On the other hand there will be those unable to adapt as quickly and who will be kept out of the European market for a certain time (even if their country has become a full member) and may even find themselves unable to market their non-standardised products in their home market.

New barriers will be established between Eastern European countries: but whom will they benefit? Enlargement is likely to move the regulatory barriers of Europe eastward. Second phase applicant countries may face difficulties in adapting to those new barriers between themselves and their former neighbours. A Slovak product usually marketed in the Czech Republic may become at some point "not European enough" to cross the Union border and enter the newly integrated Czech Republic. This question is extremely important for agriculture industry, energy, and raw materials, domains in which second phase applicant countries -as Slovakia, Romania, Bulgaria- may be competitive. European assistance, likely to be limited, will not compensate immediately for the loss of those markets. Stricter migration regulation and more efficient border management by the newly integrated states may worsen the impact of enlargement in the countries left outside the new Union. Neighbouring countries -Romania, Slovakia, Ukraine- which depend on the repatriation of immigrant workers (and the revenues of black markets) may suffer from that change.

On the other hand, Eastern European countries outside the Union borders will have more freedom in the domain of monetary and social policies. Competitive devaluation, low cost production, free zones may be considered alternatives to the long bureaucratic process of accession. Being outside the barriers may finally prove an advantage for second or third wave countries.

CONCLUSION

Tremendous progress had been achieved in Eastern Europe before the enlargement process actually started. Many articles in this book describe and explain those achievements, which may seem astonishing when compared with the situation in 1988. Throughout that first phase of transition, European Union's economic practices and regulations as well as Western style monetary and macro-economic policies have been models of efficient governance. The same impact of European styles, technologies, management practices are to be found in Eastern European companies. The association agreements have had a stimulating effect on economic transition and European assistance has started to have a certain influence in the field of professional training, higher education, culture, and the environment.

With the enlargement process started in 1998, the relationships between the Union and the applicant member states are likely to be changed as well as having an impact on local companies. As resources, public support, and political consensus are very limited over the issue of enlargement, European governance has decided that enlargement should be inexpensive, selective and monitored through a bureaucratic process of regular assessment. In order not to irritate those in favour of a more political approach, agendas, deadlines, contractual assistance for specific tasks, and sanctions have not been made explicit.

As a large margin of negotiation is left to each country, the enlargement process may finally strongly differentiate Eastern European countries according to the path and pace chosen for accession. New barriers may be established at the end of the process. European Union first played a unifying role as a model and promoter of free trade. With enlargement, Europe is likely to accelerate economic differentiation in Eastern Europe.

Europe as a legal and economic governance model, as a partner for training and technological transfer, as an opening market, has until now rather facilitated the improvement of the business environment and helped in reducing the risks associated with post-communist transition.

On the contrary, this "unpredictable conditionality" in the enlargement process, is likely to create, at least for some time, additional risks and strategic uncertainty for companies operating in Eastern Europe. The end result of the enlargement process makes it worth trying, but the stabilising role of Europe may be over for a while.

REFERENCES

Agenda 2000, Brussels, Commission Européenne, Document 97/16

O. Blanchard, The Economics of post-communist transition, Oxford, Clarendon Press, 1997

A. Frémont, L'Europe entre Maastricht et Sarajevo, Paris, Reclus, 1996

O. Gille- Belova, Les enjeux de l'élargissement de l'Union européenne dans l'opinion publique, Bruxelles, Commission européenne, 1998

C. Kupchan, Nationalism and nationalities in the New Europe, Ithaca, Cornell University Press, 1995

M.A. Landesmann, P Szekely, Industrial Restructuring and Trade Reorientation in Eastern Europe, Cambridge University Press, 1995

J. Levy, Europe, une géographie, Paris, Hachette, 1997

E. Lhomel, L'Europe centrale, orientale et balte, Paris, La Documentation française, 1998

M.-C. Maurel (dir), Recomposition de l'Europe médiane, Paris, Sedes,1998

OECD, Lessons from the Economic Transition : Central and Eastern Europe in the 1990's, Londres, Kluwer, 1997

Privatisation and Restructuring in Central and Eastern Europe, Washington, World Bank, 1997

F. de la Serre, Christian Lequesne, Jacques Rupnik, L'Union européenne : ouverture à l'Est, Paris, PUF,1994

J. Segard, "L'élargissement de l'Union européenne et la divergence entre les économies en transition", Revue française d'économie,3.1997, p. 177-201

L'Union européenne et les pays en transition, Courrier des Pays de l'Est, Documentation française, 1997

P. Van den Bempt, G.Theelen, From Europe agreements to accession : the integration of the Central and Eastern European countries into the European Union, Bruxelles, European University Press, 1996

G. Wackermann, La nouvelle Europe Centrale, Paris, Ellipses, 1997

W. Weidenfeld, Central and Eastern Europe on the Way into the European Union : Problems and Prospects in 1996, Bertelsmann Foundation, 1996

Index

A

ABB
  CEE development by, 12–13
  in Poland, 108
Agriculture, in Romania, 155–157
Alessandrini, Sergio, on Romania, 125–160
Amoroso-Robinson rule, 169
Attractiveness, as factor in foreign direct
    investment, 104
Austrian managers, *vs.* Hungarian managers,
    98–99
Automobile industry, 14

B

Baltic Republics
  political and economic independence of, 1–2
  political transition of, 2
Bank reform, in Romania, 141–143
Banking sector, in Hungary, 85–86
Berlin Wall, fall of, 1
Brasov riots, 126
Bucharest Stock Exchange, 132, 151
Business ethics, in Hungary
  communist heritage on, 93–94
  company ethics in, 99–101, 101t
  future prospects for, 101–102
  management ethics in, 98–99
  religious institutions on, 93–94
  social reception of market economy in, 94–98
Business modes, of Swedish multinationals,
    178–180, 179f
Business strategies, for transitional economies,
    1–17
  conclusions in, 16–17
  economic environment in, 6–8
  foreign direct investment in, 9–11
  foreign trade in, 8–9
  international companies in, 11–16 (*See also*
      International companies, in business
      strategies for transitional economies)
  privatization in, 4–6

'return to Europe' policy in, 1–4
social environment in, 6–8
Buyers' market, 74

C

Capital alliances, in Polish foreign direct
    investment (FDI), 110–111
Capital markets, in privatization methods, 26–27
Caritas, 131
Ceausescu
  de-villagization policy of, 126, 129
  fall from power of, 126–127
CEFTA (Central European Free Trade
    Agreement), 9
Central Europe. *See also* Privatization, in CEE;
    specific countries
  growth rates of, 6
  Swedish multinationals in, 177–191 (*See also*
      Swedish multinationals)
Central European Free Trade Agreement
    (CEFTA), 9
Chikán, Attila, on Hungarian competitiveness
    and industry restructuring, 71–92. *See also*
    Hungary, competitiveness and industry
    restructuring in
Ciorbea, Victor, 128, 133
Collectivized farm land, in Romania, 138
Commerce and Industry Chamber for Foreign
    Investors, 122
Company co-operations, between Eastern and
    Western Europe, 163–174
  analytical framework of, 165–168
  innovation in, 168–169, 169f
  macroeconomic analysis of, 163–165, 164f
  SME and development in, 169–170
  SME co-operations with Eastern Europe in,
      170–174
  strategic choices in, 168–169, 169f
Company restructuring, in CEE, 21–35. *See also*
    Privatization, in CEE
Company valuation, in privatization methods, 27
Competitiveness